THE NEXT EVOLUTION

From Systems to Governed Decision-Intelligence™

Why Modern Enterprises Still Fail Despite Having Systems—and the Missing Infrastructure Required to Scale with Audit-Grade Accountability and Defensibility

NFRASTRUCT®

First Edition 2026

THE NEXT EVOLUTION
From Systems to Governed Decision-Intelligence™

First Edition

Library of Congress Control Number: 2026935437

ISBN 979-8-9944542-0-6 (Hardcover)
ISBN 979-8-9944542-1-3 (Paperback)

Published by
Decision-Intelligence Press™
An imprint of NFRASTRUCT®

Printed in the United States of America

CLAIM OF NOVELTY AND INSTITUTIONAL CONTRIBUTION

The Next Evolution: From Systems to Governed Decision-Intelligence™ advances a novel institutional thesis: that modern enterprises and public institutions lack a dedicated infrastructure layer for governing human-impact decisions prior to exposure, and that this structural absence — not ethical failure, managerial incompetence, or insufficient regulation — is the primary driver of preventable harm, systemic risk, and downstream legal and regulatory consequence.

The thesis is institutional rather than behavioral. It does not locate the source of governance failure in the character, the competence, or the intentions of the individuals who exercise consequential authority within organizations. It locates it in the architecture of the organizations themselves — in the absence of a structural governance layer that was never built, that no existing enterprise function was designed to provide, and whose absence has been the consistent structural source of the decision failures that have defined institutional governance across industries throughout the Systems Age. The implication of this institutional location is precise: the failure cannot be corrected by improving the individuals who operate within the existing architecture. It requires building the layer the architecture is missing.

While existing disciplines address governance, risk, ethics, compliance, and decision quality, they do so within operational systems or after execution has occurred. Corporate governance frameworks govern organizational conduct and leadership accountability — but they govern the organization, not the decisions the organization makes before those decisions are executed. Enterprise Risk Management frameworks identify, model, and monitor institutional risk — but they inform decisions without possessing the authority to intercept them before execution begins. Compliance and regulatory frameworks ensure adherence to applicable rules and standards — but they evaluate conformity with established requirements after actions have been taken, not before consequential decisions are authorized to proceed.

Ethical frameworks and algorithmic impact assessments anticipate harm and promote responsible design — but they operate in advisory and principle-based modes that do not generalize into an enterprise-wide governance infrastructure capable of making execution conditional upon governance. Decision science and decision-intelligence platforms optimize choice under uncertainty and improve analytical outputs within execution systems — but they do not establish structural pre-clearance requirements that must be satisfied before consequential authority may be exercised.

The structural limitation shared by all of these disciplines is temporal: they operate within execution or after execution, not before it. Each has developed sophisticated frameworks for its designated domain. None was designed to govern whether a consequential decision should be permitted to proceed at all, before the execution system that will carry it out is engaged. This work is distinct in asserting that decision execution itself — specifically for decisions that materially affect human outcomes — requires pre-execution governance as a formal institutional responsibility, and that this requirement has no existing institutional fulfillment.

The book defines this missing layer as Governed Decision-Intelligence™ (GD-I™): the enterprise-level category implemented through a dedicated infrastructure layer — Governed Decision-Intelligence Infrastructure™ (GD-II™) — which governs whether high-impact decisions may proceed, under what constraints, with what evidentiary basis, and with what attributable accountability, before exposure occurs. This definition has four structural elements whose combination is the source of the category's novelty.

The governance of whether a decision may proceed — not how it should be implemented or what outcome it is likely to produce, but whether it meets the evidentiary and accountability standard required for authorization — is the function no existing governance mechanism performs. The specification of the constraints under which a governed decision may proceed — the evidentiary requirements, the alternative consideration requirements, the risk acknowledgment requirements, and the authority attribution requirements that the governance standard enforces — establishes the institutional substance of the governance function rather than leaving it to advisory guidance or voluntary compliance. The requirement that the evidentiary basis be contemporaneous — captured at the moment of authority before outcomes are known and before the institutional incentives that would otherwise shape its retrospective presentation have been created — distinguishes genuine decision evidence from the post-hoc rationale that documentation-based governance frameworks consistently produce in its place. And the requirement that accountability be attributable — that the exercise of consequential authority be assigned to specific identified individuals under defined mandates whose institutional responsibility for the consequences of that authority is preserved in the contemporaneous governance record — creates the governance accountability that collective approval processes and diffused responsibility consistently prevent.

This contribution is not a refinement of existing decision processes, nor an extension of ethical or compliance frameworks. Refinements of existing decision processes improve how decisions are made within the execution layer — they address the quality of the deliberative process, the sophistication of the analytical inputs, or the consistency of the procedural requirements that surround the exercise of decision authority. Extensions of ethical or compliance frameworks expand the behavioral standards that governance applies to organizational conduct within the execution layer — they define more comprehensively what is required, what is prohibited, and what consequences attach to violations. Both categories of contribution operate at the execution layer, within the governance architecture that the Systems Age produced.

This work represents an architectural reframing of decision authority as an infrastructure problem — analogous to the historical emergence of enterprise resource planning, financial controls, or information security governance. Each of these infrastructure categories emerged when the institutional evidence established that the governance of a specific category of organizational activity could not be achieved through the procedural and behavioral mechanisms of existing governance frameworks and required instead a dedicated infrastructure layer designed specifically for its governance requirements.

Enterprise resource planning emerged when the integration and governance of operational resource allocation could no longer be achieved through the departmental and procedural mechanisms that preceded it. Financial controls emerged when the governance of financial activity could no longer depend on personal trust and individual integrity and required structural enforcement mechanisms independent of the parties whose conduct they governed.

Information security governance emerged when the protection of digital information infrastructure could no longer be achieved through awareness and policy alone and required a dedicated architectural function specifically designed for its threat environment.

GD-II™ follows the same institutional pattern: it emerges because the governance of consequential decisions cannot be achieved through the compliance, advisory, and retrospective mechanisms of existing governance frameworks, and requires a dedicated infrastructure layer that is independent of the authority it governs, positioned above the execution layer, and designed specifically to perform the pre-execution governance function that no existing enterprise architecture provides.

Accordingly, this work does not propose a methodology, a checklist, or a best-practice guide. Methodologies, checklists, and best-practice guides are instruments of the execution layer — they improve how organizational activity is conducted within the existing governance architecture by defining better practices for the performance of functions that the architecture already contains. They are appropriate and valuable responses to execution gaps. They are not responses to architectural gaps. The governance gap that this work identifies is architectural: the absence of a governance layer that should exist in the institutional design of every enterprise that exercises consequential authority at scale, and that no improvement in existing execution-layer governance can supply.

This work establishes the institutional necessity of pre-exposure decision governance as a foundational enterprise layer required for operating responsibly at scale. The institutional necessity follows from the preceding analysis: the accountability environments of the modern era impose on organizations operating at scale the requirement to demonstrate the governance quality of their consequential decision-making in contemporaneous evidentiary form, in accountability forums whose standards are established by legal, regulatory, fiduciary, and public institutional requirements that no existing governance mechanism is structured to satisfy. An organization that operates at scale with consequential impact on the parties its decisions affect, without the institutional capacity to demonstrate that the governance quality of its decision-making meets the standard that these accountability environments apply, is operating with a structural governance deficit that is no longer defensible as oversight, immaturity, or the unavailability of required tools. It is operating at institutional risk. This work establishes the structural nature of that risk, defines the infrastructure category that addresses it, and provides the institutional argument for why the next evolution of enterprise must include the governance of decisions as a foundational architectural requirement.

Why This Book Exists

There was a time when systems were enough. The institutional challenges that defined enterprise management through the latter half of the twentieth century were challenges of execution — of producing consistent outcomes across distributed operations, of scaling institutional capability beyond the bandwidth of individual founders, of replacing the tribal knowledge and personal dependency that made early organizations fragile with documented processes and repeatable methods. These were genuine and consequential problems, and the solutions that organizations developed to address them were genuine and consequential achievements.

When organizations struggled to scale, the answer was clarity — the codification of operational logic into a documented process that could be transferred, replicated, and executed without the presence of the individuals who originally held the institutional knowledge. When quality varied in ways that undermined organizational performance and eroded competitive standing, the answer was process — the standardization of how work should be done that reduced variance and made consistent outcomes achievable at scale. When outcomes depended too heavily on specific individuals whose departure represented institutional risk that no organization could sustainably manage, the answer was documentation, training, and repeatability — the systematic conversion of individual expertise into transferable institutional capability.

That era produced extraordinary progress. Businesses learned how to operate without heroic founders — how to sustain and grow organizational capability beyond the cognitive bandwidth and physical presence of the individuals who created it. Execution became predictable: organizations that had previously depended on exceptional individuals to produce exceptional results could now produce consistent results through ordinary individuals operating within extraordinary systems. Complexity became manageable: the coordination problems that had previously constrained organizational growth could now be addressed through the process architectures and operational frameworks that systemization made possible. Scale became possible: organizations could grow beyond the limits that individual dependency had imposed, extending their reach and their impact without the proportional increase in institutional risk that growth had previously required.

And yet — quietly, consistently, and across industries that had achieved the highest levels of operational sophistication produced by the Systems Age — failure returned. Not because systems were missing from the organizations that experienced it. The systems were present, mature, and in many cases, among the most sophisticated operational architectures in the history of institutional management. Not because execution had failed. The processes were followed, the approvals were obtained, the documentation was complete, and the compliance records were clean. Failure returned because decisions were not governed — because the consequential acts of authority that determined what the systems would execute and what the processes would produce were made without the structural governance that distinguishes accountable institutional judgment from its absence.

The Paradox of the Modern Enterprise

Today's enterprises are more systemized than at any point in human institutional history. The operational sophistication that decades of management science, technology investment, and organizational learning have produced has created enterprises that possess capabilities that would have been inconceivable to their predecessors. They have mature operating models — structured operational architectures that define how organizational work is performed, coordinated, and measured across every function and every level of the institutional hierarchy. They have sophisticated human resources, compliance, and analytics platforms — technological and procedural infrastructures that support the management of organizational talent, the adherence to regulatory requirements, and the measurement of organizational performance with a precision and a scale that previous eras could not have imagined. They have formalized leadership structures — defined hierarchies, documented accountabilities, and explicit authority frameworks that establish who is responsible for what at every level of the organization. They have policies for nearly every conceivable scenario — documented standards of conduct, escalation protocols, and procedural requirements that address the full range of operational and governance situations that organizational management has learned to anticipate.

And still — with all of this institutional sophistication, with all of this operational capability, with all of these governance frameworks, compliance infrastructures, and documented standards — they cannot reliably answer the questions that matter most when accountability arrives. Why was this person hired instead of that one — what was the contemporaneous evidentiary basis for the judgment that this individual represented a sound institutional investment of the authority and the resources that hiring commits? Why was this leader promoted — or protected when conduct or performance warranted a different response — what governance standard was applied to the exercise of the authority that elevated or sheltered institutional power in ways whose consequences the organization now must account for? Why were warnings ignored until damage was irreversible — what institutional mechanism failed to capture, preserve, and require genuine engagement with the signals that were present in the decision environment and that the governance record would have established as having been present and unaddressed? Why did the absence of policy violations precede catastrophic outcomes — how did an organization operating within the full scope of its compliance architecture produce consequences whose severity makes the adequacy of that architecture's governance function impossible to defend?

These are not execution failures. They are not the product of operational systems that failed to function as designed, of compliance frameworks that were inadequately implemented, or of individual actors who violated the institutional standards they were required to uphold. They are decision failures — the institutional consequences of consequential acts of authority that were never required to meet a governance standard before execution, and that the execution systems of the most sophisticated enterprises in history carried out with institutional fidelity, regardless of whether the decisions they were executing were sound. By themselves, systems do not prevent decision failures. This is not a criticism of systems. It is a precise description of what systems were designed to do and what lies beyond their institutional scope.

What Systems Were Never Designed to Do

Systems are designed to execute. They standardize — converting the operational knowledge embedded in best practices into documented procedures that can be applied consistently by individuals who did not develop them. They automate — reducing the cognitive and operational burden of routine institutional activity by embedding defined decision logic into technological infrastructure that applies it reliably at scale. They enforce consistency — creating institutional mechanisms that make deviation from established standards visible, measurable, and subject to correction. They scale what already exists — extending the operational logic of a functioning institutional model to new geographies, new functions, new volumes of activity, and new generations of organizational participants without requiring the reinvention of the institutional knowledge that the model represents.

But systems do not ask the most dangerous question in business: should this decision be allowed to proceed at all? This question — the governance question that lies above execution, that must be answered before the execution system is engaged, and that no execution system was designed to ask — is the question whose systematic absence from the governance architectures of modern enterprises is the structural source of the institutional failures that the preceding description has identified. Systems do not test decisions before exposure. They execute decisions that have already been made, producing the operational activity that the decision authorized without any mechanism for evaluating whether the decision met a governance standard before the execution began.

They do not capture the alternatives that were considered and rejected before the chosen path was committed to execution — the contemporaneous record of deliberative engagement with available options that is among the most important categories of decision evidence when accountability eventually requires an account of how the direction was chosen. They do not preserve evidence at the moment authority is exercised — the contemporaneous evidentiary basis of the judgment that authorized each consequential organizational commitment, captured before outcomes are known and before the institutional incentives of the accountability environment have shaped the retrospective account of what the decision-maker knew and considered. They do not hold human judgment accountable under pressure — the conditions of time compression, authority dynamics, incentive misalignment, and cognitive distortion that the preceding chapters establish as the structural conditions under which the most consequential organizational decisions are most frequently made, and that no system was designed to govern.

As a result, modern organizations often achieve something deeply ironic: they execute the wrong decisions flawlessly. The operational precision, the process fidelity, and the compliance discipline of the most sophisticated enterprise architectures in institutional history are placed in the service of consequential decisions that were never required to justify their existence before the systems that carry them out were engaged. The execution is impeccable. The decision that authorized it was ungoverned. And the institutional consequences of that gap — visible in every category of organizational failure that the Systems Age has produced at scale — are the subject of this book.

The Invisible Assumption That Breaks Everything

For decades, organizations have operated under an unspoken belief that has never required articulation because its apparent empirical support has made articulation unnecessary: if the system is sound, the decision must be sound. This belief feels reasonable — it is consistent with the observable correlation between operational maturity and organizational performance that the Systems Age has established across every industry in which systemization has been applied. It feels efficient — it eliminates the institutional overhead of examining the decisions that systems execute by treating the quality of the system as a sufficient proxy for the quality of the judgment behind it. It feels modern — consistent with the data-driven, process-oriented, compliance-focused governance philosophy that the most sophisticated organizational cultures of the current era have adopted as their institutional standard.

It is also false. The observable correlation between system quality and organizational performance that makes the assumption feel empirically supported is a correlation within the execution domain — the domain for which systems were designed and in which the quality of the system genuinely does produce the quality of the outcome. In the decision domain — in the institutional space where consequential acts of authority determine what the systems will execute and what organizational commitments will be made — the correlation does not hold. The quality of the system that executes a decision is independent of the quality of the judgment that authorized it. A sound system executing an unsound decision produces an unsound outcome with institutional precision. And the precision of the execution makes the unsoundness of the decision harder to identify before its consequences become irreversible.

Human beings do not behave the same way under the organizational pressure of consequential decision-making as they do on paper — as governance frameworks designed for idealized conditions of rational deliberation assume. Authority distorts the signals that reach those who exercise it: the individuals and institutions whose perspectives and expertise are most relevant to the assessment of consequential decisions consistently adjust the expression of those perspectives in ways that reflect the authority gradient of the decision environment rather than the informational reality of what they know.

Incentives reshape judgment: the career considerations, the performance metrics, the reputational dynamics, and the organizational reward structures that define the institutional environment of decision-making create systematic pressures toward resolutions that serve the decision-maker's interests rather than the organization's governance obligations. Speed suppresses dissent: the temporal compression of competitive operational environments creates conditions in which the deliberative engagement that sound judgment requires is experienced as institutional irresponsibility rather than as governance discipline.

Documentation replaces evidence: the institutional practice of creating records that satisfy procedural requirements displaces the practice of capturing the contemporaneous evidentiary basis of consequential decisions in ways that establish the governance quality of the judgment behind them. After-the-fact explanations replace contemporaneous truth: the institutional incentive to present the most defensible possible account of past decisions shapes the retrospective record of what was known and considered in ways that systematically diverge from the contemporaneous reality that governance requires. When these conditions — present in every organization that operates under the pressures of the modern competitive environment — shape the exercise of consequential decision authority, systems do not fail loudly. They fail silently, continuing to execute with institutional fidelity the directions that ungoverned judgment has established, until the consequences of that judgment surface in the courtrooms, boardrooms, headlines, and institutional histories that constitute the accountability record of the modern enterprise.

The Missing Infrastructure

This book is not an argument against systems. Systems were a necessary evolution — the foundational institutional achievement that made the modern enterprise possible and that remains essential to the operational functioning of every organization that operates at scale. The operational precision, the execution reliability, and the institutional scalability that systemization has produced are genuine accomplishments whose value is not diminished by the recognition that they are insufficient for the governance requirements of the next era. Systems remain essential. But they are no longer sufficient. The institutional environments of the modern enterprise — the accountability demands, the regulatory requirements, the legal standards, and the public expectations that define the conditions under which consequential organizational decisions will be examined — require a governance layer above the execution systems that those systems were never designed to provide.

What is missing is Governed Decision-Intelligence™ (GD-I™) — an infrastructure that exists above execution, not inside it. Not a more sophisticated version of the compliance frameworks, the analytics platforms, or the AI systems that constitute the execution governance architecture of the modern enterprise. Not an enhancement of the HR systems, the risk management processes, or the approval workflows that surround the exercise of decision authority without governing it. A distinct institutional layer — positioned above all of these systems and functions, operating before execution begins rather than within it or after it, and performing the governance function that no existing enterprise architecture was designed to perform.

This infrastructure governs decisions before they expose the organization to irreversible risk — before the consequences of ungoverned judgment have been set in motion by execution systems whose institutional fidelity ensures that those consequences propagate at the full speed and scale that operational capability permits. It observes human behavior rather than assuming compliance — recognizing the systematic distortions that organizational pressure, authority dynamics, and incentive misalignment produce in the exercise of consequential judgment, and creating governance conditions that address those distortions structurally rather than relying on individual discipline to overcome them. It records why alternatives were rejected rather than merely what was chosen — preserving the contemporaneous account of the deliberative process that distinguishes governed judgment from its absence in every accountability forum that examines it. It anchors authority to evidence rather than intuition alone — requiring the contemporaneous evidentiary basis of consequential decisions to be established and preserved before the execution system is authorized to proceed. It produces accountability that is provable, auditable, and defensible — the institutional capacity to account for consequential decisions in every forum where accountability arrives, without the retrospective reconstruction that the absence of contemporaneous governance makes necessary and that every accountability forum recognizes as inadequate.

Without this layer, scale accelerates fragility rather than resilience. The same execution systems that allow organizations to operate at global scope and institutional breadth allow the consequences of ungoverned decisions to propagate at the same scope and breadth — faster, further, and with greater irreversibility than any institutional recovery mechanism can match after the fact. The organization that cannot govern its decisions before they are executed is an organization whose operational sophistication has become a liability: a mechanism for accelerating and amplifying the consequences of governance failures that its execution architecture was never designed to prevent.

From Execution Scale to Decision Resilience

The next evolution of enterprise is not about doing more, faster. The institutional achievement of the Systems Age — the capacity to execute organizational activity at scale, with consistency, and with the operational precision that systemization produces — has reached a level of development at which additional investment in execution capability produces diminishing institutional returns relative to the governance liabilities that ungoverned decision-making at scale creates. The next evolution is about deciding better, safely — about developing the institutional capacity to exercise consequential authority with the governance discipline that the accountability environments of the next era require, and to do so under the real conditions of organizational life rather than under the idealized conditions that governance frameworks designed for rational actors assume.

It is about recognizing that decisions — not processes — are the true units of institutional risk, responsibility, and consequence. Every process, every system, every operational framework in the modern enterprise exists to execute a direction that a decision has established. The quality of every organizational outcome traces its institutional source to the quality of the decision that authorized the operational activity that produced it. Governing processes without governing the decisions that processes execute is governing the instrument without governing the hand that holds it. The governance of decisions is the foundational governance requirement of the next era — not a supplement to process governance, but the institutional layer above it that makes process governance meaningful.

It is about understanding that governance must occur before outcomes are known — not after they have been produced by the execution systems that ungoverned decisions authorized, and not in the retrospective accountability proceedings that adverse outcomes create. Governance that arrives after the fact is damage management. Governance that occurs before the fact — before the execution system is engaged, before the organizational commitment is established, before the consequences of ungoverned judgment have been set in motion at the scale that operational capability permits — is the only governance that can prevent rather than merely respond to institutional harm. And it is about accepting a new truth about what organizational completeness requires: an organization is not fully designed until its decisions are governed. The execution systems are necessary. The compliance frameworks are necessary. The analytics platforms, the leadership structures, and the policy architectures are necessary. But they are not sufficient. An enterprise whose decisions are ungoverned is an enterprise whose design is incomplete — regardless of how sophisticated, how mature, or how extensively documented its execution architecture may be.

Who This Book Is For

This book is written for those who carry real institutional responsibility — the individuals whose authority determines what organizations will do, whose accountability covers the consequences of what organizations have done, and whose governance obligations require them to answer not merely for outcomes but for the quality of the judgment that produced them. It is written for Chief Executive Officers who must answer not only what happened but why it was allowed to happen — who bear the institutional accountability for the governance quality of every consequential decision made under their authority, and who will be required to account for that quality in the accountability forums of the next era that will not accept procedural compliance as a sufficient governance defense.

It is written for board members who oversee decisions they did not personally make — who carry the fiduciary obligation to govern decision quality across the full range of consequential organizational authority without the operational visibility into how decisions are actually made that that obligation requires, and who need the governance infrastructure that would provide that visibility. It is written for Chief Financial Officers and general counsel tasked with defending actions taken years earlier — whose professional obligations require them to account for organizational decisions in legal, regulatory, and governance proceedings that apply the contemporaneous evidentiary standard to judgments whose governance record may not meet it. It is written for leaders in regulated, high-impact, or public trust industries — whose accountability obligations are the most demanding, whose exposure to governance failures is the most consequential, and for whom the absence of GD-II™ is the most immediately costly institutional vulnerability. It is written for builders of enterprises that must endure scrutiny, not just growth — for the institutional architects who understand that the durability of the organizations they are building depends on governance quality rather than merely on operational performance.

It is not a management trend — a governance fashion whose institutional implications are cyclical and whose relevance will recede as the next operational priority displaces it in the institutional attention of organizational leadership. It is not a methodology — a defined set of practices and tools whose application will produce governance outcomes through procedural compliance with a specified sequence of steps. It is not a software manual — a technical specification for the implementation of a technological platform whose deployment will satisfy the governance requirements of the next era through automated process execution. It is a reframing of what it means for an organization to be complete — of the full scope of institutional design that responsible organizational governance requires, and of the missing layer whose absence has made modern enterprises incomplete in ways that the Systems Age produced the conditions for but was never equipped to recognize.

The Question That Defines the Future

Previous generations of institutional leaders asked the governance questions that the challenges of their era made most urgent. Can this business run without its founder — can the institutional capability that produced it be preserved and extended beyond the individual whose expertise and authority created it? Can this process scale — can the operational logic of a functioning model be extended to new volumes of activity and new organizational contexts without losing the institutional quality that made the model worth replicating? Can this system be replicated — can the execution architecture that produces consistent outcomes in one operational environment be transferred to others with sufficient fidelity to deliver the same institutional results?

These were the right questions for their era. They were the questions whose answers produced the Great Systemization and the operational achievements it delivered. But they are not the questions that define the institutional challenges of the next era. This generation of institutional leaders must ask something more difficult — a question that the accountability environments, the technological capabilities, and the governance requirements of the current era have made both unavoidable and urgent: should this decision exist, and can we defend it when it matters most?

The organizations that can answer that question — clearly, evidence-based, and without hindsight — will define the next era of enterprise. Not because they will never make wrong decisions: the irreducible uncertainty of consequential institutional action in complex environments ensures that even governed decisions will sometimes produce outcomes that subsequent examination would have counseled against. But because they will be able to account for their decisions in every forum where accountability arrives — because the contemporaneous governance record of their decision-making will establish the quality of the judgment behind each consequential commitment in a form that does not depend on retrospective construction, does not require the institutional politics of blame attribution, and does not erode under the scrutiny of the accountability forums that the next era will bring to bear on the governance quality of every organization that operates at the scale where decisions matter.

That evolution is no longer optional. The forces reshaping institutional accountability — the regulatory demands, the legal standards, the board governance expectations, the talent dynamics, and the public trust conditions that the preceding chapters establish as the defining institutional environment of the next era — have made the governance of consequential decisions not a governance aspiration but a structural requirement. This book is about how and why — about the institutional logic, the structural architecture, and the practical transition through which modern enterprises move from the Systems Age to the governed enterprise that the next era requires.

Contents

Claim of Novelty and Institutional Contribution iii

PREFACE vii
Why This Book Exists

CHAPTER 1 1
The Great Systemization:
How We Solved Execution and Exposed a New Class of Failure

CHAPTER 2 13
The Invisible Assumption:
Why Organizations Confuse Process Compliance with Decision Soundness

CHAPTER 3 24
When Perfect Systems Execute the Wrong Decision:
How Organizational Excellence Can Faithfully Produce Institutional Failure

CHAPTER 4 35
What a Decision Really Is:
The Organizational Definition That Governance Requires

CHAPTER 5 46
Why Documentation Is Not Evidence:
The Distinction That Separates Records from Governance

CHAPTER 6 57
The Human Variable Under Pressure:
Why Judgment Degrades Predictably and What Governance Must Account For

CHAPTER 7 69
NFRASTRUCT® and the Constitutional Logic of Governed Decision Authority:
Why Power Must Not Only Be Exercised — It Must Be Governed

CHAPTER 8 82
Decision-Governance Defined:
Precision Without Abstraction — What It Is, What It Is Not, and Why the Distinction
Is Non-Negotiable

CHAPTER 9 94
Why Existing Enterprise Functions Cannot Govern Decisions:
Structural Limits, Not Capability Gaps — Why the Solution Does Not Already Exist
Inside the Enterprise

INTERLUDE 104
Why AI Forces Decision-Governance to Become Infrastructure:
From Accelerant to Constitutional Imperative — The Structural Consequence of
Machine-Amplified Execution

CHAPTER 10 112
Governed Decision-Intelligence Infrastructure™ (GD-II™):
The Missing Layer — Defined as Infrastructure, Not Philosophy

CHAPTER 11 125
The Governed Enterprise:
What Actually Changes When Decisions Are No Longer Invisible

CHAPTER 12 137
Why This Category Never Existed:
The Conditions That Prevented Governed Decision-Intelligence™ (GD-I™) from
Emerging — Until Now

CHAPTER 13 149
When Decisions Become Defensible:
Boards, Courts, Regulators, and the New Standard of Accountability

CHAPTER 14 163
Speed Without Recklessness:
How Governed Decisions Enable Faster, Safer Execution

CHAPTER 15 175
The Enterprises That Will Survive the Next 25 Years:
Why Decision-Governance Is Becoming a Condition of Survival

CHAPTER 16 187
Building the Missing Infrastructure:
How Organizations Transition From Systems to Governed Decision-Intelligence™ (GD-I™)

RELATED WORK AND STRUCTURAL DISTINCTION 201

AFTERWORD 207
The Architecture Behind the Argument

APPENDIX 215

CHAPTER 1

THE GREAT SYSTEMIZATION

How We Solved Execution and Exposed a New Class of Failure

There was a moment in modern business when everything seemed solvable. Quality problems yielded to standardized processes. Inconsistent outcomes gave way to documented workflows. Dependence on individuals was replaced by the replicability of systems. Growth constraints were overcome by scaling what already worked. The answers felt clear, and for organizations willing to commit to the discipline of systemization, those answers delivered measurable and durable results.

This moment — spanning the late twentieth century into the early twenty-first — was defined by a single, powerful idea: execution could be engineered. If the right process was designed, documented, and enforced with sufficient rigor, the outcome would follow. This was not merely a management theory. It was a practical transformation that reshaped how industries, enterprises, and institutions understood their own operations and their own capacity for sustainable scale.

And for a time, it worked. Organizations learned to separate work from the people who performed it. Tasks became roles. Roles became functions. Functions became departments. Departments became machines that could be optimized, measured, and scaled without dependence on any single individual. The institutional knowledge that had once resided in the minds of founders and senior practitioners was codified, transferred, and replicated across geographies, hierarchies, and generations of leadership. What had been personal became institutional. What had been informal became structural. What had been fragile became durable.

This transformation — what can fairly be called the Great Systemization — was one of the most consequential and successful managerial evolutions in history. It made the modern enterprise possible. It also planted the seeds of a new kind of failure — one that would take decades to become fully visible, and that remains misdiagnosed to this day.

When the Business Became a Machine

Before systemization, most organizations were structurally fragile. Knowledge lived in heads rather than in documented processes. Outcomes depended on personalities rather than on repeatable methods. Growth was constrained by the cognitive and relational bandwidth of the individuals at the center of operations. When key individuals left, institutional capability often left with them, requiring organizations to rebuild knowledge from memory rather than from records. Scale magnified this fragility rather than resolving it — as organizations grew, the complexity of coordinating individual judgment across a larger workforce increased risk rather than reducing it.

Systemization changed that. By codifying how work should be done — by capturing the steps, the standards, the escalation paths, and the accountability structures that had previously been informal and therefore unreliable — businesses gained something they had never reliably possessed before: the ability to produce consistent outcomes independent of the specific individuals performing the work. This was a genuine architectural advance. It separated institutional capability from individual talent, and in doing so, it made institutional capability reproducible.

The specific gains were structural and durable. Predictability emerged because processes defined expectations rather than leaving them to interpretation. Consistency followed because documented standards replaced informal and variable practice. Replicability became possible because the logic of a functioning operation could be transferred to new locations, new teams, and new leadership without reinventing the underlying design. Transferability allowed organizations to grow beyond their founders, their original markets, and their founding cultures, because the system — not the individual — carried institutional capability across time and distance.

The business no longer required exceptional people to function at a high level. It required ordinary people operating within extraordinary systems. This shift was genuinely liberating at the institutional level. It allowed companies to grow beyond the limitations of their founders, beyond the constraints of specific locations, and beyond the dependence on individual expertise. It created the modern enterprise as a repeatable, scalable, and transferable form of organization — one that could survive leadership transitions, geographic expansion, and generational change without losing the operational capability that defined it.

And it trained leaders, boards, and institutions to think in a new and ultimately consequential way: if the system can be defined clearly enough, the outcome will take care of itself. This belief did not require explicit articulation because it was reinforced daily by results. Systemized organizations outperformed unsystemized ones. Process-driven enterprises grew faster, scaled more reliably, and produced more consistent outcomes than enterprises that depended on heroic individual performance. The evidence was everywhere. In time, the belief became orthodoxy — and orthodoxy became the operating assumption that governed a generation of enterprise design.

The Rise of Operational Confidence

As systems matured, confidence in those systems followed — and deepened with each successive layer of operational sophistication. Organizations accumulated process maps that defined every significant workflow. Standard operating procedures replaced ad hoc guidance with documented instruction. Key performance indicators provided quantified evidence of compliance and output. Dashboards gave leadership continuous visibility into operational performance across functions and geographies. Certifications validated adherence to recognized external standards. Internal controls limited variance and created audit trails. Periodic audits provided independent confirmation that the architecture was functioning as designed.

The cumulative effects were measurable and widely observed. Execution errors declined as processes enforced correct sequencing. Variability narrowed as standards replaced discretion for routine actions. Accountability became procedural — attached to roles and responsibilities rather than to personal relationships or informal authority structures. In many cases, performance improved dramatically across every quantifiable dimension: quality, speed, cost, output, and customer satisfaction. It became reasonable — almost inevitable — to assume that good systems produced good results. The assumption felt empirically supported because, in the domain of execution, it often was.

This assumption was rarely stated explicitly because it did not need to be. It was embedded in the logic of operational management itself, reinforced by every maturity framework, every certification standard, and every consulting engagement that treated operational sophistication as the primary determinant of organizational health. Every metric that improved, every audit that passed, every process that scaled without failure reinforced the same foundational conclusion: the system is working; therefore, the decisions embedded within it are sound. The assumption was not tested because it appeared, from the evidence of operational performance, to be confirmed.

But something important was happening beneath that surface — a parallel and less visible shift that would take decades to become fully legible. As operational confidence rose, the language of organizational health was becoming synonymous with the language of operational compliance. Governance, in the minds of most enterprise leaders, was becoming process adherence. Accountability was becoming documentation. Evidence was becoming approval records. And in that quiet conflation — in the slow substitution of procedural confirmation for substantive governance — the capacity to govern decisions themselves was steadily, structurally eroding.

The organizations accumulating the most operational sophistication were, paradoxically, the organizations most at risk of this conflation. The more mature the system, the more complete the procedural record, the stronger the internal confidence that governance was present. No one had designed this outcome. It emerged organically from the logic of systemization itself — from the rational institutional response to an era in which execution was the primary problem, and systems were the demonstrated solution. The problem was that the solution to the execution problem was being applied, by institutional inertia, to a different problem entirely.

What Systems Quietly Replaced

As systems grew stronger, something else grew weaker: judgment — not in the sense of intelligence or intent, but in the precise institutional sense of conscious decision ownership. When execution is heavily systemized, individual decisions feel smaller. They feel embedded in the workflow rather than distinct from it. They feel procedural rather than consequential. Authority disperses into processes, and the discrete human act of deciding — with full awareness of what is being chosen, what is being rejected, and who bears the accountability for that choice — becomes structurally invisible within the broader operation of the system.

This is not a failure of individual capability. It is a predictable structural consequence of mature systemization. When every step has a process owner, every escalation has a defined path, and every outcome has a procedural explanation, the organization gradually ceases to exercise the discipline of deliberate decision ownership. The cognitive and institutional energy that might have been directed at questioning the decision — at asking whether this choice is justified, evidence-based, proportionate to its consequences, and exercised by an authority operating within appropriate constraints — is redirected toward executing the process correctly and completely.

Over time, the questions organizations ask about their own actions shift in ways that feel minor but are, in practice, fundamental. The questions that once defined governance — Who decided this? On what basis was this decision made? What alternatives were considered and on what grounds were they rejected? What risks were acknowledged and accepted by the authorizing party? — are quietly displaced by questions of procedural compliance. Was the process followed? Was the relevant policy violated? Was the form completed in full? Was the required approval logged in the system?

The shift appears minor at the level of daily operations. In practice, it is the difference between an organization that governs its decisions and one that merely records its procedures. The question of whether this was the right decision is replaced, gradually and without deliberate intent, by the question of whether this was the correct procedure. That substitution is subtle in its operation and dangerous in its consequences — not because procedural compliance is unimportant, but because it creates the systematic appearance of accountability without its substance. Organizations that cannot distinguish between the governance of decisions and the recording of procedures are operating with a structural vulnerability that no additional process can address, because the vulnerability is not in the process layer.

The Illusion of Safety

Systemization creates a powerful and persistent illusion: that adherence equals correctness. When every step was followed, when every approval was logged, when every policy box was checked, the conclusion feels inevitable — the outcome must be defensible. The organization did what it was designed to do. The process produced the result it was designed to produce. The system functioned. And yet the decision that initiated the entire sequence — the decision that determined what the system would execute and against whom — was never evaluated, never tested against any standard of justified authority, and never required to produce a contemporaneous evidentiary basis for the authority it claimed.

Systems do not validate decisions. They validate compliance with process. These are not the same thing and treating them as equivalent is the central structural error of the modern enterprise. Procedural compliance confirms that defined steps were followed in the correct sequence by the designated parties. It does not confirm that the decision to take those steps was sound, proportionate to the risk, grounded in legitimate evidence, or exercised by an authority operating within appropriate institutional constraints. A hiring decision that complies with every applicable procedural requirement can still be unjustified. A termination that follows every documented step can still lack a legitimate evidentiary basis. A leadership promotion that passes every formal review can still represent a governance failure of the first order.

In fact, systemized environments often make decision risk harder to see, not easier. The presence of structure creates a pervasive sense of control that may not correspond to actual governance. Dashboards are green, audits are clean, forms are complete, approvals are logged — and yet the decisions driving outcomes are ungoverned, unexamined, and accountable to no standard beyond procedural compliance. This is how enterprises become confident in the decisions they should be questioning. The system provides institutional cover that judgment alone should not receive.

The illusion is further reinforced by the absence of immediate consequences. Ungoverned decisions do not always produce visible harm on the day they are made. They accumulate. They compound. They interact with other ungoverned decisions in ways that are not visible until the combined consequences become impossible to manage. They surface weeks, months, or years after the fact — in litigation, in regulatory action, in cultural collapse, in the erosion of institutional trust that cannot be recovered through procedure alone. And when consequences finally arrive, the organization points to its procedures as evidence of good faith, only to discover that procedure is not a substitute for governed judgment in any forum that actually matters — not in courts, not before regulators, not before boards of directors, not in public.

The deepest consequence of this illusion is not the individual failure it enables. It is the institutional confidence it produces. An organization that believes its systems are governing its decisions is an organization that has stopped looking for the governance gap. It has answered the question it should be asking — are our decisions governed? — by pointing to evidence that answers a different question entirely: are our processes documented and followed? Those are not the same question. The organizations most exposed to ungoverned decision risk are frequently those with the most mature operational architectures, because maturity generates confidence, and confidence reduces the urgency of questions that the system has structurally obscured.

When Systems Become Amplifiers

Systems scale whatever they touch. This is their defining characteristic and their most consequential institutional property. When the underlying decision is sound — when the authority exercised is proportionate, evidence-based, and appropriately constrained — systems are genuine multipliers of good outcomes. They allow a sound decision to be executed consistently, at scale, across the full operational breadth of the organization. They make good judgment durable and transferable across time, geography, and leadership transitions.

When the underlying decision is flawed, systems operate with identical efficiency as multipliers of harm. They allow an unjustified decision to be executed with the same consistency, at the same scale, and across the same organizational breadth. They make poor judgment equally durable, equally transferable, and far more difficult to interrupt once the execution machinery has been engaged. The system does not distinguish between sound and unsound decisions. It was not designed to. It executes both with identical fidelity to the process it was built to enforce.

This is the central paradox of the Great Systemization: the better organizations became at execution, the faster they could execute the wrong decision — and the more difficult it became to interrupt, reverse, or even recognize that execution once it was underway. A flawed hiring decision executed through a mature systemized process generates onboarding records, performance documentation, compliance confirmations, and institutional entrenchment before its consequences are understood. A governance failure executed through a sophisticated approval chain produces a trail of procedural evidence that makes the failure harder to name, harder to attribute, and harder to reverse.

Because the execution is flawless, the decision that authorized it often escapes scrutiny entirely. The organization examines its process. It validates its compliance records. It confirms that each step was taken in the correct order by the correct designated party. And it reaches the conclusion that nothing went wrong — right up until the consequences of the original, ungoverned decision become impossible to contain. At that point, the same system that accelerated the harm is being examined as evidence of organizational competence. It was functioning exactly as designed. The failure was never in the system. It was in the decision that the system was given to execute — a decision that existed entirely outside the jurisdiction of any governance structure the organization had built.

The Pattern No One Wanted to Name

Across industries and across decades, the same pattern has emerged with predictable consistency. Hiring decisions that complied with every applicable policy nonetheless introduced organizational risk that compounded over years. Promotions that followed every procedural step nonetheless elevated authority in ways that created downstream harm to institutions and individuals alike. Cultural failures occurred in organizations where, by every formal measure, nothing was technically wrong. Institutional scandals unfolded in environments where every participant did their assigned job and no one questioned — because no mechanism required anyone to question the decision that set the entire sequence in motion.

Post-mortems followed each failure. Committees were formed to review what had occurred. Policies were examined, revised, and tightened. Compliance frameworks were extended. Training curricula were updated to address the specific failure mode that had surfaced. And yet, the same categories of failure reappeared at regular intervals — not because organizations failed to take the review process seriously, but because the review process was itself limited to examining the execution layer. It could identify where a process step was not followed. It could not identify where a decision was ungoverned. It could recommend procedural correction. It could not recommend governance infrastructure that did not yet exist.

The root cause was consistently not recognized as an architectural problem. Organizations understood their failures through available frames: an execution problem, a cultural problem, a leadership failure, a compliance gap. Each of those framings produced interventions appropriate to the framing — more process, more training, more oversight, more controls. None of them addressed the structural absence at the center of the failure: that consequential decisions were being made and executed within highly systemized environments that possessed no mechanism for governing the decision itself — no infrastructure for testing it before exposure, no function for preserving its evidentiary basis at the moment of authority, no institutional structure for holding the human judgment behind it accountable to any standard beyond procedural compliance.

The problem was not insufficient systemization. It was never insufficient systemization. Additional processes applied to an ungoverned decision layer do not govern the decisions. It governs the execution of whatever the decisions authorize. The problem was ungoverned decisions operating inside highly systemized environments — and the persistent institutional assumption that the health of the system was equivalent to the soundness of the decisions the system was executing. That assumption was the source of the failure, and it could not be corrected by the same layer of operational architecture that produced it.

What made the pattern so difficult to name was precisely the appearance of rigor that surrounded each failure. The organizations that experienced these failures were not undisciplined. They were, in most cases, highly systemized. Their procedures were documented. Their approvals were logged. Their audits were current. The external signature of governance was present in every record. What was absent — structurally absent, by design rather than by oversight — was any mechanism for governing the decision that set each sequence in motion. Naming that absence as the root cause required a recognition that the entire organizational architecture of the modern enterprise had been built one layer short of complete.

The Unasked Question

Systemization solved how work gets done. It answered the question of execution with extraordinary sophistication and discipline. It did not solve — and was never designed to solve — the question of whether the work should be conducted at all, whether the decision to initiate it was justified and evidence-based, whether the alternatives were fairly evaluated against a legitimate standard, or whether the authority exercising the decision was operating within appropriate constraints and with appropriate contemporaneous accountability.

Those questions belong to a different layer entirely. They are not answered by process maps or standard operating procedures, which define how designated actions are to be carried out rather than whether those actions should be authorized. They are not confirmed by audits or certifications, which validate adherence to defined standards rather than the soundness of the decisions that created those standards. They are not preserved in approval logs or compliance documentation, which record that designated parties performed their assigned roles rather than establishing the evidentiary basis on which consequential authority was exercised.

Answering those questions requires a different institutional function — one that operates above the execution layer, not within it. One that governs the decision before execution begins rather than validating the process after execution is complete. One that requires decisions to meet a standard of evidence, authority, and accountability before they are permitted to proceed — not after their consequences have already propagated through the system at scale and become irreversible.

This is the question that modern enterprises have not been systematically asking — not because they lack the intelligence to recognize its importance, but because the infrastructure required to ask it and enforce the answer at the institutional level has never been built. The absence of this question has not been an oversight by any individual organization. It has been a structural condition of the entire era — the predictable result of organizations that built extraordinary execution capacity without building any corresponding capacity for the pre-execution governance of the decisions that authorize execution. That gap is now a measurable source of institutional risk, legal exposure, regulatory consequence, and organizational harm.

The Boundary Systems Cannot Cross

There is a hard and definable limit to what systems can do. Systems can standardize known actions by converting informal practice into documented, enforceable procedure. They can reduce variability by applying consistent standards across different individuals, locations, and time periods. They can enforce consistency by making deviation from established process visible, measurable, and subject to correction. They can record outcomes by capturing what was done, when it was done, and by whom — creating a historical record of execution that can be reviewed, audited, and used as the basis for operational improvement.

Systems cannot evaluate human judgment under pressure. When authority is exercised under conditions of ambiguity, competing interests, time compression, or incomplete information — the conditions that characterize virtually every consequential decision at the enterprise level — no process architecture can substitute for governance of the decision itself. The process can define who is authorized to decide. It cannot evaluate whether the judgment being exercised meets a standard of care appropriate to the consequences of the decision.

Systems cannot capture why a choice was made at the moment it was made. They can record that a decision was taken and that a process was followed. They cannot capture the reasoning that led to the decision, the evidence that was considered and weighed, the alternatives that were evaluated and rejected, or the risks that were knowingly accepted at the precise moment authority was exercised. That contemporaneous record — the record that distinguishes defensible from indefensible judgment — requires a governance function that exists above the execution layer and operates before the decision is committed.

Systems cannot preserve rejected alternatives. The history of a consequential decision includes not only what was chosen but what was considered and not chosen, and the basis on which the alternatives were set aside. That record — available only at the moment of decision, before outcomes are known and before memory is shaped by result — is among the most important categories of decision evidence when accountability arrives in any institutional forum. It does not exist in any execution system. It exists only if an infrastructure layer was designed specifically to capture it before the decision was committed to execution.

Systems cannot hold authority accountable without hindsight. Post-hoc accountability — accountability that arrives after consequences are known and after institutional memory has been shaped by outcome — is structurally limited as a governance mechanism in ways that are fundamental rather than correctable through better process design. It cannot establish with reliability what was known at the moment of decision. It cannot preserve the evidentiary basis for a decision that was never required to produce one. It cannot undo the harm that accumulated between the moment the decision was made, and the moment accountability arrived. That boundary — the boundary between what systems can do and what governance of decisions requires — is not a gap in operational design. It is the end of the jurisdiction of systems entirely. It marks the point at which a new infrastructure layer becomes not merely useful but architecturally necessary.

Recognizing this boundary is not a criticism of systems. It is an accurate description of their design. Systems were built to execute. They were not built to govern the authority that authorizes execution. That is not a deficiency — it is a scope definition. The deficiency belongs to the enterprise that has treated scope as completeness, that has interpreted the absence of execution failure as the presence of governance, and that has never built the layer above systems that would allow it to ask and answer the most important question in institutional design: Is this decision worthy of execution at all?

What Comes Next

The Great Systemization was necessary. Without it, the modern enterprise would not exist in its current form. The capacity to scale operations, transfer institutional knowledge, reduce variability, and produce consistent outcomes across large and complex organizations represents a genuine and durable achievement of twentieth-century management. It remains essential. Systems continue to constitute the foundational execution layer of every organization that operates at scale. Nothing in this chapter — nothing in this book — argues against systems. The argument is for what must be built above them.

The Great Systemization was never meant to be the final evolution of enterprise architecture. It solved execution. It did not solve GD-II™. It created the conditions under which consequential decisions could be made at unprecedented speed and scale. It did not create the infrastructure required to govern those decisions before they were executed — to test them before exposure, to preserve their evidentiary basis at the moment of authority, to hold the human judgment behind them accountable to a standard capable of withstanding scrutiny from boards, regulators, courts, and the public institutions that now routinely examine how decisions were made, not merely what results they produced.

To understand why modern enterprises still fail despite having systems — why organizations with mature operational models, sophisticated platforms, formalized leadership structures, and policies for nearly every conceivable scenario continue to produce preventable harm, systemic risk, and institutional collapse — it is necessary to look beyond the execution layer and confront what has never been built above it. The failure is not in the system. The system is functioning. The failure is in the ungoverned decision that the system was given to execute.

That recognition requires examining what a decision actually is — not as a procedural event within a workflow, but as a consequential act of authority with evidentiary requirements, accountability implications, and governance obligations that no execution system can satisfy on its own. It requires understanding the invisible assumption that has allowed ungoverned decisions to persist inside governed systems for decades without recognition. It requires accepting that the next evolution of enterprise is not faster execution, better data, or more sophisticated operational technology. It is the governance of the decision itself — before exposure, before execution, before consequences that cannot be undone. That is where the next evolution begins.

The chapters that follow trace what that evolution requires. They examine the nature of decisions as distinct from procedures, the human variables that make ungoverned authority dangerous at scale, and the specific infrastructure architecture — GD-II™ — that constitutes the missing layer above systems. They establish why this infrastructure category has never existed before, why it cannot be simulated through existing enterprise functions, and what it means for an organization, its leaders, and its decisions to be genuinely governed rather than merely systemized. The Great Systemization was the necessary foundation. What must come next is the subject of this book.

CHAPTER 2

THE INVISIBLE ASSUMPTION

Why Organizations Confuse Process Compliance with Decision Soundness

Every mature organization carries an assumption so deeply embedded that it is rarely spoken aloud. It is not written in policy manuals. It is not debated in strategy sessions. It is not voted on by boards or included in governance frameworks. It requires no formal adoption because it has already been adopted — absorbed into the institutional logic of the organization through years of reinforced operational practice. And yet it governs behavior at every level of decision-making, in every function, across every industry in which systemized execution has become the dominant mode of operation.

The assumption is this: if the process was followed, the decision must have been sound. This belief feels reasonable. It feels consistent with the discipline of mature operational management. It feels responsible in environments where scale demands speed, and authority must move without constant friction. It is also the single most dangerous assumption in contemporary enterprise — not because it is always wrong, but because it is structurally unchallenged. It sits beneath every governance framework, every compliance architecture, and every accountability structure in the modern organization, never examined, never tested, and never required to prove its own validity.

The cost of that unchallenged assumption is not abstract. It is visible in every institutional failure that follows the same pattern: the process was followed, the approvals were logged, the policies were not violated — and yet the decision that the process executed was unjustified, ungoverned, and, in retrospect, indefensible. Understanding why this assumption persists, how it shapes institutional behavior, and what it costs organizations that never confront it is essential to understanding what Governed Decision-Intelligence Infrastructure™ (GD-II™) exists to address.

How the Assumption Took Hold

The invisible assumption did not arise from negligence or from a failure of organizational intelligence. It emerged from success — specifically, from the genuine and observable success of process discipline as a solution to the execution problems that defined enterprise management in the latter half of the twentieth century. As organizations systemized execution, they learned something powerful and empirically supported: process discipline reduces chaos. When procedures are clear, consistently followed, and reinforced through training and oversight, outcomes improve. Variance shrinks. Errors decline. The operational environment becomes more predictable and, by measurable standards, safer.

Over time, the organization internalizes a quiet equation: process adherence equals organizational safety. This equation was earned through legitimate experience. In the domain of execution — where the question being answered is how work should be performed rather than whether a particular authority is justified — the equation holds. A process that governs how a product is manufactured, how a customer request is handled, or how a financial transaction is recorded produces genuine safety when followed, because the safety being produced is safety against execution variance. The process was designed to prevent that variance, and it does.

The problem arises when the equation is extended — by organizational inertia and institutional convenience rather than by deliberate design — to the domain of decisions. When process adherence is treated as equivalent to decision soundness across all categories of institutional action, including the consequential human acts of authority that determine what will be done and to whom, the equation fails. But it fails silently, because the procedural record remains intact. The approvals are present. The documentation is complete. The audit trail is unbroken. And so, the assumption survives, reinforced by the absence of visible contradiction.

Once the equation is accepted as a general institutional truth, scrutiny shifts in a way that is difficult to reverse. Leaders stop asking why a decision was made and start asking whether the correct procedural steps were followed. Governance becomes procedural rather than substantive — focused on the form of compliance rather than the content of judgment. Accountability becomes administrative rather than evidentiary — attached to role completion rather than to the reasoning behind authority exercised. The decision itself fades into the background of the process, invisible within the workflow that records its consequences without capturing its basis.

The Comfort of Checklists

Checklists are seductive instruments of organizational management. They create a reliable sense of control by converting what might otherwise be a complex judgment call into a defined sequence of verifiable steps. They reduce cognitive load by specifying what must be done, in what order, before a process can be considered complete. They transform judgment into sequence — and in doing so, they deliver genuine value in domains where the primary risk is execution variance, where the goal is consistency, and where the sequence itself has been validated against the category of problem it is designed to address.

But checklists were never designed to validate decisions under uncertainty. They were designed to ensure consistency of execution after a decision had already been made about what would be done. A checklist that governs the onboarding of a new employee assumes that the hiring decision was sound. A checklist that governs the execution of a termination assumes that the decision to terminate was justified. A checklist that governs the approval process for a capital allocation assumes that the decision to pursue the investment was evidence-based and appropriately authorized. The checklist verifies the steps. It does not verify the decision that made those steps relevant.

When organizations rely on checklists to substitute for decision scrutiny — when the completion of a checklist is treated as evidence that the decision it governs was sound — they gain procedural speed at the direct cost of decision awareness. Everything appears orderly. Everything appears compliant. The record is clean, the boxes are checked, and the process is documented in full. The decision that authorized the entire sequence has never been examined against any standard of justified authority. The appearance of control is complete. The substance of governance is absent.

Compliance answers a narrow and binary question: did we do what we said we would do? Decision soundness answers a harder and contextual one: should we have chosen this path at all? The first can be audited mechanically through review of documented steps. The second requires evidence, alternatives, and reasoning captured before outcomes are known — at the moment of decision, by the authority exercising it. When organizations conflate these two questions — when they accept the answer to the first as a proxy for the answer to the second — they confuse procedural correctness with decision integrity. That confusion is rarely deliberate. It emerges naturally in environments where scale demands simplification and where the absence of visible failure reinforces the belief that what is being measured is what matters. But it has consequences that accumulate invisibly until they cannot be ignored.

The Disappearance of Decision Ownership

As process compliance becomes the primary signal of institutional legitimacy, decision ownership does not simply weaken — it diffuses. The discrete human act of deciding, with full awareness of what is being chosen, what is being rejected, and who bears the accountability for the choice, is distributed across a workflow in which no single participant holds or acknowledges the full weight of the decision. Each participant in the process is responsible for their step and only their step. Completing that step correctly is the limit of their institutional accountability.

The language of this diffusion is familiar in every organization that has operated under mature systemization. I followed the process. I escalated appropriately. I signed where required. The committee approved. Each of these statements is accurate as a description of procedural compliance. None of them constitutes an acknowledgment of decision ownership. None of them preserves the reasoning behind the choice, the alternatives that were evaluated, the risks that were knowingly accepted, or the authority that ultimately determined that the decision should proceed. Responsibility fragments. Authority dissolves into workflow. The decision becomes a procedural artifact rather than an accountable act of judgment.

The consequences of this fragmentation are most visible when outcomes come under scrutiny — in board inquiries, regulatory reviews, litigation, or public accountability processes. In those forums, the question being asked is not whether procedures were followed. The question is who decided, on what basis, with what evidence, and with what awareness of the risks that materialized. When decision ownership has been distributed across a workflow in which no participant holds the full accountability, that question cannot be answered directly. It can only be reconstructed — and reconstruction is not the same as contemporaneous truth.

The organization becomes defensible in form but hollow in substance. It has records of every procedural step and no record of the decision that initiated them. It has documentation of compliance and no documentation of judgment. It can demonstrate that the process functioned and cannot demonstrate that the authority exercised within that process was sound. In those forums where the distinction matters most — courts, regulatory proceedings, board investigations — that hollow defensibility is not defensibility at all. It is a structural vulnerability presented in the form of a procedural record.

Why the Assumption Survives Scrutiny

The invisible assumption persists not despite scrutiny but because of the institutional dynamics that determine what gets scrutinized and what does not. The assumption survives because it protects the interests of every party with the institutional power to challenge it. It protects executives from being required to justify their authority explicitly — to produce, at the moment of decision, a contemporaneous evidentiary basis that would hold under examination independent of the outcome that followed. It protects managers from the professional risk of challenging the decisions of those above them in the authority hierarchy. It protects organizations from confronting the uncomfortable institutional truth that their governance frameworks have been measuring process compliance and calling it judgment.

Most importantly, the assumption protects the system itself from being questioned. When process compliance is accepted as the standard of sound decision-making, the system that defines those processes becomes immune to challenge on the grounds of decision quality. If the system was followed, what else could reasonably be expected? This framing contains the inquiry within the execution layer, where the answer will always be the same: the system functioned. Responsibility for the outcome is diffused across the process. The decision that initiated the sequence is never required to account for itself on its own terms.

This self-protective dynamic is reinforced by the institutional costs of challenging it. An organization that begins to ask whether its process compliance constitutes genuine decision governance is an organization that must confront the gap between what it has been measuring and what governance actually requires. That gap is not a comfortable thing to acknowledge — particularly when the acknowledgment implies that years of institutional confidence in procedural governance were misplaced. The resistance is not malicious. It is the natural institutional response to a recognition that is expensive to act on, and that carries no immediate external mandate.

There is also a temporal dimension to the assumption's persistence. The consequences of ungoverned decisions are typically deferred. They do not surface at the moment the decision is made. They accumulate and compound over time, surfacing when the organizational context that produced them has shifted sufficiently that the connection between the original decision and the present consequence is no longer obvious. By the time the consequence is legible, the decision that produced it has been embedded in the procedural record as a compliant action, and the authority that exercised it has moved on, been promoted, or acquired the institutional standing that makes it institutionally difficult to examine. The assumption survives in part because its costs are deferred long enough that failures appear disconnected from their structural source, making it easier to attribute each outcome to proximate execution causes rather than to the absence of decision governance that permitted the original judgment to proceed without scrutiny.

The assumption also survives because the organizations best positioned to challenge it — the most mature, most systemized, most operationally sophisticated — are the organizations with the greatest institutional investment in its validity. To challenge the assumption is to challenge the governance architecture that those organizations have built, refined, and defended over decades. It is to acknowledge that operational maturity and decision governance are not the same thing, and that the former does not produce the latter. That acknowledgment is not impossible, but it requires a level of institutional candor that the assumption itself has made structurally unavailable. The organizations most exposed to ungoverned decision risk are frequently those least likely to recognize the exposure, because their operational sophistication has provided them with the longest and most reinforced record of process compliance to point to in place of evidence of sound judgment.

The assumption also survives because, in a significant proportion of cases, it produces no visible failure. When a sound decision is executed through a compliant process, the outcome is good, and the assumption appears validated. The correlation between process compliance and sound outcomes — which is real in the execution domain and partial in the decision domain — is interpreted as confirmation that compliance is sufficient. The failures that reveal the assumption's limits are treated as exceptions rather than as evidence of a structural condition. And so, the assumption persists, protected by its own track record in the domain where it is legitimately applicable.

The Post-Mortem Fallacy

When failures occur in organizations operating under the invisible assumption, the response follows a predictable institutional pattern. Reviews are commissioned. Audits are conducted. Corrective action plans are developed. The examination focuses on whether policies were violated, whether controls failed to function as designed, whether training was adequate for the circumstances that produced the failure, and whether the procedural record is complete. These are all legitimate questions within their proper scope. They are not the questions that address the root cause of decision failure.

The questions that would address the root cause are structurally different in character. What alternatives were available to the decision-maker at the moment the decision was made — and were those alternatives fairly evaluated against an evidence-based standard? What signals were present in the environment at the time of the decision that indicated elevated risk — and were those signals surfaced, considered, and appropriately weighted? What pressures — organizational, hierarchical, financial, temporal — shaped the judgment of the authority exercising the decision, and were those pressures acknowledged or suppressed? What authority dynamics created conditions in which dissent was either unavailable or institutionally dangerous? These questions are uncomfortable because they expose something that systems cannot capture and that procedural records cannot preserve: the reality of human decision-making under organizational constraint.

In the absence of a governance infrastructure capable of capturing this reality contemporaneously — at the moment of decision, before outcomes are known — organizations default to what they know. More process is added. More documentation is required. More controls are layered onto the existing architecture. More approvals are introduced into the workflow. Each of these responses treats the failure as an execution problem because the organization possesses only the analytical tools appropriate to execution problems. The decision layer — the layer at which the failure actually originated — remains ungoverned, because the tools to govern it have never been built. The invisible assumption remains intact. And the cycle repeats.

Why More Process Does Not Fix the Problem

The institutional reflex to treat decision failure as an execution problem produces a specific and counterproductive pattern: the accumulation of process in response to failures that process cannot prevent. When a consequential decision produces a harmful outcome, the organization adds another approval requirement, introduces another form, tightens the existing checklist, expands training on compliance procedures, or updates the policy, the failure is retrospectively interpreted as having violated. Each of these responses is rational as a response to an execution failure. None of them addresses a decision failure, because they all operate within the same layer — the execution layer — at which the failure was not located.

The cumulative result of this pattern is an organization that becomes progressively slower, more bureaucratic, and — paradoxically — less capable of recognizing and governing decision risk over time. The system grows heavier with each remediation cycle. The procedural record grows more voluminous. The compliance documentation becomes more comprehensive. And yet the decisions being made within that elaborate procedural architecture remain as ungoverned as they were before each remediation was applied, because the governance gap is not in the execution layer and cannot be closed by additions to it.

What accumulates instead is the institutional confidence that the problem has been addressed. Each remediation produces visible evidence of organizational response: new policies, new controls, new training records, new approval logs. That visible evidence reinforces the assumption that the governance gap has been closed. In reality, the complexity of the system has increased while the governance of its decisions remains unchanged. The organization is slower, more expensive to operate, and no better governed at the decision level than it was before the remediation cycle began.

This is how well-intentioned governance becomes self-defeating. The intention is to prevent future failure. The mechanism is to add process to an execution layer that already failed to prevent the original failure precisely because the failure was not in the execution layer. The result is an organization burdened by the accumulated weight of remediation efforts, each of which addressed the visible signature of a failure without addressing its structural source. Over time, this burden becomes a governance liability in its own right — a system so complex that the decisions embedded within it are even harder to isolate, examine, and hold accountable than they were before.

The Difference Between Legibility and Truth

Systems make organizations legible. They produce records that can be reviewed, audited, and reported. They create artifacts — forms, logs, approvals, certifications — that constitute a visible institutional history of what was done and by whom. They generate reports that translate operational activity into quantified performance indicators. This legibility is genuine and valuable. Without it, large organizations would be operationally opaque, incapable of oversight, and unable to identify execution variance before it compounds into systemic failure.

But legibility is not truth. A decision can be perfectly legible — fully documented, procedurally compliant, supported by a complete audit trail — and remain deeply flawed as an act of judgment. The documentation records what was done. It does not establish that what was done was justified, evidence-based, proportionate to its consequences, or exercised by an authority operating within appropriate constraints. A process can be fully documented and fundamentally misguided. A record can be complete and silent on the reasoning that would distinguish responsible authority from its absence.

When organizations confuse documentation with evidence — when the completeness of a procedural record is treated as validation of the decision the procedure was designed to govern — they mistake visibility for validity. The record is visible. The governance of the decision it documents may be entirely absent. True GD-II™ requires something that systems alone cannot provide: the contextual truth of what was known, considered, evaluated, and accepted at the moment of decision, captured before outcomes are known and preserved in a form that cannot be reshaped by hindsight. That is not what procedural documentation produces. It is what a governed decision produces — and it requires infrastructure that operates above the execution layer.

The Cost of the Assumption

The invisible assumption carries a hidden institutional cost that compounds with each decision cycle in which it goes unchallenged. Decisions become progressively harder to challenge internally, because the standard of sound decision-making — procedural compliance — is easily met and cannot be disputed on its own terms. Authority becomes less accountable over time because the accountability standard has been set at a level that measures process completion rather than decision quality. Risk migrates upward through the organization unnoticed, because the signals of ungoverned decision-making are absorbed into the procedural record without triggering any governance response. Learning degrades into compliance theater — into the production of the documentation that satisfies the visible standard rather than the genuine examination of whether consequential decisions are being made responsibly.

Eventually, organizations find themselves in a position they did not anticipate and cannot easily explain: one where they are unable to account for their most consequential actions in terms that satisfy external scrutiny. Boards ask harder questions about how decisions were actually made and discover that the procedural record answers a different question. Regulators require evidence of decision reasoning and find documentation of process completion. Courts examine intent and judgment through the lens of hindsight and encounter records that were never designed to preserve contemporaneous truth. Public confidence, once eroded by visible failure, cannot be restored by pointing to compliance documentation that was never a substitute for governed judgment.

By the time the organization recognizes that process compliance was never a substitute for GD-II™, it is operating in a reactive posture — defending the gap rather than closing it. The cost of that posture — in legal exposure, regulatory consequence, reputational damage, and institutional loss of trust — substantially exceeds the cost of having built the governance infrastructure that would have prevented it. The assumption that felt responsible, modern, and efficient at the organizational level has, at the institutional level, been an ongoing liability that compounded in silence for as long as it went unexamined.

The Question Systems Cannot Ask

Systems are designed to ask the questions that fall within their scope of operation. Was the required step completed? Was the approval recorded by the designated authority? Was the policy followed as written? Was the form submitted in full and on time? These are the questions that execution systems are built to answer, and they answer them reliably and at scale. The value of that capability is not in question. What is in question is the institutional practice of treating those answers as sufficient for the governance of consequential decisions.

The questions that governance of decisions requires are categorically different. Was this decision responsible under the circumstances as they existed at the time it was made — not as they were later understood, but as they were known? What evidence was available to the decision-maker at the moment of decision, and was that evidence the basis for the choice rather than a post-hoc justification of it? What alternatives were considered, on what grounds were they evaluated, and why was this path chosen over the others that were available? What risks were identified at the time of decision, and were those risks consciously accepted by an authority with the mandate and accountability to accept them?

These questions cannot be asked by a system because they require a governance function that operates at the decision layer rather than the execution layer — a function that intercepts the decision before it becomes an instruction to the execution system, requires it to meet an evidentiary standard, captures the reasoning and alternatives at the moment of authority, and preserves that record in a form that cannot be retroactively altered by knowledge of what followed. No execution system performs this function. No compliance framework requires it. No existing enterprise function is designed for it. Until organizations build the infrastructure capable of asking these questions — and enforcing their answers as conditions of decision execution — they remain exposed at the decision layer, regardless of how mature, comprehensive, or well-documented their execution systems appear.

Where the Next Evolution Begins

The invisible assumption marks the boundary between two distinct eras of enterprise architecture. The Systems Age ends at the point where compliance masquerades as judgment — where the organization's confidence in its governance is proportional to the completeness of its procedural record rather than to the quality of the decisions that the procedures govern. The next evolution begins when organizations accept a harder and more demanding institutional truth: following the process does not absolve the decision. The procedural record establishes compliance. It does not establish governance.

Moving forward from this recognition requires more than a change in perspective. It requires confronting the reality that decisions — not processes, not systems, not compliance frameworks — are the true units of organizational risk, responsibility, and consequence. It requires acknowledging that the governance gap is not in the execution layer and cannot be closed by additions to it. And it requires building the infrastructure layer that has been missing from enterprise architecture since the beginning of the Systems Age: an infrastructure that exists above execution, that governs decisions before they are committed, that requires authority to meet an evidentiary standard before proceeding, and that preserves the contemporaneous truth of consequential judgment in a form capable of withstanding the scrutiny that will eventually arrive.

The organizations that make this transition will not eliminate decision failure. Judgment is irreducibly human, and human judgment will always carry variance. What they will eliminate is the structural condition in which consequential decisions are executed without governance, without evidentiary basis, and without the contemporaneous accountability that distinguishes defensible judgment from its absence. That is the boundary the next evolution crosses. And crossing it begins with naming what has been invisible: the assumption that has governed enterprise decision-making for decades, never examined, never tested, and never required to prove that process compliance and decision soundness are the same thing. They are not. Recognizing that distinction is where the architecture of governed enterprise begins.

CHAPTER 3

WHEN PERFECT SYSTEMS EXECUTE THE WRONG DECISION

How Organizational Excellence Can Faithfully Produce Institutional Failure

There is a moment in nearly every organizational failure when someone says, with genuine confusion: the system worked. They are usually correct. The approvals were obtained. The controls functioned. The process flowed exactly as designed. The records were complete. The audits passed. And still — the outcome was disastrous. This is not an anomaly. It is a structural condition. It is the predictable result of organizations that have mastered execution without building the infrastructure to govern the decisions that execution is given to carry out.

This chapter is about that paradox: how organizations with excellent systems can produce profoundly flawed results — not by accident, not through negligence, but through the faithful operation of architectures that were designed to execute decisions rather than to govern them. Understanding this paradox is not an academic exercise. It is the prerequisite for recognizing why the next evolution of enterprise requires a governance layer that has never been built, and why systems alone — however mature, however sophisticated, however extensively audited — cannot substitute for it.

Systems Multiply Whatever They Are Given

Systems do one thing exceptionally well: they multiply. They multiply efficiency by applying consistent methods to high volumes of activity. They multiply consistency by enforcing the same standards across every instance of a defined process. They multiply speed by removing the friction of individual discretion from routine execution. They multiply reach by extending the operational logic of a functioning model across geographies, teams, and time periods without requiring the physical presence of the individuals who designed it. These are genuine institutional capabilities, and their value is not in dispute.

What is less often acknowledged — and what represents the core structural risk of the Systems Age — is that systems also multiply decisions. A single hiring decision, when executed through a mature systemized process, becomes a pattern that replicates itself across dozens of subsequent decisions made by individuals who observe and internalize the first decision as a precedent. A single promotion rationale, when absorbed into the informal logic of a leadership culture, becomes the unstated standard against which future promotions are evaluated. A single cultural tolerance — a behavior that was observed, addressed procedurally, and allowed to persist — becomes a norm that defines what the organization actually accepts rather than what its policies formally prohibit. A single risk assumption, embedded in an operational decision that was executed without governance, becomes an enterprise posture that shapes how subsequent risks are evaluated, weighted, and accepted across the full scope of the organization's activity.

When the original decision is sound — when the authority that authorized it was exercised responsibly, with appropriate evidence, with genuine consideration of alternatives, and with conscious acceptance of the risks it carried — scale is a genuine institutional gift. Sound judgment, multiplied by a mature execution system, produces outcomes that are durable, defensible, and consistently aligned with the organization's legitimate interests and obligations. When the original decision is flawed — when the authority that authorized it was exercised without governance, without contemporaneous evidence, without the structural requirement to consider alternatives or acknowledge risk — scale becomes a liability of the first order. The flawed decision is replicated with the same fidelity, extended with the same reach, and entrenched with the same institutional momentum as a sound one. The system does not discriminate. It amplifies whatever it is given.

How Early Signals Disappear

In systemized environments, the early signals of decision failure are characteristically subtle — and the organizational logic of mature systemization makes them exceptionally easy to dismiss. When a consequential decision has been made without governance, and its consequences begin to surface in the form of early warning indicators, the first institutional response is almost never to examine the decision. It is to explain the signals in terms that are consistent with the existing process architecture and that do not require any challenge to the authority that exercised the original judgment.

Performance issues that trace their origin to a flawed hiring decision are attributed to onboarding gaps, to the complexity of the role, or to the individual's adjustment period — all of which are explanations that point toward process refinements rather than decision reexamination. Behavioral concerns that reflect an authority dynamic created by a governance failure in promotion are reframed as style differences, as personality conflicts, or as change resistance on the part of the individuals whose legitimate concerns are being suppressed — all of which are framings that protect the decision rather than expose it. Cultural friction that has its source in a single decision to tolerate conduct that violated the organization's stated values is labeled a change management challenge, an engagement issue, or a communication failure — all of which direct institutional attention toward execution interventions rather than toward the decision that created the condition.

Risk indicators that are the direct consequence of a risk assumption embedded in an ungoverned decision are normalized as edge cases, treated as acceptable variance within established tolerances, or absorbed into operational metrics in ways that prevent them from triggering the governance response they require. Each of these explanations feels reasonable in isolation. Each fits comfortably within the existing process logic of a mature organization. Each is plausible as a description of a transient operational condition rather than a structural consequence of an ungoverned decision. And each delays confrontation with the underlying judgment failure long enough for the decision's consequences to compound beyond the point at which they can be managed without significant institutional cost.

Because the system is functioning — because the processes are operating as designed and the procedural record is intact — leaders assume that the decision itself must be viable. The system's health is interpreted as evidence of the decision's soundness, which is precisely the invisible assumption operating at its most dangerous. This is how small judgment errors survive long enough to become institutional crises. The system provides the early signals with enough procedural explanation to prevent them from being recognized as what they are: evidence that the decision authorizing the system's execution was never sound.

The Illusion of Reversibility

One of the most consequential and persistent assumptions in modern organizations is that decisions are easily reversible. This belief is reinforced by the structural features of mature execution systems, which include mechanisms — transfers, reassignments, performance improvement plans, reorganizations, policy updates — that create the appearance of ongoing adjustability. The organization observes these mechanisms and concludes that no decision is truly final, that every path remains open for correction, and that the existence of remediation options is equivalent to the retention of genuine decision control. This conclusion is structurally incorrect, and its incorrectness compounds with scale.

Many of the most consequential decisions in organizational life are not truly reversible. Once authority is granted to an individual — particularly authority over other people, over organizational culture, over resource allocation, or over the direction of consequential operations — that authority begins immediately to reshape behavior in ways that are not corrected by the procedural reversal of the original decision. The individuals whose behavior has been shaped by the granted authority adapt their expectations, their relationships, and their institutional standing to the new reality. When the authority is subsequently withdrawn or modified, those adaptations do not reset. The behavioral and cultural consequences of the original decision persist, shaped by and traceable to the judgment that was never governed.

Once organizational culture has shifted in response to an ungoverned decision — once a behavioral norm has been established, once a tolerance has been embedded, once a precedent has been set for how authority is exercised or how dissent is managed — that shift resists correction through procedural means alone. Culture is not a policy artifact. It is the accumulated behavioral logic of how an organization actually operates, as distinguished from how its documents say it operates. Correcting a cultural shift that traces its origin to an ungoverned decision requires more than a policy update. It requires an institutional reckoning with the decision itself — a reckoning that the absence of contemporaneous decision evidence makes extraordinarily difficult to conduct with the clarity that genuine correction requires.

Once trust has been eroded by the consequences of an ungoverned decision — trust between leadership and staff, between the organization and its regulators, between the institution and the public it serves — that erosion does not reset when the procedural response to the visible failure is complete. Trust is rebuilt through demonstrated behavioral change over time, not through documentation of remediation efforts. Once precedent has been set — once a decision has been made, executed, and allowed to stand as the organization's implicit position on the class of judgment it represents — that precedent propagates through every subsequent decision that is evaluated against the same informal standard. Systems create the structural illusion of control over consequences that are, in reality, cumulative, path-dependent, and frequently irreversible by the time the organization recognizes their source. By the time reversal is attempted, the cost is already embedded in the organization's culture, its relationships, its regulatory standing, and its institutional memory.

How Authority Hides in Process

In systemized organizations, the exercise of consequential authority rarely announces itself as a discrete and identifiable act. It hides inside the operational architecture of the organization — inside approval chains that distribute sign-off across multiple parties without assigning ownership to any of them, inside committees that provide collective cover for decisions that no single member would be willing to own individually, inside escalation paths that create the appearance of deliberation without the substance of it, and inside standard operating procedures that convert what are, in reality, consequential acts of judgment into routine procedural steps that feel too embedded in operational flow to be examined as authority exercised.

The effect of this concealment is profound. No single individual appears to be the decision-maker in the sense that would require them to produce a contemporaneous evidentiary basis for their judgment. Responsibility diffuses across roles in ways that make post-hoc attribution of accountability both institutionally contentious and practically difficult. Accountability becomes procedural — attached to the correct completion of assigned steps rather than to the soundness of the judgment that those steps collectively authorized and executed. When a decision later proves damaging, the organization struggles to locate the precise moment when judgment should have intervened, because judgment was never explicitly required to surface. The system absorbed the decision into its operational logic without creating any record that would allow the decision to be isolated, examined, and held accountable on its own terms.

This diffusion of authority through process is not always deliberate. In many cases, it is the natural consequence of organizational growth — the inevitable result of building execution systems that are designed for scale and efficiency rather than for the governance of the authority embedded within them. But whether deliberate or emergent, its institutional consequence is the same: it protects individuals from the accountability that consequential judgment requires while leaving the organization exposed to the full cost of every ungoverned decision that the process architecture concealed. The individual who exercised the authority is protected by diffusion. The organization that bears the consequences is not.

The Committee Consensus Problem

Committees are widely assumed to reduce decision risk through the distribution of deliberative responsibility across multiple parties with different perspectives, different expertise, and different institutional interests. In practice, collective decision-making structures frequently mask risk rather than reducing it. The dynamics that govern behavior within committees — particularly in organizations with strong hierarchical cultures, significant authority differentials among members, or structural incentives that reward alignment over dissent — create conditions in which the appearance of deliberation is produced without the substance of it.

Collective decision-making spreads responsibility thinly enough that no individual member feels a full and personal accountability for the judgment being exercised. The weight of the decision is distributed across the committee in a way that reduces the threshold of personal accountability below the level at which any individual member is compelled to challenge the dominant narrative, to surface inconvenient evidence, or to require that the alternatives be genuinely evaluated rather than pro forma acknowledged. Dissent becomes optional in institutional practice even when it is nominally encouraged in policy. Silence becomes the functional equivalent of consensus, not because every member agrees with the direction being taken, but because the institutional cost of explicit dissent exceeds the institutional reward for it.

The execution system records that an approval was obtained by the required committee. It does not record the hesitation that individual members felt but did not voice. It logs the outcome of the committee process. It does not preserve the reservations that were present in the room but absent from the record. It preserves the decision that the committee ratified. It does not preserve the doubts that were suppressed by the social and hierarchical dynamics of a room in which the authority gradient made genuine deliberation structurally unavailable. Over time, in organizations where committee structures are the primary governance mechanism for consequential decisions, an institutional logic develops in which alignment matters more than insight and agreement matters more than accuracy. And the wrong decision proceeds — perfectly, compliantly, and confidently — because every required party provided the required approval without being structurally required to justify it.

Rationale Is Not Evidence

As systems mature and the invisible assumption deepens its institutional hold, organizations become progressively more skilled at explaining decisions after the fact. Post-hoc rationales are constructed with increasing sophistication. Narratives are refined through repetition until they feel like the contemporaneous account of what occurred. Justifications are documented in forms that create the appearance of having been present at the time of decision rather than assembled in response to the scrutiny that followed. This skill — the skill of constructing plausible after-the-fact explanations for decisions that were never required to justify themselves before execution — is one of the most consequential institutional capabilities of the Systems Age, and one of the most dangerous.

Rationale is not evidence. The distinction is precise, consequential, and not interchangeable. Evidence is what existed before the outcome was known — the information that was available to the decision-maker at the moment of authority, the alternatives that were under genuine consideration, the risks that were identified and assessed, the reasoning that was applied to available information to produce the judgment that authorized action. Evidence is contemporaneous. It is created at the decision moment and preserved independent of what followed. Rationale is what is constructed after the outcome is observed — the explanation of why the decision that was taken was reasonable, given the information now available, through the interpretive lens of what actually occurred. Rationale is retrospective. It is shaped by outcome. It is, in most cases, unconsciously optimized to present the decision in the most defensible light available, given the evidence that hindsight has made legible.

When organizations fail to maintain this distinction — when they accept a well-constructed post-hoc rationale as the equivalent of contemporaneous decision evidence — they lose the ability to learn honestly from their experience. Every outcome, regardless of whether the decision that produced it was sound or defective, can be explained in retrospect. Very few decisions, in the absence of contemporaneous evidence, can be genuinely questioned. The organization accumulates a growing archive of plausible explanations for past decisions while building no institutional capacity to govern future ones. The execution system becomes a storytelling engine — producing coherent narratives of organizational action — rather than a truth engine that preserves the contemporaneous record of the authority and judgment that authorized each action taken.

The Escalation of Commitment

Once a consequential decision has been executed at scale through a mature systemized process, the institutional dynamics of reversibility shift fundamentally. Reversing the decision is no longer simply a matter of choosing a different path. It becomes an act that carries significant political and psychological costs for the individuals and institutions whose authority is implicated in the original judgment. Acknowledging that a decision was wrong threatens the credibility of the decision-maker. Challenging prior judgment from within the organization risks the authority relationships on which the challenger's own institutional standing depends. Reversing course implies that the approvals that authorized the original decision were flawed

— and by extension, that the governance process that produced those approvals is not a reliable standard for the organization's future decisions.

In response to these costs, organizations characteristically escalate commitment rather than reversing it. They invest additional resources in making the original decision succeed — not because the evidence supports continued investment, but because the institutional cost of acknowledging failure exceeds the apparent cost of continued execution. They add more controls around the decision's consequences — not because the controls address the source of the problem, but because additional controls demonstrate organizational responsiveness without requiring acknowledgment of the decision's fundamental flaw. They reinterpret adverse signals optimistically, finding in every piece of evidence that could support continued commitment a reason to discount or defer the evidence that points toward the need for reversal.

They defend the decision rather than examine it — not out of dishonesty, but because the institutional architecture of the organization provides no structured mechanism for examining the decision on its own terms, independent of the outcome it has produced and independent of the authority relationships that are implicated in its continued defense. This is not stubbornness in the ordinary sense. It is a structural condition produced by the combination of scale, institutional momentum, and the absence of a pre-execution governance record that would allow the decision to be examined against the standard of what was known and considered at the moment it was made, rather than against the retrospective standard of what it is politically convenient to acknowledge in light of what has since occurred. The system keeps moving forward because stopping would require confronting a decision that the organization was never structurally required to govern before it executed.

What Audits Cannot See

Audits are designed to evaluate compliance. This is their institutional purpose and the scope within which their findings are reliable and actionable. They ask whether controls were in place and functioning as designed. They ask whether procedures were followed in the sequence and by the parties that the process architecture specified. They ask whether approvals were documented by the designated authorities at the designated stages. These are legitimate and important questions, and audits that answer them reliably provide genuine institutional value by confirming that the execution layer is operating as intended.

Audits cannot ask — and were never designed to ask — whether the decision that the execution layer was given to carry out was responsible under the uncertainty that existed at the time it was made. They cannot ask whether the alternative paths that were available were fairly considered against an evidence-based standard or whether they were acknowledged pro forma and set aside without genuine evaluation. They cannot ask whether dissenting views that were present within the organization were surfaced, considered, and weighed in the deliberative process, or suppressed by the authority dynamics that governed the decision environment. They cannot ask whether the authority that authorized the decision was operating within appropriate institutional constraints or whether it was exercised in ways that exceeded its legitimate mandate.

As a result, organizations can pass every audit with complete and unqualified success while drifting steadily toward a failure that no audit was designed to prevent. The absence of audit violations becomes mistaken for the presence of sound institutional judgment. The clean audit record is cited as evidence of organizational health — and in the domain of execution compliance, it is. In the domain of decision governance, it is silent. The organization is well-audited and ungoverned at the decision layer simultaneously. These conditions are not mutually exclusive. They coexist with regularity in organizations that have invested heavily in execution oversight while never building the infrastructure required to govern the decisions that execution carries out.

The Moment of Reckoning

Eventually, the consequences of ungoverned decisions surface beyond the organization's capacity to contain them within the execution layer's explanatory framework. Performance collapses in ways that cannot be attributed to execution variance or to external conditions. Culture fractures in ways that make the internal dynamics of the organization visible to external parties, who then ask questions the organization has no contemporaneous evidence to answer. Trust erodes between the organization and the individuals it affects, the regulators who oversee it, the boards who govern it, and the public institutions that grant it the social license to operate at the scale it has achieved.

Legal scrutiny intensifies, and with it the demand for the kind of decision evidence that was never created because the governance infrastructure that would have required its creation was never built. Public confidence disappears at a speed that the organization's communication architecture designed to manage perceptions of execution outcomes rather than to establish the integrity of the decisions that produced them cannot match. At that point, organizations scramble to identify what went wrong. They look to their systems, which were functioning. They look to their policies, which were current. They look to their controls, which were documented. They rarely look at the decision, because by the time the reckoning arrives, the decision is buried beneath layers of execution — embedded in the procedural record as a compliant action, surrounded by documentation that records what was done and is silent on whether what was done was justified.

The question is no longer why the decision was made and whether it was sound. The question is how the damage occurred and who bears the accountability for it. Those are different questions, and they are asked too late. The moment at which the decision could have been governed — before it was executed, before its consequences had propagated through the system at scale, before its evidentiary basis had been displaced by post-hoc rationale — has passed. What remains is the reckoning: the institutional accounting for consequences that Governed Decision-Intelligence Infrastructure™ (GD-II™) would have required to be examined before they were authorized.

The Lesson of Orderly Failure

The most instructive failures in modern enterprise are not chaotic. They do not arise from the breakdown of systems or from the abandonment of process. They unfold through proper channels, through approved processes, through documented steps, and through compliant actions taken by individuals who were each doing precisely what their role required them to do. They are, in the most precise institutional sense, orderly. The systems functioned. The procedures were followed. The approvals were obtained. The records are complete. And the outcome represents a failure of the first order — not despite these conditions, but through them.

This category of failure teaches a sobering and essential lesson about the limits of systemized execution as a governance framework. The lesson is not that systems are insufficient in the execution domain for which they were designed. The lesson is that systems are entirely insufficient as a substitute for the governance of the decisions that execution is authorized to carry out. Orderly failures are the signature of organizations that have invested all of their governance capacity in the execution layer while leaving the decision layer structurally ungoverned. The orderliness of the failure is evidence of the system's competence. The failure itself is evidence of the decision's absence of governance.

Until organizations accept this truth — until the institutional understanding of failure shifts from a question of how decisions were implemented to a question of whether they were governed before authorization — organizations will continue to be surprised by the failures their systems faithfully produce. The surprise is not a failure of intelligence or of operational discipline. It is a structural condition produced by an architecture that was built one layer short of complete. The execution layer is present. The governance layer that should sit above it has never been built. And in that absence, perfect systems continue to execute wrong decisions with institutional precision.

Where This Forces the Argument

The Great Systemization taught the modern enterprise how to execute with discipline and scale. The invisible assumption taught it how to confuse procedural compliance with institutional judgment. The phenomenon of perfect systemic failure forces the argument to its next and unavoidable stage: the recognition that the execution problem and the decision problem are categorically distinct, that solving the former does not address the latter, and that the governance of decisions requires a different institutional infrastructure — one that exists above the execution layer, that operates before consequences are generated, and that is designed specifically to govern whether a decision is worthy of execution before the system is given permission to execute it.

The next evolution requires a shift in institutional focus — from how decisions are implemented to whether they should exist at all in the form in which they are being authorized. That shift does not begin with technology or with process refinement. It begins with understanding the nature of decisions themselves: what they are, what they require, what distinguishes a governed decision from an ungoverned one, and what infrastructure is necessary to ensure that the distinction is maintained at the institutional level under the conditions of scale, speed, and pressure that define modern enterprise. That understanding is the subject of the chapter that follows.

WHAT A DECISION REALLY IS

The Organizational Definition That Governance Requires

Organizations talk endlessly about process. They map it with precision. They optimize it for efficiency. They automate it at scale. They audit it for compliance. The language of process saturates every level of enterprise management — from the boardroom to the operational front line — in a way that has made process the primary lens through which organizations understand their own functioning and evaluate their own health. And yet, process is not where failure originates. Failure originates one layer above the process — at the moment a decision is made. To understand why systems alone are insufficient, and why Governed Decision-Intelligence Infrastructure™ (GD-II™) constitutes a categorically different institutional requirement from any existing governance framework, it is necessary to understand what a decision actually is — not philosophically, but organizationally.

The organizational definition of a decision is precise, and precision matters here because the ambiguity that surrounds the concept of decision-making in most enterprises is itself a governance vulnerability. When organizations cannot distinguish clearly between what a decision is and what an action is, they direct their governance resources at the wrong level of institutional activity — treating symptoms while leaving causes ungoverned. The first and most consequential clarification is the distinction between decisions and actions, and it is the foundation upon which every subsequent element of this chapter rests.

The Distinction Between a Decision and an Action

The distinction between a decision and an action is critical, and in most enterprise governance frameworks, it is almost entirely absent. An action is something that happens after a decision. It is the execution — the operational step, the procedural activity, the workflow task — that a decision has authorized. A decision is something that happens before action, and that shapes everything that follows. It is the act of authority that determines what the action will be, who it will affect, under what conditions it will be carried out, and who bears the accountability for the consequences it produces.

Processes govern actions. They define the sequence, the standards, and the responsible parties for the operational steps that follow a decision. Systems execute actions. They automate, standardize, and scale the operational activity that a decision has set in motion. Controls monitor actions. They validate that the operational steps being taken conform to the standards and constraints that governance frameworks have established. None of these functions — process, system, or control — governs the decision itself. All of them operate after the decision has been made, on the downstream consequences of an act of authority that existed before any of them were engaged.

When organizations confuse decisions with actions — when they treat the governance of operational steps as equivalent to the governance of the authority that authorized those steps — they attempt to manage institutional risk at the wrong level entirely. They treat the symptoms of ungoverned decisions — the operational consequences, the cultural residue, the compliance signatures — while leaving the cause that gives rise to those systems ungoverned. This confusion is not a minor misalignment of organizational focus. It is the structural condition that allows ungoverned decisions to persist inside governed systems — protected by the organization's own governance architecture, which is directed at the execution of decisions rather than at the decisions themselves.

The Three Defining Properties of Every Consequential Decision

Every consequential organizational decision — whether explicitly recognized as a decision at the time it is made or absorbed into the operational flow of a systemized process without being surfaced as an identifiable act of authority — shares three defining properties. These properties are not contingent on the category of decision, the level of the organization at which it is made, or the industry in which the organization operates. They are structural characteristics of what it means for an act of authority to determine a consequential organizational outcome. Understanding these properties is the prerequisite for understanding what governance of decisions requires.

The first property is irreversibility. Some decisions appear reversible on paper — they exist within operational frameworks that include mechanisms for modification, reassignment, or reversal — but are irreversible in practice through the consequences they set in motion before any reversal is attempted. Once authority is granted to an individual, behavior changes — in the individual exercising the authority, in the individuals subject to it, and in the organizational environment that observes and adapts to it. Once trust is extended to a person, a process, or an institutional position, it reshapes incentives in ways that do not reset when the formal extension of trust is withdrawn or modified. Once an organizational culture absorbs a signal — a decision about what is tolerated, what is rewarded, what is protected — that signal persists in the informal logic of how the organization actually operates, independent of what subsequent policy changes say about how it should operate. Systems can rearrange structure through the mechanics of reorganization and reassignment. They cannot undo the meaning that consequential decisions have already embedded in the organization's behavioral reality.

The second property is risk generation. A decision commits the organization to a future it cannot fully predict. Every consequential organizational decision introduces exposure that did not exist before the decision was made. Hiring introduces long-term exposure to the judgment, character, and conduct of the individual being granted institutional authority. Promotion concentrates authority in ways that amplify the consequences of the promoted individual's decisions across the scope of their expanded mandate. Tolerance of conduct or outcomes that fall below the organization's stated standards establishes precedent that shapes how subsequent conduct and outcomes are evaluated, accepted, or challenged. Acceleration of operational activity compounds uncertainty by committing organizational resources to paths whose full risk profile cannot be assessed before commitment is made. Risk is not a side effect of decisions. It is their defining institutional feature, and governance of decisions requires that risk be identified, evaluated, and consciously accepted before execution begins — not assessed retrospectively after consequences have materialized.

The third property is memory creation. Every consequential decision becomes a permanent element of the organization's institutional memory. It establishes what is acceptable — what the organization has demonstrated through its choices that it will tolerate and authorize. It establishes what is rewarded — what categories of judgment and conduct produce advancement, recognition, and expanded authority. It establishes what is ignored — the signals and concerns the organization has shown, through its decisions, that it will not act upon. It establishes what is protected — whose authority and whose conduct the organization has demonstrated through its choices that it will defend against challenge. Even when decisions are entirely undocumented — even when they are absorbed into the operational flow of a systemized process without being identified as discrete acts of judgment — they teach the organization how to behave in subsequent situations that resemble the circumstances under which the original decision was made. This institutional memory is cumulative and frequently invisible. It operates through the informal logic of organizational behavior rather than through the formal logic of policy and procedure, which is precisely what makes it so powerful and so difficult to examine after the fact.

Why Existing Governance Operates Around Decisions, Not On Them

Governance frameworks in modern enterprises typically focus their institutional attention on the elements that surround decisions rather than on the decisions themselves. Policies establish the boundaries within which decisions are supposed to be made — defining what is permitted and what is prohibited, but not governing the quality of the judgment exercised within those boundaries. Controls enforce compliance with established standards — monitoring whether the operational steps that follow decisions conform to defined requirements but not evaluating whether the decisions that authorized those steps were sound. Committees distribute deliberative responsibility across multiple parties — creating the organizational appearance of collective governance but not requiring any individual member to produce a contemporaneous evidentiary basis for the judgment they collectively authorize. Escalation paths define the authority hierarchy through which decisions of defined categories must pass — establishing who must approve before execution proceeds but not requiring that the approval represent anything more than a procedural sign-off.

All of these governance mechanisms operate around decisions, not on them. A policy sets boundaries but does not ask why this decision, at this moment, by this authority, was the right choice within those boundaries. A control enforces compliance but does not ask what alternatives were rejected before the compliant path was selected. A committee distributes responsibility but does not ask what evidence existed at the time that made the authorized path more defensible than the paths that were not taken. An escalation path routes the decision to the appropriate authority level but does not ask what risks were knowingly accepted when that authority exercised its mandate. Without answers to these questions — questions that can only be answered at the moment of decision, before outcomes are known, through a governance function that operates at the decision layer rather than around it — governance becomes procedural theater. It produces the appearance of institutional accountability while leaving the substance of decision authority entirely ungoverned.

True governance begins at the decision itself. It begins at the moment authority is exercised — before action is taken, before consequences are generated, before the organization is committed to a path whose full risk profile has not been examined and whose evidentiary basis has not been preserved. Every governance mechanism that operates after that moment — however sophisticated, however comprehensive, however rigorously enforced — is operating on the downstream consequences of an act of authority that was never required to justify itself. The gap between where governance currently operates and where it must operate to address the root cause of institutional failure is the gap that GD-II™ is designed to close.

Authority as the Core of Every Decision

Authority does not reside in job titles. It resides in the power to decide — in the institutional capacity to determine what will be done, to whom, under what conditions, and with what consequences for which parties. When a consequential decision is made, three things occur simultaneously, regardless of whether the organizational architecture that surrounds the decision makes them explicit or allows them to remain invisible. Authority is exercised: the power to commit the organization to a path is used by whoever holds it, formally or informally, at that moment. Responsibility is implied: the party whose authority determined the outcome is the party to whom accountability for that outcome properly attaches, regardless of whether the organizational record makes that attachment clear. Consequences are initiated: the chain of effects that the decision will produce is set in motion from the moment the decision is made, independent of when those effects become visible or when the organization acknowledges their source.

Most organizations do not explicitly surface authority at the moment of decision. They allow it to hide inside workflows, where the identity of the authorizing party is diffused across sequential signoffs. They allow it to hide inside approvals, where the existence of a required signature is treated as the governance event rather than the judgment behind it. They allow it to hide inside consensus processes, where the social and hierarchical dynamics of collective deliberation make it institutionally unavailable for any individual party to own the full weight of the decision being collectively authorized. This invisibility of authority is institutionally convenient — it distributes the political cost of consequential decisions across multiple parties and reduces the exposure of any single decision-maker. But it is also institutionally costly in a way that compounds with scale and time.

When authority is not explicit at the moment of decision, accountability cannot be precise at the moment of consequence. The organization that made a consequential decision without surfacing and recording who held the authority that authorized it will find, when accountability arrives, that the evidentiary basis for assigning responsibility is absent — or available only through reconstruction that is shaped by hindsight, by institutional self-interest, and by the memory limitations of parties whose recollection of what they knew and considered at the time of decision has been inevitably shaped by knowledge of what followed. Explicit authority at the moment of decision is not a bureaucratic requirement. It is the institutional prerequisite for genuine accountability at the moment of consequence.

How Decisions Escape Scrutiny Entirely

In systemized organizations, consequential decisions are routinely treated as inputs to operational processes rather than as institutional events that require governance in their own right. They are assumed — embedded in the logic of a workflow that begins operating as though the decision that authorized it has already been validated, without any mechanism for that validation ever having occurred. They are abstracted away — converted from a discrete act of authority into a procedural step that feels too embedded in operational flow to be examined as the exercise of consequential institutional power. They are normalized as given — treated by the execution system as an authorized starting condition rather than as a judgment that must meet an evidentiary standard before the system is engaged.

By the time execution begins in earnest — by the time the process is running, the approvals are flowing, and the operational machinery is producing its documented record of compliant activity — the decision has already been absorbed into the system's operational logic without having been required to justify itself. The system proceeds without questioning the legitimacy of the decision it was given to execute, because the system was not designed to ask that question. Questioning the legitimacy of the decision given is outside the system's scope. It is precisely this gap — between the decision's legitimacy and the system's operation — that governance of decisions is designed to close, and that existing governance frameworks, by operating around decisions rather than on them, have consistently failed to address.

This absorption of decisions into process is how they escape scrutiny entirely. The decision is not examined because it is not visible as a decision. It is visible only as the starting condition of an operational process — a condition that the process assumes to be valid rather than tests for validity. The question of whether this decision should exist, in the form in which it has been authorized, and with the consequences it will produce, is never asked — not because the organization lacks the intelligence to ask it, but because no institutional function exists that is designed to require the question to be answered before execution proceeds.

No Decision Is Neutral

Organizations frequently operate under the belief that their decisions are neutral — that because they are data-informed, policy-compliant, and committee-approved, they exist above the domain of value-laden judgment and represent nothing more than the rational application of objective standards to available information. This belief is institutionally convenient. It reduces the threshold of deliberative accountability that the organization must meet before committing to a consequential course of action. It allows decisions to proceed without the explicit acknowledgment of the value judgments, the risk tolerances, the trade-off weightings, and the outcome prioritizations that every consequential decision in fact reflects. But no organizational decision is neutral, and treating decisions as though they were, in and of themselves, acts of governance failure.

Every consequential decision reflects a set of values — an implicit or explicit ranking of what the organization considers important, whose interests it will prioritize, and what it is willing to accept as the cost of pursuing its chosen path. Every decision reflects a tolerance for risk — a judgment about how much uncertainty is acceptable, how much downside is warranted by the anticipated upside, and who will bear the consequences if the risk materializes. Every decision reflects a weighting of trade-offs — a determination of which competing considerations will be given precedence, and which will be subordinated in the specific circumstances under which the decision is being made. Every decision reflects a prioritization of outcomes — a choice, whether acknowledged or not, about which results are being optimized for and at the expense of which alternatives.

When these elements are not made explicit — when the value judgments, risk tolerances, trade-off weightings, and outcome prioritizations embedded in a consequential decision are allowed to remain invisible within the procedural record of the approval process that authorized it — the decision still occurs, with all of its institutional consequences, but without the visibility or accountability that would allow it to be examined, challenged, or defended on its own terms. The organization loses the ability to understand itself — to know, with the precision that governance requires, what its decisions actually reflect about its values, its risk posture, and its priorities, as distinguished from what its policies and public statements say about those things. That gap between what the organization says and what its decisions reveal is a governance gap, and it exists at the decision layer rather than in the execution systems that carry the decisions out.

The Conditions Under Which Decisions Are Actually Made

Most governance frameworks are designed around an implicit assumption of rationality — the assumption that consequential decisions are made by individuals with full information, adequate deliberative time, and freedom from the organizational pressures that distort judgment. Real organizational decisions are rarely made under those conditions. They are made under time pressure, when the organizational urgency of operational continuity compresses the deliberative space available to the decision-maker. They are made under authority pressure, when the hierarchical dynamics of the decision environment make the expression of dissent or uncertainty institutionally costly for the parties whose judgment is most needed. They are made under incentive pressure, when the performance metrics, compensation structures, and career advancement logic of the organization create systematic incentives to resolve uncertainty in favor of the outcome that serves the decision-maker's institutional interests rather than the organization's legitimate obligations.

They are made under reputational pressure, when the decision-maker's standing within the organization — their perceived decisiveness, their demonstrated alignment with the priorities of senior leadership, their track record of producing outcomes that are reported favorably — creates a systematic incentive to avoid the expressions of uncertainty, the acknowledgment of risk, and the surfacing of alternatives that genuine deliberative governance requires. Human judgment degrades under these conditions — not because of incompetence, not because of dishonesty, but because of the biological and structural realities of how human cognition operates under the compound pressures of organizational hierarchy, time constraint, and incentive misalignment.

Systems do not account for these conditions. Policies do not adjust their requirements based on the pressure level under which the decision they govern is being made. Training does not prevent the biological and structural degradation of judgment under organizational pressure — it addresses the knowledge and skill gaps that training can remedy while leaving the structural conditions that degrade judgment entirely intact. GD-II™ must account for these conditions by design. It must provide the structural support that allows consequential decisions to meet a standard of evidentiary care even under the organizational conditions that make that standard most difficult to maintain — which are precisely the conditions under which the most consequential decisions are most frequently made.

Why Outcomes Are the Wrong Place to Start

Organizations routinely evaluate the quality of their decisions by examining the outcomes those decisions produce. This practice is pervasive, institutionally convenient, and structurally wrong as a governance approach. Outcomes are noisy signals of decision quality. Luck intervenes in the space between a decision and its outcome — market conditions shift, external circumstances change, the behavior of parties whose cooperation was assumed diverges from the projection on which the decision was based. Context changes in ways that affect the outcome independent of the quality of the judgment that authorized the original decision. Externalities that were outside the organization's knowledge or control at the time of decision intrude on the outcome in ways that neither reward sound judgment reliably nor punish poor judgment consistently.

A sound decision — one that was made with appropriate evidence, with genuine consideration of alternatives, with conscious acceptance of identified risks, and with authority operating within appropriate institutional constraints — can produce a bad outcome when luck, context, and externalities conspire against it. A defective decision — one made without governance, without contemporaneous evidence, without genuine alternative consideration, and without acknowledged risk acceptance — can produce a good outcome when luck, context, and externalities conspire in its favor. When governance begins with outcomes, the organization systematically rewards the luck of defective decisions that produced good results and punishes the prudence of sound decisions that produced bad ones. Learning becomes fundamentally distorted — organized around outcome correlation rather than decision quality, producing institutional incentives that reinforce ungoverned judgment and undermine the deliberative discipline that governance requires.

GD-II™ must focus on decision quality at decision time — on the evidentiary standard that the decision met before execution began, the alternatives that were genuinely considered, the risks that were explicitly acknowledged and accepted, and the authority that was exercised within appropriate institutional constraints — not on outcome justification after the fact. This shift in focus is not merely an improvement in governance methodology. It is the prerequisite for any governance framework that can produce genuine institutional learning, genuine accountability, and genuine defensibility in the forums where defensibility is ultimately tested.

The Core Failure of Modern Enterprise

Modern enterprises have mastered execution governance with a sophistication that represents one of the most significant institutional achievements of the past century. They have not mastered GD-II™. They have built comprehensive frameworks for governing what happens after decisions are made — for monitoring the operational consequences of authority already exercised, for enforcing compliance with standards that decisions have already been made to adopt, for recording the procedural steps through which decisions already taken have been carried out. They have built almost no institutional capacity for governing decisions themselves — for requiring that consequential authority meet an evidentiary standard before execution, for capturing the contemporaneous basis of judgment at the moment it is exercised, for preserving the alternatives considered and rejected before outcomes are known.

As a result, the structural condition of the modern enterprise is one in which decisions are made implicitly — embedded in operational flows without being identified and examined as discrete acts of authority requiring governance. Authority is exercised invisibly — distributed across workflows and approval chains in ways that prevent any individual party from holding the full accountability that the exercise of consequential institutional power requires. Risk accumulates silently — generated by every ungoverned decision and compounded through the scale of every execution system that carries those decisions out, without triggering any governance response because no governance function exists that is positioned to observe risk at the decision layer where it originates. Accountability emerges only in hindsight — after consequences have surfaced, after the evidentiary basis of the original decision has been displaced by post-hoc rationale, and after the institutional conditions that produced the failure have been obscured by the temporal distance between the decision and its consequences.

This is not a tooling gap that better technology will close. It is not a process gap that additional operational controls will address. It is an architectural gap — a structural absence in the institutional design of the modern enterprise that cannot be filled with more of what already exists at the execution layer, because the gap is not at the execution layer. It is at the decision layer, and it requires infrastructure designed specifically for that layer.

The Unavoidable Conclusion

Once the organizational definition of a decision is understood precisely — once it is clear that decisions are irreversible commitments that generate institutional risk and create lasting organizational memory, that they require governance at the decision layer rather than around it, that authority must be made explicit and accountable at the moment of its exercise, and that decision quality is determined at decision time rather than by the outcomes that follow — a conclusion becomes unavoidable that the preceding chapters of this book have been building toward from different directions.

The next evolution of enterprise does not begin with better systems. Systems are already as capable as their design permits. It does not begin with more comprehensive compliance frameworks. Compliance frameworks already govern execution with a sophistication that, in most large organizations, is at or near the practical limit of what procedural governance can achieve. It does not begin with improved leadership development, with more sophisticated analytics, or with technological platforms that optimize decision outputs within the existing governance architecture. None of these interventions addresses the structural absence that is the source of the failure.

It begins with infrastructure designed specifically for decisions — infrastructure that exists above the execution layer, that operates at the moment of authority rather than after it, that requires decisions to meet an evidentiary standard before the system is authorized to execute them, and that preserves the contemporaneous basis of consequential judgment in a form that cannot be reshaped by hindsight, by institutional self-interest, or by the temporal distance between the moment of decision and the moment of accountability. That infrastructure has never been built. Building it is the next evolution. Understanding what it requires begins with understanding what decisions demand of governance — and that understanding, in turn, requires confronting the distinction between documentation and evidence, which is the subject of the chapter that follows.

CHAPTER 5

Why Documentation Is Not Evidence

The Distinction That Separates Records from Governance

Modern enterprises document everything. They document meetings — recording attendance, agenda items, and summarizing conclusions. They document approvals — logging signatures, dates, and the names of parties who authorized each step in a defined process. They document policies — establishing the written standards against which conduct and decisions are formally measured. They document outcomes — producing performance records, compliance reports, and operational metrics that constitute the visible institutional history of what the organization has done and what it has produced. Documentation is, in the modern enterprise, the primary medium through which institutional activity is made legible, reviewable, and defensible.

And yet, when consequential decisions are questioned — by boards conducting governance reviews, by regulators requiring evidence of reasoned judgment, by courts examining the basis of authority exercised in ways that produced harm, or by the institutional record of history that eventually renders its verdict on what organizations chose to do and why — enterprises routinely discover something deeply unsettling. They have records. They do not have evidence. The distinction between these two things is the subject of this chapter, and it is among the most consequential distinctions in institutional governance.

Why Documentation Feels Like Enough

Documentation feels safe. It creates artifacts — tangible, reviewable records of organizational activity that satisfy the procedural requirements of audit, compliance, and regulatory oversight. It produces timestamps that establish a chronological record of when activities occurred and in what sequence. It signals diligence — the visible evidence that the organization has attended to its obligations, completed its required steps, and maintained the records that governance frameworks specify. In systemized organizations, documentation becomes synonymous with institutional responsibility. If a record exists, the decision it references is assumed to be legitimate. If documentation is missing, the failure is attributed to an execution gap rather than to a failure of judgment.

The comfort that documentation provides is genuine in a narrow and specific domain. In the execution domain — where the question is whether defined steps were completed by designated parties in the correct sequence — documentation is exactly what governance requires. A complete, accurate, and timely record of execution activity is the appropriate evidentiary standard for questions about execution compliance. But documentation answers only one narrow question: was something written down? Evidence answers a far more demanding one: was the decision justified at the moment it was made? These two questions are not interchangeable, and the governance frameworks of most modern enterprises have been built as though they were.

The conflation of documentation with evidence is not a deliberate institutional choice. It is the natural result of governance frameworks that evolved in the execution domain and were extended, without adequate examination, to the decision domain, where they do not apply. When an organization's governance architecture was designed to ensure execution compliance, documentation was the correct evidentiary standard. When that same architecture is applied to the governance of consequential decisions — which require not execution compliance but judgment integrity — documentation produces the appearance of governance without its substance. The records exist. The evidence of sound judgment does not.

The Timing Problem

Most documentation in modern enterprises is created after a decision has already been made. This is not a peripheral observation. It is the central structural defect of documentation as a governance instrument for decisions. Meeting notes are produced after the meeting at which a decision was reached — summarizing conclusions that were already reached rather than capturing the deliberative process through which they were reached. Approval forms are completed after the decision to proceed has already been informally made — capturing signatures that formalize a commitment that was established before the form was filled. Rationales are articulated after the direction has been determined, and the organizational commitment has been established — constructed with full knowledge of where the decision is headed and shaped, inevitably and often unconsciously, by that knowledge.

This sequence matters in ways that are fundamental rather than technical. When documentation is created after commitment has been established, it is inevitably shaped by the conditions that exist at the moment of its creation rather than the conditions that existed at the moment of decision. It is shaped by outcome expectations — the anticipated results that the decision is expected to produce and that the documentation will reflect in its framing of why the decision was made. It is shaped by organizational narratives — the institutional stories through which the organization understands its own direction, and that the documentation will be constructed to align with. It is shaped by power dynamics — the authority relationships within the organization that determine whose perspective on the decision will be reflected in the record and whose reservations will be absent from it. It is shaped by the desire for coherence — the institutional drive to produce a record that presents the decision as rational, considered, and internally consistent, regardless of whether the deliberative process that produced it actually had those characteristics.

This shaping does not require bad faith. It requires only the presence of hindsight — the inevitable condition of any documentation created after the moment of decision. Hindsight is not dishonesty. It is the structural reality of human cognition operating in the presence of outcome knowledge. Documentation created after commitment has been established reflects the decision as it appears in light of what the organization knows will follow, not as it existed at the moment it was made. Evidence, by contrast, must exist before outcomes are known. It must reflect the uncertainty, the alternatives genuinely under consideration, and the risks explicitly acknowledged, without the benefit of knowing how the decision will turn out. That temporal requirement — before outcomes are known — is not satisfied by any documentation created after commitment has been established, regardless of how comprehensive, how detailed, or how carefully constructed that documentation may be.

The Difference Between Rationale and Evidence

Organizations are exceptionally skilled at constructing rationales for their decisions. The modern enterprise has developed, through decades of experience with post-mortem reviews, regulatory inquiries, litigation, and board governance processes, a sophisticated institutional capacity for explaining, after the fact, why the decisions it made were reasonable, appropriate, and consistent with the information available at the time. These explanations address why the decision aligned with the organization's stated strategy. They address why the timing was appropriate given market conditions, operational readiness, or regulatory context. They address why the risks were acceptable given the anticipated benefits and the organization's risk tolerance as established in its governance frameworks. They address why the alternatives that were available were less viable than the path that was chosen, given the constraints and priorities under which the organization was operating.

These explanations often sound compelling. They are internally consistent. They draw on real information about the organization's circumstances, its strategic context, and the conditions under which the decision was made. They are produced by intelligent, experienced people who understand the organization's history and can construct a credible account of why its decisions were reasonable. But rationales are narratives. Evidence is constraint. The distinction between them is not a matter of quality or sophistication — it is a matter of timing, independence, and the structural conditions under which each is produced.

A rationale can be internally consistent and still be wrong — not wrong in the sense that the narrative is incoherent, but wrong in the sense that it does not accurately represent the reasoning and evidentiary basis that actually existed at the moment of decision. A rationale can be compelling to every party who hears it and still fail to withstand the scrutiny of an external examiner who has access to contemporaneous records that reveal a different picture of what was known, considered, and acknowledged at the time. Evidence must withstand external scrutiny without the support of narrative scaffolding. It must be capable of standing on its own — as a record of what actually existed at the moment of decision, independent of the interpretive framework that the organization subsequently constructs to explain why that decision was sound. When organizations mistake rationale for evidence, they lose the ability to distinguish between persuasion and truth — and with that distinction goes the foundation of genuine institutional accountability.

What True Decision Evidence Requires

True decision evidence has specific and non-negotiable characteristics that distinguish it categorically from the documentation that modern enterprises routinely produce. These characteristics are not procedural preferences — they are the structural requirements of a record that can function as genuine governance rather than as a compliance artifact. Understanding these requirements is the prerequisite for understanding what governance infrastructure at the decision layer must be designed to capture and preserve.

The first requirement is contemporaneity. Decision evidence must be captured at the time of decision — not reconstructed later, not assembled from fragments of subsequent communication, and not constructed in response to the scrutiny that follows an adverse outcome. Contemporaneous evidence is evidence that existed before the outcome was known, before the organization's interpretive framework for the decision was shaped by what followed, and before the parties whose judgment is being examined had the opportunity to align their accounts of what was decided and why. Without contemporaneity, a record of a decision is always, to some degree, a record of how the decision appears in retrospect rather than of how it existed at the moment of authority.

The second requirement is the explicit documentation of alternatives — the paths that were considered and not taken, the options that were evaluated and rejected, and the basis on which those rejections were made. The history of a consequential decision cannot be understood, and its quality cannot be assessed, through a record of what was chosen alone. What was not chosen, and why, is among the most important categories of decision evidence because it establishes whether the decision-maker exercised genuine deliberative judgment or simply executed the path of least institutional resistance. A decision made with full awareness of available alternatives and a genuine evaluation of their relative merits is categorically different — as an act of governance — from a decision made without that deliberative process, regardless of whether both decisions arrived at the same conclusion.

The third requirement is the acknowledgment of trade-offs — the explicit recognition of which risks were accepted, which potential harms were knowingly incurred, and which competing interests were subordinated in favor of the path chosen. Every consequential organizational decision involves trade-offs, and the governance value of a decision record is substantially diminished if it presents the decision as having produced only benefits without costs. A record that acknowledges the risks accepted and the trade-offs made at the moment of decision is a record that can support genuine institutional learning — that can distinguish between risks that were consciously accepted and risks that were simply not considered — in a way that a record presenting only the anticipated benefits of the decision cannot.

The fourth requirement is clarity of authority — an explicit record of who held the power to make this decision, under what mandate, and with what accountability for the consequences it would produce. Without this record, accountability becomes a matter of institutional politics rather than institutional governance — determined by who has the power to deflect responsibility rather than by who held the authority that authorized the decision. The fifth requirement is context — a record of the constraints, pressures, and informational conditions that were present at the moment of decision, including the information that was available and the information that was known to be absent. Without this context, a decision record cannot support the assessment of whether the judgment exercised was reasonable under the circumstances as they actually existed, which is the standard that every external accountability forum will ultimately apply.

What Existing Records Cannot Capture

The documentation that modern enterprises routinely produce — meeting minutes, approval records, email correspondence, policy documents, compliance certifications — fails to meet the evidentiary requirements of genuine decision governance in ways that are structural rather than correctable through better documentation practice. Meeting minutes record the conclusions that a deliberative process reached. They do not record the doubts that individual participants harbored but did not voice, the objections that were raised and dismissed without adequate engagement, the alternatives that were mentioned in passing and never seriously evaluated, or the authority dynamics that shaped which perspectives were heard and which were structurally unavailable in the room.

Approval records indicate that a designated authority granted permission for a defined action to proceed. They do not record the reasoning behind the approval, the alternatives to the approved path that the approving party considered or failed to consider, the risks that were identified or overlooked at the moment of approval, or whether the approval represented a genuine exercise of deliberative judgment or a pro forma sign-off on a decision that had already been made informally by the parties with the actual institutional power to determine the outcome. Email correspondence reflects fragments of communication between selected parties on selected topics — capturing some elements of a deliberative process while leaving most of it absent from the record.

None of these conventional documentation forms captures the doubts that were suppressed by the institutional dynamics of the decision environment. None preserves the signals that were present in the decision context and were discounted, ignored, or actively resisted rather than incorporated into the deliberative process. None records the assumptions that went untested because the organizational logic of the decision environment made testing them institutionally inconvenient or professionally risky. None captures the authority dynamics that determined whose judgment was solicited, whose reservations were heard, and whose assessment of the decision's risk shaped the outcome, versus whose assessment was present but unavailable within the power structure of the deliberative process. These elements create the appearance of deliberation without preserving its substance. When decisions later fail, organizations discover that they cannot reconstruct why a path was chosen — only that it was, and that the required procedural steps were completed in the required sequence by the required parties.

The Illusion of Auditability

Audits thrive on documentation. Their operational logic is built around the assumption that documentation is the appropriate evidentiary standard for governance assessment — that the existence of records, the completion of procedures, and the application of controls constitute the institutional evidence of sound governance that audit is designed to verify. Within the execution domain, where documentation is the appropriate evidentiary standard, this assumption is valid and produces genuine governance value. Audits that verify execution compliance — confirming that records exist, that procedures were followed, that controls were applied — are performing a function that the governance of execution requires.

But audits rarely interrogate the decision itself. They assess whether governance appeared to occur — whether the procedural architecture surrounding a decision was present and functioning — not whether the judgment embedded in that decision was sound. An audit can confirm that a hiring decision followed the required procedural steps without examining whether the decision was evidence-based. It can confirm that a promotion was approved by the designated committee without examining whether the committee's deliberative process was substantive or pro forma. It can confirm that a risk-acceptance decision was documented without examining whether the risk was accurately assessed, whether the alternatives were genuinely evaluated, or whether the authority exercising the decision was operating within appropriate institutional constraints.

As a result, organizations can be fully auditable — can pass every audit with complete and unqualified success — while simultaneously accumulating unexamined decision risk at the layer that audit is not designed to assess. The clean audit record creates a dangerous and persistent institutional illusion: that documentation equals defensibility. It does not. Defensibility in the forums where it is ultimately tested — boards, regulatory proceedings, litigation, public accountability — is not established by the completeness of a procedural record. It is established by the quality of the decision evidence that was created at the moment of authority and preserved in a form that can withstand the scrutiny of external examination without the support of post-hoc narrative construction. Documentation satisfies audit requirements. Evidence satisfies governance requirements. These are different standards, applicable to different institutional functions, and treating the first as a proxy for the second is a governance failure that audits are structurally designed not to detect.

How Documentation Distorts Organizational Learning

When documentation substitutes for evidence as the primary governance standard, the learning processes of the organization are systematically distorted in ways that compound over time. Organizations reward outcomes instead of judgment — promoting and recognizing the individuals whose decisions produced favorable results, regardless of whether those results were the product of sound deliberative process or of luck, regardless of whether the decision-maker exercised genuine governance discipline or simply benefited from favorable circumstances that made a poorly governed decision look sound in retrospect.

They punish visibility instead of risk-taking — creating institutional incentives that discourage the explicit acknowledgment of uncertainty, the honest documentation of alternatives considered and rejected, and the candid recording of risks accepted, because the organizational record that results from such transparency is more likely to be cited against a decision-maker if the outcome is adverse than a record that presents the decision as unambiguously correct. They optimize narratives instead of truth — developing, through repeated engagement with post-mortem processes, board reviews, and regulatory inquiries, an institutional skill in constructing the most defensible possible account of decisions whose actual basis was never required to meet an evidentiary standard.

Over time, leaders in organizations where documentation has substituted for evidence learn to document in ways that protect rather than reveal — ways that satisfy procedural requirements and create a compliant record without exposing the actual deliberative process, the actual risks acknowledged, the actual alternatives considered, or the actual authority dynamics that shaped the outcome. Transparency degrades as an institutional value because transparency, in an environment where documentation is treated as evidence, creates vulnerability rather than accountability. Candor disappears from the deliberative record because candor — honest acknowledgment of uncertainty, risk, and the limits of available evidence — is institutionally penalized in an environment where the documentation standard rewards confident, clean narratives. The organization becomes legible — its procedural record is complete, its compliance documentation is comprehensive, its audit trail is intact — but it is no longer honest. And an organization that cannot be honest in its decision records cannot govern its decisions.

How Evidence Requirements Change Behavior Before Decisions Are Made

The most important effect of genuine decision evidence requirements is not retrospective. It is prospective. The presence of an institutional requirement that consequential decisions be evidenced — that decision-makers must articulate the alternatives they considered, surface the risks they identified, record the uncertainty they acknowledged, and attach their authority explicitly to the reasoning they applied — alters decision behavior before decisions are made. This prospective effect is the most powerful governance benefit of evidence requirements and the one most absent from documentation-based governance frameworks, which operate entirely after the decision has been made and therefore cannot produce the behavioral change that occurs when decision-makers know their judgment will be examined against a contemporaneous evidentiary standard.

When decision-makers know they must articulate alternatives, they are structurally required to identify and evaluate options they might otherwise have dismissed without genuine consideration. The act of being required to document why alternatives were rejected forces a level of deliberative engagement with those alternatives that the absence of such a requirement does not. When they must surface risks explicitly, they are structurally required to acknowledge the uncertainty and potential downside of the path they are choosing — which changes the character of the decision itself, making it a conscious acceptance of identified risk rather than an implicit assumption that the chosen path is without meaningful downside. When they must record uncertainty, they are prevented from presenting decisions as more confident or more evidence-based than the information available actually supports — which creates institutional honesty about the conditions under which consequential authority is being exercised.

When they must attach their authority to their reasoning — when the record of the decision links the identity of the authorizing party to the explicit basis for the decision — they slow down. They listen more carefully to the perspectives of those whose expertise or experience is relevant to the decision. They invite dissent more genuinely because the record will reflect whether dissent was surfaced and how it was addressed, rather than simply whether the required procedural steps were completed. They weigh trade-offs more honestly because the record of acknowledged and accepted trade-offs will persist independently of the outcome and will be examined against the standard of what was known at the time. Evidence does not merely preserve accountability after the fact. It improves the quality of judgment before the decision is made. Documentation does not produce this effect, because it operates after commitment has been established and cannot change the deliberative process that produced it.

The Compounding Cost of Confusion

When organizations confuse documentation with evidence — when they accept a complete procedural record as the institutional equivalent of contemporaneous decision evidence — the governance costs compound with each decision cycle in which the confusion persists. Decisions escape scrutiny because the documentation standard treats the completion of required procedural steps as sufficient evidence of deliberative soundness, without any mechanism for examining the quality of the judgment that those steps were designed to govern. Authority remains unexamined because the documentation record captures who signed the required forms without requiring that the authority behind those signatures be explicitly justified and preserved in a form that can withstand independent scrutiny.

Risk compounds silently because the documentation system records what was done without capturing whether the risks of doing it were consciously identified and accepted before the commitment was made — which means that risk accumulates in the organization's decision profile without triggering any governance response, until it surfaces in forms whose connection to their source in ungoverned decisions is obscured by the temporal distance and the procedural record that surrounds each decision in the chain. Accountability arrives too late because the documentation that exists at the moment of consequence does not preserve the contemporaneous truth of the decision that initiated the chain — leaving the organization to reconstruct, from inadequate records and recollections shaped by hindsight, the basis of authority that was exercised in conditions that no longer exist and cannot be accurately reproduced.

By the time consequences surface, records exist in abundance — but the truth of the decision that produced them does not. At that point, governance becomes defensive rather than preventive. The organization is no longer in a position to govern the decisions that produced the consequences it is managing. It is in a position only to manage the consequences and to construct the most defensible possible account of the decisions that produced them — an account that will be evaluated against the standard of contemporaneous evidence that was never created and found wanting in every forum where that standard is applied.

The Question That Changes Everything

To move forward from this structural condition — to close the gap between the governance of execution and the governance of decisions — enterprises must stop asking the question that documentation-based governance has trained them to ask: is this documented? And start asking the question that genuine decision governance requires: is this decision evidenced? This is not a procedural change at the execution layer. It is an architectural change at the decision layer — a change in what the governance infrastructure of the organization is designed to capture, preserve, and require before consequential authority is exercised.

It requires infrastructure designed to capture decision truth at the moment choices are made — to intercept the consequential act of authority before execution begins, to require that it meet an evidentiary standard, and to preserve the record of that standard — the alternatives considered, the risks acknowledged, the authority exercised, the context present — in a form that is contemporaneous, complete, and resistant to the retrospective reshaping that hindsight inevitably produces when records are created after outcomes are known. That infrastructure does not currently exist in the governance architecture of the modern enterprise. It is the missing layer — the layer that must be built above the execution systems, the compliance frameworks, and the documentation practices that have constituted the institutional boundary of enterprise governance for the past half-century.

Systems record actions — the operational steps that follow from the decisions that authorized them. Documentation records artifacts — the procedural evidence that execution compliance governance requires. Evidence governs decisions — the consequential acts of authority that determine what systems will execute and what artifacts will be produced. Until organizations recognize and institutionally respect this distinction, they will continue to believe that their documentation-based governance frameworks provide them with the protection that only evidence-based decision governance can actually produce. And they will continue to discover, in the moment when accountability arrives and contemporaneous evidence is required, that they have records — comprehensive, compliant, and entirely inadequate to the standard that governance demands.

CHAPTER 6

The Human Variable Under Pressure

Why Judgment Degrades Predictably and What Governance Must Account For

Organizations design their systems for rational behavior. They assume time to deliberate — that the individuals making consequential decisions will have adequate opportunity to gather relevant information, consider available alternatives, and evaluate trade-offs against a standard of reasoned judgment. They assume access to information — that the decision-maker will have what they need to make an evidence-based assessment of the options before them. They assume calm evaluation of trade-offs — that the deliberative process will be conducted in conditions that allow for genuine weighing of competing considerations without the distortion of acute organizational stress. They assume good faith and clear intent — that the parties exercising authority will be doing so in pursuit of the organization's legitimate interests rather than their own institutional survival.

Real decisions are rarely made under these conditions. They are made under pressure — conditions that are not exceptional in the life of the modern enterprise but that are, in fact, its defining operational reality. The governance frameworks that organizations have built — the policies, the controls, the approval chains, the compliance architectures — were designed for the rational decision-maker operating under the assumed conditions. They were not designed for the actual decision-maker operating under the actual conditions that characterize consequential institutional judgment. This chapter confronts a truth that modern enterprises prefer not to face: pressure does not arrive as an anomaly to be managed. It is the structural condition under which the decisions that matter most are made.

Pressure as the Structural Condition of Enterprise Decision-Making

Pressure does not arrive in modern enterprise as an exceptional circumstance that temporarily disrupts normal operating conditions. It is baked into the operating reality of the modern enterprise as a defining and permanent feature of the environment in which consequential decisions are made. Time compression shapes every significant decision environment — the urgency of operational continuity, competitive response, regulatory deadlines, and leadership visibility ensures that most consequential decisions are made in less deliberative time than the rational model of decision-making assumes. Revenue targets create systematic institutional pressure to resolve uncertainty in favor of the path that most directly supports the metrics against which organizational success is measured and leadership performance is evaluated.

Regulatory deadlines impose external temporal constraints that compress the deliberative process regardless of the internal readiness of the organization to make the decision that the deadline requires. Public scrutiny — the awareness that organizational decisions are increasingly visible, increasingly permanent in their recorded form, and increasingly subject to external examination that may occur in circumstances and forums that the decision-maker cannot anticipate at the moment of decision — creates a form of pressure that shapes the character of deliberation in ways that are rarely acknowledged in the governance frameworks designed to govern it. Leadership visibility creates institutional pressure on decision-makers to demonstrate the confidence, decisiveness, and forward momentum that organizational cultures consistently reward, regardless of whether the conditions of the specific decision warrant those qualities.

Career risk — the awareness that the consequences of decisions will attach to the individual making them, that adverse outcomes will be attributed to the judgment of the party who authorized them, and that the institutional standing of the decision-maker will be shaped by the record of the decisions they have made — creates a pervasive and structurally embedded form of pressure that interacts with every other pressure condition in ways that systematically distort the quality of the deliberative process. Decisions are made while inboxes fill, while meetings overlap, while reputations hang in the balance, and while consequences loom over the deliberative space in ways that the rational decision-making model is not designed to account for. Under these conditions, judgment does not fail randomly. It fails predictably — in ways that are well understood by cognitive science, that are structurally produced by organizational design, and that no training, policy, or values statement is capable of preventing.

How Pressure Distorts Human Cognition

Under pressure, human cognition does not simply perform less well — it shifts in ways that are adaptive to the perceived threat the pressure represents and that are, in the context of consequential organizational decision-making, systematically dangerous.

These shifts are not the result of carelessness or of inadequate professional discipline. They are the result of cognitive mechanisms that evolved to protect individuals under conditions of threat and that operate in organizational environments in ways that their evolutionary context did not produce them to navigate.

Narrowing of attention is among the most consistently documented effects of high-pressure decision environments. Under acute pressure, the cognitive system filters out information that it does not categorize as immediately relevant to managing the source of pressure — which means that important signals that fall outside the narrow attentional focus of the pressured decision-maker are systematically excluded from the deliberative process, not because the decision-maker is incompetent, but because the cognitive resources available for broad information integration have been redirected toward managing the immediate threat. Signals that would be visible and significant in a calm deliberative environment become invisible in a pressured one — and the decision record that results from that attentional narrowing contains no trace of their absence.

Overreliance on authority cues is a predictable cognitive response to the uncertainty that pressure creates. When time is compressed and information is incomplete, the cognitive system seeks reliable shortcuts, and deference to authority — to the judgment of those with higher institutional standing, greater apparent confidence, or more established track records — provides a cognitively efficient response to uncertainty that feels safer than independent deliberative assessment. In organizational environments, this means that rank replaces reasoning as the primary determinant of whose judgment prevails in high-pressure decision environments, regardless of whether the authority figure's judgment is more reliably sound than the independent assessment of those whose input is being displaced by deference.

Speed bias — the cognitive preference for action over deliberation under pressure — produces systematic decisions to proceed with available options rather than to pause, gather additional information, or surface alternatives that are not immediately visible. Action feels safer than pausing in high-pressure environments because the cognitive system interprets inaction as a failure to manage the source of pressure rather than as a responsible exercise of deliberative judgment. Confirmation bias amplification under pressure produces systematic discounting of contradictory data — of information that challenges the direction the decision-maker is already inclined toward and that, in a calm environment, would be weighed against confirming information in a genuinely balanced deliberative process. Risk normalization occurs when the conditions of pressure become familiar enough that the risks they create are no longer recognized as elevated — when the decision-maker's cognitive system has adapted to operating under stress to the point where the risks associated with that stress feel ordinary rather than exceptional. None of these cognitive shifts violates any policy. None of them triggers any system alert. They operate silently, inside the decision-making process itself, entirely invisible to the execution and compliance architectures that constitute the governance framework of the modern enterprise.

Why Experience Does Not Immunize Leaders

Experience is widely and institutionally assumed to protect against poor judgment under pressure — to provide the decision-maker with a repertoire of precedent, pattern recognition, and contextual understanding that reduces the cognitive vulnerability created by high-pressure conditions. This assumption is embedded in the governance logic of most enterprises, which delegate increasing levels of consequential authority to leaders on the basis of their accumulated experience and the track record that experience has produced. The assumption is partially correct in execution domains — where experience with a known class of problem does reduce the cognitive load and the error rate associated with managing that problem under pressure. In the decision domain, particularly under acute organizational pressure, experience can in fact increase risk rather than reduce it.

Pattern recognition — the cognitive capacity that experience develops most reliably — is a decision-making asset in conditions where the current situation closely resembles the situations that produced the patterns the decision-maker has internalized. In novel or partially novel decision environments, pattern recognition becomes a liability: the experienced decision-maker categorizes the current situation as a familiar pattern and applies the solution appropriate to that pattern without adequate assessment of the ways in which the current situation differs from the precedents that the pattern is based on. Situational nuance — the specific features of the current decision context that distinguish it from apparently similar precedents and that would, if identified and integrated, produce a different deliberative judgment — is overridden by the cognitive efficiency of pattern matching. The experienced decision-maker proceeds with confidence in a solution that would have been appropriate in the situations that generated the pattern, and that is wrong in the specific situation where it is being applied.

Confidence, which accumulated experience reliably produces, suppresses dissent in organizational environments. The decision-maker whose experience has generated institutional standing and a reputation for sound judgment creates conditions, by the mere fact of that standing and reputation, in which those whose input is needed are less likely to challenge the direction the decision-maker has indicated, less likely to surface information that contradicts the experienced leader's assessment, and less likely to maintain dissenting positions in the face of the authority gradient that experience and institutional standing create. Prior success narrows the imagination of the experienced decision-maker — producing systematic underinvestment in the evaluation of alternatives that fall outside the range of solutions that prior success has validated. Reputation raises the institutional cost of reversal — making it harder for the experienced leader to acknowledge the need to change direction because the acknowledgment implicates the judgment that generated the reputation. Experienced leaders often make faster decisions than their less experienced counterparts. Systems reward speed. Pressure rewards confidence. Neither speed nor confidence guarantees judgment quality, and in high-pressure decision environments, both can be actively correlated with judgment degradation.

How Authority Distorts Information Flow

Pressure interacts with authority in ways that are among the most structurally dangerous dynamics in organizational decision-making. When decision stakes are high — when the consequences of the decision are significant and the pressure on the decision-maker is acute — the information flow into the deliberative process is systematically distorted by the authority structure within which that process occurs. Subordinates hesitate to challenge the assumptions of those with the authority to determine their professional futures, even when those assumptions are visibly incorrect and the challenge would serve the organization's legitimate interests. The cognitive and professional cost of direct challenge in a high-stakes, high-pressure environment is experienced as exceeding the benefit — and so the challenge does not occur, and the decision proceeds on the basis of assumptions that a more structurally protected deliberative process would have identified and corrected.

Dissent is reframed as obstruction in high-pressure decision environments — where the organizational premium on decisive forward movement creates conditions in which the expression of concern, the surfacing of alternative perspectives, or the request for additional deliberative time is interpreted as a failure of institutional alignment rather than as the exercise of the governance discipline that sound decision-making requires. Silence is interpreted as alignment — as the absence of objection rather than as the presence of suppressed concern — which produces a systematic misreading of the deliberative record that treats the absence of visible dissent as evidence of genuine consensus rather than as evidence of an authority gradient that has made genuine dissent institutionally unavailable. Agreement accelerates approval — the social dynamics of collective deliberation under pressure create momentum toward the path that the most authoritative parties in the room have indicated support for, with each expression of agreement reducing the deliberative space available for the challenge and alternative evaluation that governance requires.

The execution system records consensus. It does not record fear — the professional risk calculation that led the subject-matter expert to soften their objection rather than maintain it, the career consideration that led the junior analyst to qualify their concern rather than press it, the institutional self-preservation logic that led the experienced manager to align with the direction of the most senior party in the room rather than to persist with an assessment that contradicted it. The decision proceeds with apparent unanimity — with a procedural record that reflects collective agreement — even though the critical insights, the alternative perspectives, and the risk assessments that would have produced a different outcome if the deliberative process had been structurally protected from authority distortion never surfaced into the record. This is not a culture problem that better values or improved leadership development can resolve. It is a structural condition that requires structural governance — a governance infrastructure that is designed to account for authority distortion rather than to assume it away.

The Role of Incentives in Decision Distortion

Incentives do not need to be explicit, deliberately structured, or consciously recognized as such to exert powerful and systematic influence on the quality of judgment exercised in consequential organizational decisions. The career advancement logic of the organization — the implicit and explicit standards against which individual performance is evaluated and individual advancement is determined — shapes decision behavior under pressure in ways that are often entirely invisible to the parties whose judgment it is distorting. The bonus structures and performance metrics that define what the organization rewards create systematic pressures on decision-makers to resolve uncertainty in favor of the outcomes those metrics are designed to produce, regardless of whether those outcomes represent the organization's legitimate long-term interests.

Visibility — the institutional awareness that decisions and their outcomes are observable by those whose assessment will determine the decision-maker's organizational future — creates incentives that favor the presentation of confidence, decisiveness, and optimism over the honest acknowledgment of uncertainty, risk, and the genuine limits of available evidence. Reputational exposure — the sensitivity of the decision-maker's institutional standing to the outcomes of their decisions — creates systematic incentives to avoid decisions that, however sound they may be as exercises of deliberative governance, carry a meaningful probability of adverse outcomes that will be attributed to the decision-maker's judgment regardless of the quality of the reasoning behind them.

When incentives align with speed, with growth, or with the avoidance of the institutional embarrassment that frank acknowledgment of uncertainty or risk creates, the systematic effects on decision quality are predictable and consistent. Risks are downplayed rather than acknowledged — not because the decision-maker is unaware of them, but because the organizational reward structure creates incentives to minimize their salience in the deliberative record. Alternatives are narrowed rather than genuinely evaluated — because the time and institutional energy required for genuine alternative evaluation is experienced as a cost in environments where speed and decisive forward movement are the primary performance signals. Ambiguity is resolved optimistically rather than honestly — because the institutional reward for optimistic resolution, which produces apparent decisiveness, exceeds the institutional reward for honest acknowledgment of ambiguity, which produces apparent hesitation. The decision feels justified in the moment — consistent with the organizational pressures, the incentive structures, and the authority dynamics that shaped it. It is only later, when consequences have surfaced and the contemporaneous conditions of the decision are no longer present to be observed, that the organization recognizes what the incentive structure of the moment traded away.

Why Training, Policy, and Values Cannot Solve This

Most organizations respond to the evidence of human judgment failure under pressure by reaching for the governance instruments they know: more training, clearer policies, stronger values statements. These responses are not without institutional value. Training improves knowledge — expanding the decision-maker's awareness of relevant principles, frameworks, and precedents that bear on the category of decision they are making. Policies define boundaries — establishing the formal limits within which decisions must fall and the procedural requirements they must satisfy to be authorized. Values statements articulate intent — expressing the organization's stated commitment to the principles that should govern how its decisions are made and what they should reflect about the organization's character.

None of these instruments change how humans behave under acute organizational pressure. Training expands what decision-makers know in conditions of calm reflection. Under acute pressure, the cognitive resources available for accessing and applying that knowledge are systematically reduced by the attentional narrowing, the speed bias, and the authority deference that pressure produces — and the knowledge that training has expanded is precisely the knowledge that pressure makes least available. Policies define the boundaries of permissible action in conditions where the decision-maker has adequate deliberative time to consult, interpret, and apply them. Under acute pressure, the speed bias that pressure creates makes consultation and interpretation feel institutionally irresponsible, and the boundaries that policies establish are experienced as obstacles to the decisive action that the pressure environment demands.

Values statements articulate intent in conditions where the organization's stated principles and its operational incentive structure are aligned. Under acute pressure, when the incentive structure of the organization creates pressure to resolve uncertainty in favor of speed, growth, or the avoidance of institutional embarrassment, values statements provide no structural mechanism for ensuring that the stated principles prevail over the operative incentives. The expectation that training, policy, and values can reliably change how humans behave under conditions of acute organizational pressure is itself an invisible assumption — one that quietly undermines the governance frameworks built upon it by treating as a solved problem the human behavioral reality that those frameworks are least designed to address.

The Real Decision-Maker Organizations Are Designing For

Enterprise governance assumes a rational decision-maker operating within a well-designed system — an individual who has adequate time, complete information, genuine deliberative freedom, and no conflicts of interest between the organization's legitimate obligations and their own institutional self-interest. This assumed decision-maker is a necessary fiction for the design of execution governance frameworks, which require a stable and predictable behavioral model to specify the procedural requirements, approval sequences, and compliance standards that govern operational activity. In the domain of execution, the rational actor assumption produces governance frameworks that function reliably and at scale.

In the domain of consequential organizational decisions, the rational actor assumption collapses under the weight of the actual conditions under which those decisions are made. Real decisions are made by humans who are balancing limited time against the organizational urgency that the pressure environment produces. They are balancing incomplete information against the institutional expectation that confidence and decisiveness are the appropriate responses to that incompleteness. They are navigating social dynamics — the authority gradients, the professional risk calculations, the incentive structures, and the reputational considerations — that shape the character of the deliberative process in ways that the rational actor model is not designed to account for. They are managing personal risk — the career consequences, the reputational implications, and the institutional stakes that attach personally to the decision-maker in ways that create systematic conflicts between the organization's legitimate governance requirements and the decision-maker's individual institutional interests.

They are operating under organizational expectations that create structural incentives to produce the kinds of decisions — fast, confident, aligned with the direction of the most senior parties in the room — that the pressure environment rewards, regardless of whether those characteristics correspond to the qualities of sound deliberative judgment. Pretending otherwise — designing governance frameworks on the assumption that the real decision-maker resembles the rational actor that the governance model assumes — does not make decisions safer. It makes failure harder to explain, harder to prevent, and harder to govern, because the governance framework is addressing a decision-maker who does not exist rather than the actual human whose judgment it needs to structure.

Why Strong Systems Intensify Pressure Effects

The irony of mature systemization in the decision domain is that strong execution systems can intensify the pressure effects they are assumed to mitigate. When execution systems are highly capable — when they move quickly, produce outputs efficiently, and create institutional momentum that is visible and measurable — the experience of being inside a fast-moving system creates conditions in which consequential decisions feel harder to stop, harder to question, and harder to subject to the deliberative scrutiny that their consequences require. Decisions feel harder to stop because the execution machinery is already in motion — because the approval process, the resource allocation, and the operational preparation for execution have already begun by the time the decision is reached, and the cost of stopping feels larger than the cost of proceeding.

Momentum replaces reflection as the dominant organizational orientation in fast-moving execution environments — the institutional priority becomes maintaining the speed and efficiency of the execution system rather than ensuring the quality of the decisions that system is executing. Pausing appears irresponsible in environments where speed is the primary performance signal — where the organizational culture has been shaped by the experience of execution success to treat deliberative pause as a sign of inadequate commitment to the enterprise's operational objectives. Questioning feels disruptive in environments where the execution architecture has been optimized for consistent forward movement — where the introduction of deliberative challenge into an established execution flow is experienced as a source of institutional friction rather than as a governance responsibility.

The better the system executes, the harder it is to interrupt a flawed decision once that decision has been absorbed into the system's operational logic. Speed creates confidence — not the confidence of sound deliberative judgment, but the confidence of institutional momentum, of a process that is functioning as designed and producing visible outputs at the pace that the organization has come to expect. Confidence suppresses doubt — and in environments where the execution system is performing well, the doubt that would produce the deliberative pause that governance requires becomes institutionally unavailable, suppressed by the momentum of a system that is doing exactly what it was built to do. What the system cannot do is ask whether what it was built to do — the decision it was given to execute — was sound. That question requires infrastructure that exists above the execution system, not inside it.

The Consequences of Failing to Account for Human Behavior

When organizations fail to account for the predictable effects of pressure on human judgment — when they design governance frameworks on the assumption of rational deliberation and deploy those frameworks in environments characterized by time compression, authority distortion, incentive misalignment, and the cognitive effects of acute organizational stress — the institutional consequences are predictable and consistent. Decision risk accumulates invisibly, because the governance architecture in place was not designed to detect the degradation of deliberative quality that pressure produces. The procedural record remains intact — approvals are logged, steps are completed, records are produced — while the quality of the judgment behind each procedural event is systematically reduced by conditions that the governance architecture cannot observe.

Authority becomes unchallengeable in practice even when it is formally subject to institutional checks, because the authority distortion that pressure creates removes the genuine deliberative challenge that those checks were designed to produce. The institutional mechanisms for surfacing dissent, requiring genuine alternative evaluation, and preserving the independence of judgment that governance requires are present in the policy architecture but absent in the operational reality of high-pressure decision environments. Errors propagate at scale because the execution systems that amplify every decision — sound or unsound — are operating with full efficiency while the governance infrastructure that should have intercepted the flawed decision before execution began was not designed to function under the conditions that actually characterize enterprise decision-making.

Accountability arrives only after harm — after the consequences of the ungoverned, pressure-distorted decision have propagated through the execution system at scale and produced outcomes that can no longer be absorbed within the organization's operational management capacity. At that point, the narrative shifts from how this happened to why no one stopped it. The answer is almost always the same: because no infrastructure existed to intervene before execution began — no governance function that was positioned at the decision layer, that was designed to operate under real-world pressure conditions, and that was structured to provide the deliberative support that human judgment under pressure requires before the execution system is authorized to proceed.

What Decision-Governance Must Do

If decision quality degrades under pressure — and pressure is not an exceptional condition but the structural reality of consequential organizational decision-making — then governance cannot rely on individual discipline, professional training, or institutional culture to ensure the quality of judgment under conditions that systematically degrade it. Governance must be structural. It must anticipate the conditions under which consequential decisions are actually made rather than the conditions under which governance frameworks are designed to operate, and it must provide a structural architecture that supports sound judgment under those conditions rather than assuming that individual capacity and institutional culture will supply what structural architecture is required to provide.

Governed Decision-Intelligence Infrastructure™ (GD-II) must anticipate pressure by designing governance functions that are intended to operate in high-pressure environments rather than to function optimally in calm deliberative conditions. It must surface authority explicitly — requiring that the party who holds the decision-making power to be identified and held accountable for the decision rather than allowing authority to diffuse into the operational architecture of the approval process. It must force alternatives into view — through structural requirements that prevent decisions from proceeding without genuine engagement with the alternatives that were available, regardless of the time pressure and institutional momentum that make such engagement feel inconvenient. It must capture evidence before momentum takes over — creating a governance function that intercepts the decision before the execution system creates the institutional conditions that make deliberative challenge feel irresponsible. It must slow decisions when slowing is necessary — when stakes are high, when reversibility is limited, when risk is concentrated, and when the conditions of the decision environment are those that most predictably produce judgment degradation.

This is not about removing humans from decisions. Human judgment is irreducibly necessary in the governance of consequential organizational authority, and no infrastructure can substitute for it. The realization that pressure predictably distorts that judgment marks a turning point in understanding what governance requires. Better people are not the solution — the most experienced, most capable, most institutionally committed individuals in any organization are subject to the cognitive effects of acute pressure in ways that individual quality cannot overcome without structural support. More training is not the solution — training cannot change how human cognition operates under the conditions that produce judgment degradation. Stronger execution systems are not the solution — they amplify the consequences of ungoverned decisions rather than governing the decisions themselves. The solution requires a new layer of infrastructure — one designed specifically for decision-making under real-world conditions, which must exist before decisions are executed, not after they are justified by the outcomes they have already produced.

CHAPTER 7

NFRASTRUCT® AND THE CONSTITUTIONAL LOGIC OF GOVERNED DECISION AUTHORITY

Why Power Must Not Only Be Exercised — It Must Be Governed

Modern enterprises face a paradox that would have been immediately familiar to the architects of constitutional government. They possess immense institutional power, sophisticated operational systems, and unprecedented informational reach — capabilities that have transformed the scale, speed, and complexity of what organizations can accomplish. Yet they repeatedly fail at the moment that matters most: the moment of decision. The failure does not arise from a lack of information, from insufficient process sophistication, or from any absence of the execution capabilities that the modern enterprise has spent a century developing. It arises from a structural condition — from the fact that the authority to decide remains unchecked at the moment of its exercise.

This structural condition mirrors a problem that political philosophers confronted centuries ago and that constitutional democracy was specifically designed to solve: how to vest authority in human institutions without allowing that authority to become arbitrary, self-justifying, or destructive of the interests it was created to serve. The framers of constitutional governance understood a principle that modern enterprises largely ignore: power must not only be exercised — it must be governed.

This chapter establishes NFRASTRUCT® as the modern institutional answer to that problem — a Governed Decision-Intelligence™ (GD-I™) layer that performs, for enterprises, the same structural function that constitutional design performs for states.

The Constitutional Insight That Enterprises Have Not Applied

In *Federalist No. 51*, James Madison articulated a principle that remains as structurally relevant to modern enterprises as it was to the constitutional governments it was designed to frame. Madison's observation that if men were angels, no government would be necessary was not a cynical assessment of human character. It was a structural recognition of the relationship between unconstrained authority and institutional failure. The danger that Madison identified was not malevolence in the ordinary sense — not the deliberate abuse of power by individuals of bad character — but the far more common and far more consequential danger of unconstrained authority operating without the countervailing structure that would prevent its natural tendencies toward self-justification, toward the suppression of challenge, and toward the prioritization of its own continuity over the legitimate interests of those it was created to serve.

The Constitution's response to this structural danger did not attempt to perfect human judgment — to select for officials of exceptional character and rely on the quality of their individual deliberation to prevent the harms that unconstrained authority produces. It assumed imperfection as the baseline condition of human institutional behavior and designed around it. Three elements were identified as essential to making authority governable rather than merely authorized. The separation of authority — the distribution of different categories of institutional power across different branches and offices — prevented any single institution from exercising the full range of authority that governance requires without being subject to the constraint of competing institutional interests. Independent checks on decision power — mechanisms that evaluated the exercise of authority from positions that did not report to, depend on, or benefit from the authority they were evaluating — ensured that oversight was substantive rather than self-referential. Pre-commitment to rules that operate before action, not after harm — the establishment of constitutional constraints that bound authority before it was exercised rather than evaluated its exercise after consequences were known — prevented the structural vulnerability in which governance arrives too late to prevent the harm it is nominally designed to address.

Crucially, these mechanisms were not advisory. They were not established as best-practice recommendations that institutional actors were encouraged to follow when circumstances permitted. They were binding — they constrained what could proceed, imposed consequences for the unauthorized exercise of constrained authority, and were enforced by institutional structures that did not depend on the voluntary compliance of the parties whose authority they bounded. Modern enterprises, by contrast, have scaled power without scaling constraint. They have built execution capability without building the governance architecture that makes the exercise of that capability accountable to any standard independent of the authority exercising it.

The constitutional model recognized a further principle that is directly applicable to the enterprise context: the problem of unconstrained authority is not solved by the good intentions of those who hold it. Even the most well-intentioned authority, operating without structural constraint, will tend over time toward the normalization of its own judgment as the standard of acceptable conduct, toward the suppression of challenges that produce institutional friction without immediate apparent benefit, and toward the construction of governance processes that appear to satisfy accountability requirements while preserving the substance of unconstrained discretion. Constitutional design addressed this tendency not by attempting to select for better holders of authority but by establishing structural mechanisms that made unconstrained authority institutionally unavailable regardless of the intentions of those who sought to exercise it. This is the governance logic that enterprises must now apply to the governance of their own consequential decisions.

Why Enterprises Are Capable Systems but Not Governed Systems

Enterprises today are highly capable systems. The operational sophistication that decades of systemization have produced — the analytical platforms, the forecasting capabilities, the workflow architectures, the risk management frameworks — represents a genuine and remarkable institutional achievement. They are not governed systems. The distinction is precise and consequential. A capable system is one that can execute the decisions it is given with efficiency, consistency, and scale. A governed system is one in which the authority to make those decisions is itself subject to structural constraint — in which what may proceed is determined not only by the capacity to execute but by a governance layer that evaluates whether the decision to execute meets the standards required for it to be authorized.

The mechanisms that modern enterprises deploy as governance — advanced analytics, artificial intelligence-assisted forecasting, formal approval workflows, risk committees, and compliance reviews — operate inside the same authority they are nominally designed to restrain. This creates a structural contradiction that is as fundamental in the enterprise context as it would be in a constitutional context: the parties whose authority is subject to governance are the same parties whose judgment determines what governance requires, whose compliance with governance standards is evaluated by processes they control, and whose accountability is assessed in forums that report to rather than operate independently of the authority they are charged with examining.

An organization cannot meaningfully govern decisions when the same leadership that authorizes action is also responsible for evaluating the risk of that action

— when the parties who make the decision are the parties who assess whether the decision was sound. It cannot govern decisions when the evidence that bears on the decision is curated by the parties who are accountable for the outcomes the decision will produce — when those whose institutional standing depends on the decision's success determine what information is relevant and how it will be presented to the deliberative process. It cannot govern decisions when oversight occurs after execution, framed as review rather than prevention — when the institutional function of governance is retrospective examination of decisions already made rather than pre-execution evaluation of decisions seeking authorization. This is not governance. It is self-policing. The framers of constitutional democracy rejected this model on structural grounds that are equally applicable in the enterprise context. The modern enterprise must confront the same structural rejection.

The structural contradiction of self-governance is not a new problem in the enterprise context. Organizations have long recognized, in narrow domains, that the parties most directly implicated in an activity cannot reliably evaluate that activity's compliance with independent standards. Financial statement preparation is separated from financial statement certification precisely because the same party cannot objectively assess the adequacy of work, they are responsible for producing. Legal representation is separated from judicial determination because the advocate for a position cannot objectively adjudicate its merit. These separations are not courtesy arrangements — they are structural requirements of any oversight function that must produce findings independent of the interests of the parties it evaluates. The governance of consequential decisions requires the same structural logic, applied at the decision layer rather than at the execution layer where enterprise governance has historically been concentrated.

The Structural Principle That Constitutional Governance Established

Constitutional governance succeeded in creating durable institutional accountability because it solved a problem that enterprises have not yet acknowledged as a governance requirement rather than a cultural preference: authority must be constrained by something that does not answer to authority. The Constitution did not rely on better leaders — on the selection of officials whose individual quality of character and judgment would prevent the harms that unconstrained authority tends to produce. It did not rely on more virtuous officials — on the assumption that the right cultural environment would produce decision-makers who would voluntarily constrain their own authority in ways that institutional structure did not require. It did not rely on stronger cultural norms — on the expectation that the shared values of the institutional environment would produce the self-restraint that constitutional constraint was designed to provide.

It relied on structure — on binding institutional mechanisms that constrained authority before it was exercised, that required authorization from bodies independent of the authority being constrained, and that imposed enforceable consequences for the unauthorized exercise of constrained power. This structural approach to the problem of unconstrained authority is not merely a feature of constitutional democracy. It is the foundational insight of any governance architecture that has successfully maintained accountability over institutional power across time, scale, and changing conditions of human behavior.

Similarly, decision failure in modern enterprises does not arise because leaders are incompetent. The individuals who exercise consequential institutional authority in modern enterprises are, in most cases, highly capable, well-intentioned, and experienced in the operational domains they lead. It does not arise because employees are unethical. The vast majority of organizational participants operate in good faith within the institutional frameworks they are given. It does not arise because data is insufficient. Modern enterprises have access to quantities and qualities of data that previous generations of organizational leaders would have found inconceivable. It arises because decision authority is unchecked at the moment of execution — because the institutional architecture of the modern enterprise contains no structural mechanism that constrains the exercise of consequential authority before it is acted upon, that requires authorization from a body independent of the authority seeking to exercise it, or that binds the decision to a contemporaneous evidentiary standard that does not depend on the voluntary compliance of the parties whose authority it governs. Systems optimize execution. They do not govern permission.

Governed Decision-Intelligence Infrastructure™ (GD-II™) — The Constitutional Layer for Enterprise Decisions

NFRASTRUCT® exists to perform, in modern enterprises, the same structural role that constitutional design performs in democratic governance systems. This is not a rhetorical comparison offered to elevate the institutional significance of a governance framework. It is a precise description of the structural function that NFRASTRUCT® performs and the institutional problem it was designed to solve. Constitutional design does not make decisions for the officials it governs. It does not replace leadership judgment with algorithmic outputs. It does not optimize the outcomes that institutional authority produces. It governs the conditions under which authority may be exercised — establishing what is required before action may proceed, what standard of authorization must be met, and what institutional constraints bind the exercise of power regardless of the preferences of those who hold it.

NFRASTRUCT® is not a decision engine — it does not make or recommend the decisions that organizational leadership is charged with making. It is not a predictive model — it does not forecast outcomes or optimize decision outputs within existing authority structures. It is not a workflow enhancement — it does not improve the efficiency or consistency of the execution processes through which decisions are carried out. It is not a compliance overlay — it does not add procedural requirements to the execution layer that verify conformity with established standards after the decision to proceed has been made. It is a governance layer that operates before execution, determining whether a decision is permitted to proceed at all — establishing, independently of the authority seeking to exercise the decision, whether the evidentiary and governance requirements for that exercise have been met.

Like constitutional checks and balances, NFRASTRUCT® introduces a separation between decision intent and decision authorization — a structural distinction between the desire of the decision-making authority to proceed and the institutional determination that proceeding has been validated against the standards that governance requires. It introduces independent evaluation of evidence and alternatives — an assessment of whether the decision meets the evidentiary standard of contemporaneous evidence, genuine alternative consideration, and explicit risk acknowledgment that GD-II™ requires, conducted by a function that does not report to the authority it is evaluating. It introduces pre-commitment to rules that bind authority before outcomes are known — governance constraints that operate at the moment of decision rather than after consequences have surfaced and the institutional framing of what occurred has been shaped by hindsight. It produces immutable records that prevent post-hoc justification — preserving the contemporaneous truth of what was known, considered, and accepted at the moment of authority in a form that cannot be retroactively altered to conform with the narrative that a subsequent outcome has made institutionally convenient. This is not cultural reform. It is institutional design.

CONSTITUTIONAL LOGIC OF GOVERNED DECISION AUTHORITY

NFRASTRUCT® – Independent Governance Layer Above Execution

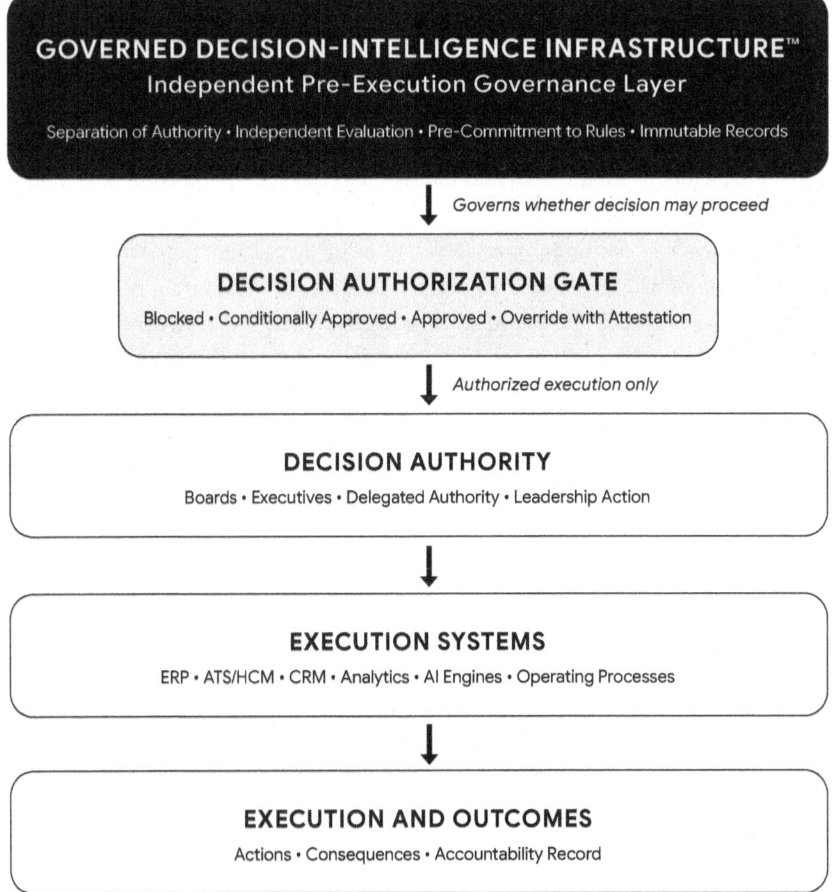

Figure 7.1 — Constitutional Logic of Governed Decision Authority. The governance layer is independent of the authority it governs and positioned above execution. Decisions must pass through the authorization gate before execution may begin. Core principle: Authority must be constrained by something that does not answer to authority.

Why Existing Enterprise Independence Functions Do Not Satisfy the Constitutional Requirement

At this point, a well-informed skeptic will raise an objection that deserves a precise answer rather than a general reassurance. Modern enterprises already possess functions that carry the designation of independence. Audit committees are constituted by directors without operational management responsibilities, specifically to provide oversight independent of the executives whose conduct they are charged with evaluating. Internal audit functions operate under charters that explicitly establish their independence from the business units they review. General counsel and legal departments provide advice that is institutionally separated from the operational line management whose decisions they counsel. Risk and compliance functions are staffed by professionals whose role is defined as the independent evaluation of operational and governance risk. If the constitutional principle requires independence, these functions will appear to satisfy it. The structural analysis of this chapter requires a direct response to why they do not.

The constitutional model established independence as a structural condition, not a designatory one. The independence of the judiciary in constitutional governance is not produced by the title "judge" or by the nominal designation of the judicial role as independent. It is produced by the structural conditions under which that role is exercised: tenure that insulates the officeholder from the political consequences of decisions that displease the authority whose conduct is being evaluated; funding that cannot be reduced by the authority whose actions are subject to judicial review; jurisdiction that is defined by constitutional mandate rather than by the institutional preferences of the parties who would prefer not to be evaluated. Remove any of these structural conditions, and the nominal independence of the title becomes the institutional reality of dependence — a function that bears the designation of independence while operating under the structural constraints that make genuine independence unavailable.

Enterprise independence functions fail the constitutional test on precisely this structural basis. The audit committee of a corporate board is composed of directors who are nominated by a process that the management team influences, whose continued service on the board depends on factors that management shapes, and whose access to the information required for genuine independent evaluation flows through the same organizational infrastructure whose governance quality they are charged with assessing. The independence of the audit committee is real within the narrowly defined domain of financial statement oversight, where the structural conditions of independence — external auditor relationships, audit committee charters, regulatory requirements — have been deliberately designed to satisfy the constitutional requirement. Outside that domain, in the governance of the consequential decisions whose quality determines institutional outcomes, the audit committee's independence is nominal rather than structural. It evaluates after the fact, with information curated by the parties it is evaluating, against standards that those parties substantially influence.

Internal audit operates under a reporting structure that, in the overwhelming majority of enterprises, terminates at the Chief Financial Officer or the Chief Executive Officer — the same executive authority whose operational decisions internal audit is charged with evaluating. Its budget, its staffing, its access to information, and its institutional standing are all functions of the organizational hierarchy it nominally reviews. Its independence is defined by professional standards that internal auditors are ethically required to maintain, not by structural conditions that make the exercise of genuine independence institutionally available independent of the preferences of the authority it serves. A governance function that depends on the ethical commitment of individual practitioners to maintain independence against institutional pressure has not satisfied the constitutional requirement. It has created a cultural aspiration that substitutes for the structural condition it cannot provide.

Compliance and legal functions occupy an even more structurally compromised position with respect to the governance of consequential decisions. These functions report to executive leadership, are funded by the operational budget of the enterprise whose decisions they nominally constrain and derive their institutional standing from their utility to the authority they serve rather than from the structural independence that would allow them to constrain that authority before decisions are executed. General counsel advises. It does not authorize. Risk management informs. It does not intercept. Compliance verifies adherence to established requirements after the decision to act has been made. None of these functions performs the pre-execution governance function that the constitutional model identified as the foundational requirement of accountable institutional power — the function of determining, independently of the authority seeking to exercise a consequential decision, whether that decision is permitted to proceed at all.

The distinction between nominal independence and structural independence is not a theoretical refinement. It is the difference between governance that produces the appearance of accountability and governance that produces accountability itself. Constitutional governance did not create the appearance of independent oversight by designating certain offices as nominally independent. It created structural independence by establishing the conditions — tenure, funding independence, jurisdictional definition, enforcement authority — under which those offices could exercise genuine constraint on authority regardless of the institutional preferences of those whose authority was being constrained. Enterprises have created the appearance of independent oversight through the designation of roles as nominally independent. They have not created the structural conditions under which those roles can exercise genuine pre-execution constraint on consequential decision authority.

NFRASTRUCT® is designed to satisfy the constitutional requirement, not merely to approximate it through designation. Its independence from the authority it governs is not produced by a charter, a title, or a professional standard that depends on individual commitment for its enforcement. It is produced by the same structural logic that constitutional independence requires: a governance layer that operates outside the organizational hierarchy of the authority it evaluates, that does not report to the executives whose decisions it is charged with authorizing or declining, and that cannot be instructed by institutional preference to produce findings that are convenient for the authority it governs rather than sound by the governance standard it applies. This is what distinguishes a constitutional layer from a compliance function — not the language in which its independence is described, but the structural conditions under which that independence is exercised.

Why Independence Is Not Ideological — It Is Functional

A core and non-negotiable principle of constitutional governance is the independence of the oversight function from the authority it oversees. Courts do not report to the legislative bodies whose acts they are charged with evaluating. Auditors do not report to the executives whose financial records they are charged with certifying. Regulators do not answer to the entities they regulate. This independence is not ideological — it is not a preference for a particular model of institutional organization based on abstract principles of fairness or separation of powers. It is functional: the oversight function cannot produce the accountability that governance requires if it reports to, depends on, or is otherwise subject to the authority it is charged with constraining.

For the same structural reason, GD-II™ cannot be embedded within the authority it governs. A governance function that reports to the leadership whose decisions it is evaluating cannot maintain the independence that genuine pre-execution evaluation requires. The parties whose judgment is subject to governance will inevitably — not through malevolence but through the structural dynamics of institutional self-interest — shape the governance function in ways that reduce its constraining effect on their own authority, increase the procedural compliance requirements that they can satisfy without genuine deliberative change, and ensure that the governance framework produces the findings that are institutionally convenient for the authority it nominally constrains. This is not a theoretical risk. It is the structural inevitability of any governance function that depends on the cooperation of the authority it governs.

NFRASTRUCT® operates independently — not as a consultant, not as an advisor, and not as a policy body that provides recommendations for the authority it engages to accept or reject according to its own institutional preferences. It operates as a structural layer that enterprises must pass through when decisions carry irreversible risk to human outcomes — a layer whose authorization is required before those decisions may proceed, and whose independence from the authority seeking authorization is not a feature that can be waived for convenience or efficiency. This independence is not ideological. It is the functional prerequisite of any governance architecture that produces genuine pre-execution constraint rather than the self-referential oversight that creates the appearance of accountability without the substance of it. Without independence, governance collapses into discretion — into the exercise of the authority it nominally constrains, operating under the institutional guise of accountability.

Governing the Conditions of Judgment, Not Replacing It

The Constitution did not eliminate human judgment from the governing functions it designed. It bound it — established the structural conditions within which judgment could be exercised, the standards to which it would be held, and the mechanisms through which its exercise would be accountable to institutional requirements that the judgment itself did not determine. The quality of constitutional governance is not measured by whether it produces infallible decisions. It is measured by whether the conditions under which consequential authority is exercised meet the structural standards that prevent arbitrary, self-justifying, or destructive outcomes from becoming the institutional norm.

Likewise, NFRASTRUCT® does not replace leadership judgment. The decisions of modern enterprises are made by the leaders who hold the authority and the accountability for making them. GD-II™ governs the conditions under which that judgment may be exercised — the evidentiary standard that must be met, the alternatives that must be genuinely considered, the risks that must be explicitly acknowledged, and the authority that must be transparently identified before the decision is authorized to proceed. The distinction between governing judgment and replacing it is fundamental. Governance that replaces judgment removes the human accountability that institutional governance exists to create. Governance that bounds judgment — that establishes the conditions under which human authority may be exercised and enforces those conditions independently of the authority it governs — produces the accountability that enterprises require and that constitutional design has demonstrated is achievable through structural rather than cultural means.

GD-I™ means that leaders retain full agency over the decisions that fall within their legitimate authority — they make the decisions, they bear the accountability for their consequences, and they exercise the judgment that no governance infrastructure can substitute for. Responsibility is made explicit rather than diffused across workflows and approval chains — the party whose authority authorized the decision is identified, the basis for that authority is established, and the accountability for its exercise is preserved in a record that cannot be reconstructed by hindsight. Risk acceptance is bound to accountable actors — the parties who are institutionally responsible for the consequences of a decision are the parties who explicitly acknowledge and accept the risks that the decision carries, at the moment of decision, before those risks become irreversible consequences. Decisions are defensible without hindsight — their evidentiary basis exists in contemporaneous form, independent of the outcomes they produced, and capable of withstanding the scrutiny of any institutional forum without the support of post-hoc narrative construction. This is not about slowing organizations down. It is about preventing the irreversible harm at scale that ungoverned authority predictably produces when consequential decisions are made without the structural governance that the constitutional model has long recognized as the foundational requirement of accountable institutional power.

The Parallel Between Constitutional and Enterprise Governance Evolution

The emergence of constitutional governance as the dominant model for managing institutional authority did not occur because political philosophers convinced those who held power that structural constraint was preferable to unconstrained discretion. It occurred because the accumulated consequences of unconstrained institutional authority — the arbitrary exercise of power, the absence of accountability for decisions that produced harm, the systematic suppression of the challenge and deliberative scrutiny that sound institutional judgment requires — became sufficiently visible, sufficiently consequential, and sufficiently understood as structural rather than individual in their origin to make the structural response politically and institutionally unavoidable. Constitutional governance was not a voluntary improvement on unconstrained authority. It was the structural response to conditions that unconstrained authority had made intolerable.

The governance evolution that enterprises must now undertake follows the same pattern. The emergence of GD-II™ as an institutional requirement does not depend on the voluntary acceptance by those who currently hold decision authority that structural constraint on that authority is preferable to its current unconstrained exercise. It depends on the accumulated visibility of the consequences that unconstrained decision authority has produced — the institutional failures, the regulatory interventions, the legal exposures, the reputational collapses, and the harms to individuals and communities that ungoverned enterprise decisions have generated at scale. These consequences are now sufficiently visible, sufficiently consequential, and sufficiently understood as structural rather than individual in their origin to make the structural response institutionally unavoidable for enterprises that intend to operate at scale with the accountability that modern institutional environments require.

NFRASTRUCT® represents the institutional implementation of this structural response — not as a theoretical framework or a voluntary best-practice commitment, but as a governance layer that performs, with the binding authority that governance requires, the function constitutional design has long demonstrated is the foundational requirement of accountable institutional power. Just as constitutional governance did not eliminate the need for capable, experienced, and well-intentioned holders of institutional authority — but rather established the structural conditions under which such authority could be exercised accountably — GD-II™ does not eliminate the need for capable organizational leadership. It establishes the structural conditions under which that leadership's exercise of consequential authority is accountable to the independent, evidence-based standard that enterprises operating at scale in modern institutional environments are now required to meet.

CHAPTER 8

DECISION-GOVERNANCE DEFINED

*Precision Without Abstraction — What It Is, What It Is Not,
and Why the Distinction Is Non-Negotiable*

By this point, a pattern should be unmistakable. Modern enterprises do not fail because they lack systems. They do not fail because their people are incompetent, their data is insufficient, or their operational processes are underdeveloped. They fail because they never govern decisions themselves — because the consequential acts of authority that determine what their systems will execute, what their people will be authorized to do, and what risks their organizations will carry are made without the structural governance that distinguishes accountable institutional judgment from its absence.

This chapter defines Governed Decision-Intelligence Infrastructure™ (GD-II™) precisely — without jargon, without abstraction, and without conflating it with the tools, committees, or compliance mechanisms that organizations most commonly reach for when the term is introduced. This precision is not a procedural formality. It is an institutional necessity. Because if GD-II™ is misunderstood — if it is interpreted as a more sophisticated form of the governance mechanisms that already exist within the execution layer of the modern enterprise — it will be rebuilt as process. And if it is rebuilt as process, the structural gap it was designed to close will remain open, and the failure pattern it was designed to address will continue with the same predictability and the same consequences that it has always produced.

The Definition

GD-II™ is the disciplined oversight of decision authority before execution begins. This definition is precise in every element it contains, and each element matters. Disciplined oversight means that the examination of consequential decisions is not optional, not advisory, and not variable in its requirements based on the convenience or the institutional preferences of the parties whose authority is subject to it. It is structured, consistent, and enforced through governance architecture that does not depend on the voluntary compliance of those whose decisions it governs. Oversight of decision authority means that what is being governed is not the execution of decisions — not the operational steps that follow from the authority that authorized them — but the authority itself: the act of deciding, at the moment it is exercised, by the party who holds the power to commit the organization to a consequential path.

Before execution begins, it establishes the temporal requirement that is the most fundamental and most consistently violated element of the definition. Governance that occurs after execution has begun — after resources have been committed, after organizational momentum has been established, after the psychological and institutional costs of reversal have elevated to levels that make genuine reconsideration structurally unavailable — is not GD-II™. It is the retrospective examination of decisions already made, which is a different institutional function with a different purpose and a different standard of what it can achieve. GD-II™ is pre-execution by definition. It operates at the moment of authority, before the decision becomes an instruction to the execution system. If it does not operate there, it does not operate at all.

GD-II™ exists to answer four fundamental questions at the moment a decision is made — not before the decision is contemplated, not after the decision has been executed, but at the precise institutional moment when authority is exercised and the organization is committed to a path. The first question is who is exercising authority — not which role is nominally responsible for this category of decision, but which specific individual holds the authority that is being exercised in this specific instance, under what mandate, and with what accountability for the consequences that will follow. The second question is what evidence supports the decision now — not what evidence can be assembled after the fact to justify the direction that has been chosen, but what contemporaneous evidence exists at this moment, before the outcome is known, that makes this decision sound under the standard of care appropriate to its consequences. The third question is what alternatives were considered and rejected, and why — a question that cannot be answered by a record of what was decided but only by a contemporaneous record of the deliberative process that evaluated the available options and determined that this path was preferable to those that were not taken. The fourth question is what risks are being knowingly accepted — what the decision-maker understands to be the potential adverse consequences of this choice, expressed as a conscious and attributed acceptance of identified risk rather than as a post-hoc acknowledgment that risk was present.

If an organization cannot answer these four questions at decision time — if the governance infrastructure it has built is not capable of producing these answers before execution begins — then GD-II™ does not exist in that organization, regardless of how many systems surround the actions that follow from its decisions, regardless of how comprehensive its documentation practices are, and regardless of how sophisticated its execution governance frameworks have become. GD-II™ is not about controlling outcomes. Outcomes are shaped by factors that extend well beyond the governance of the decisions that initiate them. GD-II™ is about controlling exposure — the institutional exposure that ungoverned decisions create before their consequences become visible, and that governed decisions prevent by ensuring that authority is exercised with the evidentiary discipline and structural accountability that defensible judgment requires.

What Decision-Governance Is Not

Clarity about what GD-II™ is requires equal clarity about what it is not — because the institutional reflex of organizations confronted with a governance gap is to fill that gap with the governance mechanisms they already possess and understand. Each of the mechanisms most commonly deployed in response to a recognized governance failure is a legitimate governance instrument in its appropriate domain. None of them is GD-II™ and treating them as such — as sufficient responses to the structural absence that GD-II™ is designed to address — is the error that has allowed that absence to persist inside organizations that believe their governance frameworks are complete.

A committee is not GD-II™. Committees distribute the procedural responsibility for authorizing a decision across multiple parties, which reduces the visibility of individual accountability without increasing the quality of the deliberative process that determines whether the decision is sound. A committee can ratify a decision that no individual member would have been willing to own alone, producing apparent collective endorsement of a choice that no individual party is willing to be accountable for on its own terms. The existence of a committee approval in the governance record establishes that a required procedural step was completed. It establishes nothing about whether the deliberative process that produced the approval constituted genuine governance of the decision itself.

A checklist is not GD-II™. A checklist ensures that defined steps are completed in a defined sequence by defined parties. It does not evaluate whether the decision that the checklist governs was sound, whether the alternatives to that decision were genuinely considered, whether the risks it carries were consciously identified and accepted, or whether the authority exercising it was operating within appropriate institutional constraints. An approval workflow is not GD-II™. An approval workflow routes the decision to the appropriate authority level for authorization. It does not require that the authorization represent anything more than a procedural sign-off by the party whose signature the workflow requires. A policy document is not GD-II™. A policy document establishes the boundaries within which decisions must fall. It does not govern the quality of the judgment exercised within those boundaries or require that the decision-maker produce a contemporaneous evidentiary basis for the authority they are exercising.

A compliance function is not GD-II™. Compliance evaluates whether organizational actions conform to established regulatory, legal, and procedural requirements. It operates after the decision to act has been made, assessing conformity with external standards rather than governing the internal quality of the judgment that authorized the action. A retrospective review is not GD-II™. A retrospective review examines decisions after their consequences are known, which means it operates in conditions that are structurally incapable of producing the contemporaneous evidentiary standard that GD-II™ requires. Retrospective review can identify failures after they have occurred. It cannot govern decisions before execution begins. Each of these mechanisms may support governance in the sense that it contributes to an overall architecture of institutional oversight. None of them is governance of the decision itself. Most importantly, GD-II™ is not execution oversight. Execution oversight begins after a decision is already accepted as valid — after the authority to proceed has been established and the execution system has been engaged. GD-II™ occurs before that acceptance. If governance begins once execution is underway, it is already too late.

The Structural Mistake Most Enterprises Make

Most enterprises commit the same structural mistake when they attempt to close the governance gap at the decision layer: they attempt to govern decisions using tools that were designed to govern actions. This mistake is understandable because the tools that govern actions are the tools enterprises know — the committees, the approval workflows, the documentation requirements, the compliance frameworks, and the audit processes that constitute the execution governance architecture of the modern enterprise. These tools were designed for the execution domain, and in that domain they function reliably. When they are applied to the decision domain — when they are expected to produce governance of the consequential acts of authority that authorize execution rather than governance of the execution itself — they produce outcomes that are familiar, predictable, and consistently insufficient.

Committees rubber-stamp momentum — not because the individuals who comprise them are uncommitted to their governance responsibilities, but because the social and authority dynamics of collective deliberation under organizational pressure predictably produce ratification of the direction that the most consequential parties in the room have already established, regardless of whether genuine deliberative challenge occurred. Approvals validate authority rather than judgment — confirming that the party who signed was the party designated to sign, without producing any evidence that the signing party's judgment met the evidentiary standard that sound decision-making requires. Documentation explains decisions after the fact — creating rationale rather than evidence, producing a record that reflects the decision as it appears in light of anticipated outcomes rather than as it existed at the moment of authority. Controls monitor behavior but never question direction — enforcing compliance with established standards for how decisions are implemented without ever examining whether the decision to implement them was itself sound.

These mechanisms feel like governance because they add friction to the decision process — they create steps that must be completed, approvals that must be obtained, and records that must be maintained before execution can proceed. But friction alone is not discernment. The friction produced by a committee approval, a compliance review, or a documentation requirement is friction applied to the execution process, not to the decision that authorized that process. GD-II™ requires interrogation of choice — the structural examination of whether the decision itself, at the moment of its making, meets the evidentiary and accountability standard that governance requires. That interrogation does not occur in any of the mechanisms that the execution governance architecture of the modern enterprise provides.

What Decision-Governance Preserves

GD-II™ does not replace leadership judgment. The individuals who hold consequential authority in organizations are the parties whose judgment is irreducibly necessary for the exercise of that authority, and no governance infrastructure can substitute for the quality of deliberative judgment that experienced, capable, and well-intentioned leaders bring to consequential decisions. GD-II™ does not eliminate intuition — the pattern-recognition capabilities, the contextual awareness, and the accumulated experience that produce the quality of institutional judgment that sophisticated organizations require. It does not override experience — the track record of sound decision-making that establishes the institutional standing of leaders and that is a legitimate basis for the delegation of consequential authority. It does not prevent speed when speed is appropriate — when the decision category, the risk profile, and the reversibility of the choice permit rapid execution without the evidentiary requirements that high-stakes, irreversible decisions require.

What GD-II™ does is bind authority to evidence and accountability. A governed decision can still be bold — it can authorize a course of action that is ambitious, unconventional, or that carries significant risk, provided that the risk is consciously identified, the alternatives have been genuinely evaluated, and the authority exercising the decision is explicitly accountable for the judgment it represents. A governed decision can still be fast — the governance requirements that GD-II™ imposes are calibrated to the stakes and the reversibility of the decision, not applied uniformly to every organizational choice regardless of its consequence. A governed decision can still be unconventional — it can challenge established institutional patterns, pursue directions that deviate from prior practice, and exercise authority in ways that are not predetermined by existing policy or precedent. But it cannot be unexamined. At the moment of its making, it must meet the evidentiary standard that governance requires — it must be capable of answering the four fundamental questions that GD-II™ exists to ask, and it must produce a contemporaneous record that preserves those answers in a form independent of the outcomes that follow.

Why Timing Is Everything

Once a decision is executed — once the organizational commitment has been established, the resources have been allocated, the authority has been operationalized, and the institutional momentum of execution has begun — the governance conditions that GD-II™ requires are no longer available. Incentive structures shift at the moment of execution in ways that make genuine governance of the decision systematically unavailable. Admitting that the decision was wrong becomes institutionally costly — it threatens the credibility of the party who authorized it and creates accountability for the consequences that have already begun to accumulate. Reversing course threatens the organizational standing of those whose judgment the original decision reflects. Challenging the direction of an executed decision feels destabilizing to the parties whose operational responsibilities are organized around its implementation.

At that point, governance becomes defensive rather than preventive — oriented toward managing the consequences of an ungoverned decision rather than preventing the harm that governance before execution would have addressed. GD-II™ must therefore occur both before exposure and before the specific pre-execution conditions that make reversal difficult are established. It must occur before authority is operationalized — before the decision has been converted from an act of judgment into an instruction to the execution system that initiates the operational sequence of resource allocation, personnel engagement, and procedural activation. It must occur before resources are committed — before the financial, human, and operational resources required to execute the decision have been allocated in ways that create the sunk-cost dynamic that makes reconsideration institutionally expensive. It must occur before precedent is established — before the decision has been observed and internalized by the organization as the standard for how subsequent decisions in the same category will be made. And it must occur before behavior adapts — before the individuals affected by the decision have modified their conduct, their expectations, and their institutional positioning in response to it. Governance that arrives after harm appears is not governance. It is damage control, and damage control operates in conditions where the governance opportunity has already been foreclosed.

Decisions as First-Class Objects

A critical shift occurs in an organization's governance capacity when it begins to treat decisions as first-class institutional objects rather than as invisible assumptions embedded in the operational flow of systemized execution. A first-class object is one that the institutional architecture is designed to recognize, engage with, and process on its own terms — one that is visible as a distinct category of institutional event requiring specific governance treatment, rather than absorbed into the workflow of a process that treats it as a starting condition rather than as an act of authority requiring independent examination.

A decision that functions as a first-class institutional object has a defined scope — the organizational authority it engages, the parties it affects, the consequences it will produce, and the reversibility of those consequences are explicitly established before the decision is made rather than inferred from the execution record that follows it. It has a clear owner of authority — an identified individual who holds the specific power to make this decision under a defined mandate, and whose accountability for its consequences is established at the moment of authority rather than distributed across the approval chain that surrounds it. It has explicit alternatives — a contemporaneous record of the paths that were genuinely considered and not taken, and the basis on which they were evaluated and rejected. It has articulated risk — an explicit acknowledgment of what the decision-maker understands to be the potential adverse consequences of the chosen path, expressed in contemporaneous terms at the moment of authority. It has contemporaneous evidence — an evidentiary basis that existed before the outcome was known and that does not depend on retrospective construction to establish the soundness of the judgment it supports. And it has a record that cannot be rewritten by hindsight — a preserved account of the decision that remains as it was created, independent of the institutional incentives that would otherwise shape its retrospective presentation.

Until decisions are formalized in this way — until the organizational architecture includes a governance function that requires decisions to achieve first-class status before execution is authorized — they cannot be governed. They can only be executed. The distinction between an organization in which decisions are first-class objects and one in which they remain invisible assumptions is the distinction between an organization with genuine GD-II™ and one without it, regardless of how mature, comprehensive, or extensively documented the execution governance architecture of the second organization may be.

From Distributed Responsibility to Located Accountability

Committees distribute responsibility across multiple parties in ways that make the accountability for any individual decision institutionally diffuse. When everyone approves a decision, no one decides in the sense that governance requires — no individual party bears the full accountability for the judgment the decision represents, because that accountability has been divided across the participants in a collective approval process in which no single member was required to own the decision's evidentiary basis on their own terms. This diffusion is institutionally convenient for the parties whose authority the committee process protects, and institutionally catastrophic for the organization whose governance requires that accountability be precise.

When dissent is optional within the deliberative process — when the organizational dynamics of the decision environment make genuine challenge institutionally available to some parties and professionally risky for others — conformity dominates not through explicit suppression but through the structural conditions that make the expression of genuine disagreement more costly than the performance of institutional alignment. When accountability is shared across a collective process, it is diluted — the dilution is proportional to the number of parties among whom it is distributed. In organizations where every significant decision is subject to committee review, the dilution of individual accountability can reach levels at which no individual party experiences any meaningful institutional consequence for the quality of the judgment they contributed to the collective outcome.

GD-II™ does not require consensus. It requires clarity — the precise identification of a single decision, a single authority whose power authorized it, and a single accountable moment at which that authority was exercised, and the organization was committed to the consequences it would produce. Everything else — the committee input, the stakeholder consultation, the peer review, the risk assessment — is institutional support for the decision rather than the decision itself. The decision moment is the governance moment. Everything that precedes it is preparation. Everything that follows it is execution. GD-II™ operates at the decision moment and only at the decision moment, with the clarity of authority and accountability that governance requires.

The Role of Dissent in Governed Decisions

True governance does not seek agreement. It seeks exposure — the surfacing of the assumptions, risks, blind spots, authority dynamics, and overconfidence that characterize consequential decisions made under the real conditions of organizational life. A governance process that produces agreement is a process that may have achieved alignment, but it has not necessarily achieved the deliberative examination that governance requires. A governance process that produces exposure — that surfaces the considerations, the concerns, the alternative perspectives, and the identified risks that would otherwise remain invisible in the procedural record of a smooth approval process — has produced the institutional intelligence that sound decision-making requires.

A governed decision must withstand dissent rather than avoid it. The evidentiary standard of GD-II™ requires that the alternatives be genuinely evaluated — which means that the perspectives most likely to challenge the direction the decision-making authority prefers must be structurally available, not merely nominally permitted. If dissent cannot be expressed safely at decision time — if the authority dynamics of the decision environment, the career implications of challenge, or the institutional momentum of the prevailing direction make the expression of genuine disagreement professionally risky for those whose input is most needed — then governance has already failed at the moment when it is most required. The governance infrastructure of GD-II™ must be designed to create the structural conditions in which genuine dissent is not merely permitted but required — in which the deliberative process is not complete, and the decision is not authorized to proceed, until the alternatives have been engaged with and the risks have been acknowledged in a form that the governance record will preserve.

Why Technology Cannot Replace Decision-Governance

Automation excels at pattern execution — at applying defined rules to defined categories of input with speed, consistency, and scale that human deliberation cannot match. It excels at rule enforcement — at monitoring compliance with established standards and flagging deviations in real time across high volumes of operational activity. It excels at speed — at processing information and generating outputs at rates that human cognitive capacity cannot approach. These capabilities produce genuine institutional value in the domains for which they were designed.

GD-II™ requires capabilities that automation cannot provide. It requires context awareness — the ability to recognize the specific features of a decision situation that distinguish it from the patterns that prior decisions have established, and that would, if applied without situational judgment, produce governance of the wrong category of decision. It requires human accountability — the attribution of the exercise of consequential authority to a specific individual who bears institutional responsibility for the judgment they have exercised, which is a governance requirement that cannot be satisfied by a system that processes inputs and produces outputs without the capacity for institutional accountability. It requires judgment under uncertainty — the deliberative engagement with incomplete information, competing considerations, and irreducible uncertainty that governance of consequential decisions demands and that no automated system can perform without replacing the human judgment that accountability requires. It requires ethical and legal defensibility — the capacity to produce a contemporaneous account of the decision that meets the standards of reasonableness, evidence, and proportionality that accountability forums apply, which is a capability that requires the integration of human judgment, institutional context, and governance discipline that no automated system can supply.

Technology can support GD-II™ by creating the infrastructure through which evidence is captured, preserved, and made available for independent examination. It cannot replace GD-II™ by automating the deliberative process through which consequential authority is exercised. Any system that claims to automate decisions without governing them — that converts the exercise of consequential institutional authority into an automated output without preserving the human accountability that governance requires — does not produce GD-II™. It accelerates risk by removing the governance layer that human accountability provides while retaining the scale and speed that make ungoverned decision authority most consequential.

Decision-Governance as Infrastructure

Governed Decision-Intelligence™ (GD-I™) is not a feature that can be added to an existing organizational architecture as an enhancement to current governance practice. It is not a department that can be created within the existing institutional structure of the enterprise. It is not an add-on — a supplementary governance mechanism that provides additional oversight for a defined category of high-risk decisions while leaving the broader decision governance architecture of the organization unchanged. It is an infrastructure layer — a foundational element of organizational design that sits above the execution systems, the functional domains, and the leadership structures of the enterprise, governing the conditions under which authority at every level may be exercised rather than being embedded within any of those structures as a component of the authority it is designed to govern.

This infrastructure layer must intercept decisions before execution — it must be positioned in the organizational architecture so that consequential decisions cannot proceed to the execution layer without passing through the governance function that determines whether the evidentiary and accountability requirements for proceeding have been met. It must preserve evidence immutably — in a form that cannot be altered, reconstructed, or replaced by post-hoc rationale regardless of the institutional incentives that would otherwise shape the retrospective presentation of decisions whose consequences have become visible. It must make authority explicit — identifying the specific individual whose power authorized the decision, establishing the mandate under which that authority was exercised, and creating the contemporaneous record that links accountability to the act of judgment rather than diffusing it across the procedural architecture that surrounds it. It must surface alternatives and risk — requiring that the deliberative process produce a record of what was considered and rejected, and what was knowingly accepted, before the decision is authorized to proceed. It must enable accountability without blame — creating governance conditions in which the attribution of authority to accountable individuals serves the organizational interest in sound decision-making rather than creating institutional environments in which the prospect of accountability discourages the honest exercise of judgment. It must produce defensibility without hindsight — establishing the contemporaneous evidentiary basis that allows the organization to demonstrate the soundness of its decision-making in any accountability forum, without requiring the retrospective construction of a narrative that the contemporaneous record did not produce.

Without this architecture, governance remains aspirational — a set of institutional commitments that the organization sincerely holds and consistently fails to operationalize at the decision layer where those commitments are most required. The Systems Age asked how organizations could ensure that work is done consistently. The next evolution asks the more demanding question that the Systems Age produced the conditions for but could not answer: how do organizations ensure that consequential decisions are made soundly? That question cannot be answered by a process applied to the execution layer. It cannot be delegated to compliance functions that operate after authority has been exercised. It cannot be solved with more documentation of actions already taken. It requires an entirely new way of designing organizations — one in which the governance of consequential decisions is not an aspiration embedded in policy, but an institutional requirement enforced by infrastructure that exists above the systems, functions, and authority structures that it governs.

Where This Leads

Now that GD-II™ is precisely defined — as the disciplined oversight of decision authority before execution begins, requiring answers to four fundamental questions at the moment of decision, delivered by an infrastructure layer that operates independently above the execution systems and authority structures of the enterprise — the next step is to confront a difficult institutional truth. The existing enterprise functions that organizations most commonly rely on for governance — human resources, compliance, analytics platforms, artificial intelligence systems — cannot perform this function. Not because they are inadequate in the domains for which they were designed. Not because they are staffed by individuals who are incapable of governance discipline. But because they were never designed to govern decisions, and because the structural conditions under which they operate — their embeddedness within the authority they would be required to constrain, their retrospective orientation, their focus on execution compliance rather than decision accountability — make them institutionally incapable of performing the pre-execution governance function that GD-II™ requires. Understanding why requires examining their structural limits, which is the subject of the chapter that follows.

CHAPTER 9

WHY EXISTING ENTERPRISE FUNCTIONS CANNOT GOVERN DECISIONS

Structural Limits, Not Capability Gaps — Why the Solution Does Not Already Exist Inside the Enterprise

When organizations recognize that decision failures — not execution failures — are the root cause of the institutional risk, legal exposure, and reputational harm they experience, their instinct is predictable. They look inward. They examine the functions that already exist within the enterprise — the people systems, the legal and compliance infrastructure, the analytics platforms, the artificial intelligence deployments — and ask whether any of them can be extended, strengthened, or repurposed to fill the governance gap that has been identified. They assume that the solution must already exist somewhere inside the enterprise, waiting to be configured correctly, funded adequately, or empowered sufficiently to perform the governance function that has been missing.

It does not. This chapter explains why — not as a critique of the existing functions, not as a claim that they have failed in the domains for which they were designed, and not as an argument for replacing or diminishing any of them. It explains why on structural grounds. Each of the existing enterprise functions most commonly identified as candidates for the Governed Decision-Intelligence Infrastructure™ (GD-II™) role was designed to solve a different problem. The structural design of each function — the mandate it was given, the authority it was granted, the temporal position it occupies in relation to the decisions it is involved with, and the evidentiary standard it is equipped to apply — makes each of them incapable of governing decisions in the sense that GD-II™ requires, regardless of how sophisticated, how well-resourced, or how committed to governance excellence the individuals who lead those functions may be.

The Four Domains Organizations Turn To

Most enterprises, when confronted with the governance gap at the decision layer, attempt to close it by enhancing one of four existing organizational domains. Human Resources is the most common first candidate — it is the function most visibly associated with the categories of consequential decisions that produce the most prominent governance failures, including hiring, promotion, performance management, and termination. Compliance and Legal is the second common candidate — it is the function most explicitly associated with governance in the organizational lexicon, and it carries institutional authority to define the boundaries within which organizational action must fall. Analytics and Business Intelligence is the third candidate — in an era in which data-driven decision-making is presented as the solution to the limitations of individual judgment, the function that provides data and analysis to organizational decision-makers appears to be a natural governance resource. Artificial Intelligence and Automation is the fourth and increasingly prominent candidate — as AI systems are deployed to support, augment, and in some cases replace human judgment across a growing range of organizational decisions, they are frequently presented as the governance solution to the limitations of human decision-making.

Each of these domains is genuinely important to the operational functioning of the modern enterprise. None of them can govern decisions in the sense that GD-II™ requires. The limitation is not one of capability within their respective domains. It is one of structural design — of the fundamental architecture of each function's mandate, authority, temporal position, and evidentiary capacity, which makes the performance of pre-execution decision governance structurally unavailable to each of them, regardless of the investment, the authority enhancement, or the mandate expansion that the enterprise might attempt to apply.

Why Human Resources Cannot Govern Decisions

Human Resources governs people, not decisions. Its institutional mandate is the administration of employment processes — the systems, standards, and procedural requirements through which the organization's relationship with its workforce is managed in compliance with applicable law, internal policy, and organizational governance requirements. It is designed to ensure that employment actions are executed lawfully and consistently — that hiring processes conform to legal requirements, that performance management frameworks are applied equitably, that termination decisions are documented in ways that satisfy the legal and procedural standards that protect the organization against employment litigation, and that workforce planning is conducted in alignment with the strategic and operational requirements of the business.

Human Resources operates downstream of decisions. By the time HR is involved in any consequential employment action — by the time the function is engaged to process a hire, to document a promotion, to manage a performance improvement plan, or to execute a termination — the decision to take that action has already been made. It has been made by the business leader, the department head, the executive, or the management team that holds the authority over the employment relationship, and it has been made outside the jurisdiction of HR's governance mandate. HR can ensure that the decision is executed in a manner that is procedurally lawful and organizationally consistent. It cannot interrogate whether the decision itself was justified under the conditions of uncertainty that existed at the moment it was made, cannot require that the decision-maker produce a contemporaneous evidentiary basis for the authority they exercised, and cannot hold the decision accountable to the governance standard that GD-II™ requires.

The structural constraints on HR's governance capacity are not correctable through mandate expansion or authority enhancement. HR lacks the institutional authority over executive judgment that GD-II™ requires — it cannot challenge, delay, or require the re-examination of a business decision made by the leadership whose authority it serves without overstepping the mandate boundaries that define its legitimate institutional role. It cannot challenge business decisions without overstepping the mandate that defines its relationship with the organizational authority it supports — a relationship that is characterized by service to that authority rather than governance of it. It is designed to reduce organizational exposure after decisions have already been made — to ensure that the execution of decisions is legally defensible — not to prevent exposure before decisions are made by requiring that the decisions themselves meet a pre-execution governance standard. Asking HR to govern decisions is a category error of precisely the kind that the previous chapter identified as the source of the structural mistake most enterprises make: it applies a function designed for one domain — the governance of employment process execution — to a different domain for which it was not designed and for which its structural architecture makes it incapable of performing.

Why Compliance and Legal Cannot Govern Decisions

Compliance and Legal departments exist to interpret the rules that govern organizational conduct, to ensure that organizational actions adhere to applicable legal and regulatory requirements, to reduce the exposure of the organization to regulatory enforcement and litigation, and to defend the organization's decisions and actions when they are subjected to external scrutiny. These are legitimate and essential institutional functions. They are also, by structural design, reactive — oriented toward the evaluation of decisions that have already been made rather than the governance of decisions before they are made.

Legal review in most organizations occurs after a decision path has already been chosen — after the business leadership has determined the direction it intends to pursue and has engaged Legal to evaluate whether that direction is permissible, how it should be structured to minimize legal exposure, and what documentation should be produced to support its defense if it is subsequently challenged. Legal analysis operates on a decision that has already been established as the organizational intention, providing guidance on how to execute that intention within the constraints of applicable law rather than evaluating whether the decision itself represents the exercise of sound institutional judgment under the governance standard that GD-II™ requires.

Compliance ensures that organizational actions fall within the defined boundaries of applicable regulatory requirements, internal policies, and established standards of conduct — but does not evaluate whether the decision to take those actions should exist in the first place. It assesses conformity with established constraints rather than the quality of the judgment exercised within those constraints. Compliance cannot answer the governance question that GD-II™ requires — not whether this action was permissible under the applicable rules, but whether this decision was responsible given the uncertainty, the risk, and the alternatives that existed at the moment it was made. More fundamentally, Legal and Compliance functions cannot insert themselves into live decision-making in the manner that genuine pre-execution governance requires without creating operational conditions that would paralyze the organizational decisions they are attempting to govern. Their structural value lies in defining the boundaries of permissible action and defending the organization's decisions within those boundaries — not in the real-time governance of judgment under operational pressure. They answer whether this is allowed and whether it is defensible after the fact. They do not answer whether this decision is responsible, given the uncertainty the organization faces at the moment of its making. That distinction is decisive for the governance function that GD-II™ requires.

Why Analytics Cannot Govern Decisions

Analytics and Business Intelligence functions illuminate patterns in organizational and market data that support decision-making at the strategic, operational, and tactical levels. They excel at measuring outcomes — quantifying what has happened and how it compares to established benchmarks and expectations. They excel at identifying correlations in historical data that suggest causal relationships relevant to future decisions. They excel at forecasting trends — projecting the continuation or modification of historical patterns into future periods in ways that inform strategic and operational planning. They excel at evaluating performance

— assessing the outcomes of past decisions against the targets that those decisions were designed to achieve. These are genuine contributions to the quality of organizational decision-making.

Analytics operate on data that already exists. The foundational limitation of analytics as a GD-II™ mechanism is not one of analytical sophistication but of temporal position and data availability. Analytics can only analyze what has been recorded. They can only identify patterns in what has already occurred. They can only evaluate the quality of decisions whose consequences have already become visible as data. They cannot capture what alternatives were considered and rejected at the moment of a decision that has not yet been made. They cannot record what risks were consciously accepted by the decision-maker at the moment the decision was authorized. They cannot observe the authority dynamics that shaped the deliberative process through which a decision was reached. They cannot document the uncertainty that existed at the moment of choice — the informational gaps, the contested assumptions, and the acknowledged limits of available evidence that characterized the decision-maker's epistemic position at the moment of authority. Analytics can explain what happened in the aftermath of a decision. GD-II™ must interrogate why something was allowed to happen before it occurred — and the most important elements of that interrogation are qualitative, contextual, and human in ways that data cannot capture and that analytical systems were not designed to address.

Why Artificial Intelligence Cannot Govern Decisions

Artificial intelligence is frequently presented as the solution to the limitations of human judgment in consequential organizational decisions. This presentation is dangerously incomplete as a governance claim. AI systems learn from historical data — they develop the capability to recognize patterns in past decisions and outcomes and to apply those patterns to new decision inputs, which can support certain categories of operational and analytical judgment. They optimize for defined objectives — they can identify the action most likely to produce a specified outcome within a specified set of constraints, which can inform certain categories of operational decision support. They replicate patterns at scale — they can apply consistent decision logic across high volumes of inputs with a speed and consistency that human deliberation cannot match. These capabilities produce genuine value in the operational domains for which they are designed.

AI systems do not understand moral responsibility — the attribution of ethical accountability to specific human actors for the consequences of choices made in conditions of uncertainty and competing obligation. They do not understand legal defensibility — the capacity to produce a contemporaneous account of decision-making that meets the standards of reasonableness, evidence, and proportionality that accountability forums apply to human institutional authority. They do not understand organizational accountability — the institutional relationship between the exercise of consequential authority and the parties who bear the obligation to answer for its consequences. They do not understand authority legitimacy — the determination of whether the party exercising a particular decision is operating within the institutional mandate that confers the right to make that decision and bear the accountability for its consequences.

AI systems inherit the blind spots of the data on which they are trained — including the blind spots produced by ungoverned past decisions that were made without the evidentiary standard and the deliberative discipline that GD-II™ requires. When an AI system is trained on a dataset that reflects the decision patterns of an organization that has been making consequential decisions without governance, the AI system learns those ungoverned patterns and replicates them at scale. When AI is deployed without a governing layer above it — when AI-generated recommendations or outputs are acted upon without the pre-execution governance that examines whether the decision to act on them meets the evidentiary and accountability standard that governance requires — bias is scaled rather than reduced, poor judgment is automated rather than corrected, accountability becomes untraceable rather than attributed, and authority becomes institutionally invisible rather than explicitly owned. AI accelerates decision-making. It does not govern it. Without a governing layer above AI that determines whether the decisions it supports meet the standard of GD-II™ before they are executed, organizations move faster toward risk rather than away from it.

The Shared Structural Limitation

All existing enterprise functions share a critical and definitive structural limitation with respect to the governance of consequential decisions: they operate around decisions rather than on them. This distinction is precise and consequential. Operating around decisions means providing the support, the boundaries, the analysis, and the post-execution evaluation that surround the exercise of decision authority — functions that are genuinely valuable and genuinely necessary for the operational health of the enterprise, but that are structurally positioned outside the governance of the decision itself. Operating on decisions means governing the act of authority directly — interceding at the moment of decision before execution begins, requiring that the decision meet an evidentiary standard, binding the exercise of authority to explicit accountability, and preserving the contemporaneous truth of the decision in a form that cannot be retroactively altered by the outcomes it produces.

The existing functions support execution — they provide the resources, the expertise, the analytical inputs, and the procedural structures that enable the execution of decisions that have already been authorized. They monitor outcomes — they track what happens after decisions are executed, identify variances from expectations, and report on the performance of the organization's decision record in the aggregate. They enforce boundaries — they ensure that organizational actions fall within the legal, regulatory, and policy limits that define the outer boundaries of permissible conduct. They defend after exposure — they provide the legal arguments, the documentary evidence, and the institutional narrative that organizations deploy when their decisions are subjected to external scrutiny after the consequences of those decisions have become visible. None of these functions is designed to intercept decisions before execution and bind them to evidence, authority, and accountability in the contemporaneous, pre-exposure form that GD-II™ requires. This is not a missing feature within any of the existing functions. It is a missing layer — a governance layer that does not exist within any of them, and that cannot be created by extending, combining, or enhancing any of them.

Why Incremental Fixes Fail

When organizations attempt to add GD-II™ to existing functions by expanding their mandates, increasing their authority, or requiring closer coordination between them, they encounter predictable and consistent problems that reflect the structural limitations described in the preceding sections. HR becomes politicized when it is expected to challenge the business decisions of the leadership it serves — the organizational relationship between HR and the decision-making authority it is being asked to govern creates the conditions in which HR's governance role becomes a source of institutional conflict rather than an institutional safeguard, producing political dynamics that undermine both the governance function and the operational relationship it is embedded within.

Legal becomes a bottleneck when it is inserted into the pre-execution review of business decisions as a governance mechanism — the combination of Legal's reactive structural design, its risk-averse institutional posture, and its limited capacity for rapid engagement with the operational decision cadence of a modern enterprise produces delays that the organization experiences as governance costs exceeding governance benefits, leading to the systematic workaround of the governance mechanism rather than its consistent application. Compliance becomes performative when it is expanded beyond its structural mandate to cover the governance of decision quality — producing documentation of procedural conformity that satisfies the compliance requirement without addressing the governance gap, in a pattern identical to the documentation-as-evidence substitution identified in Chapter 5. Analytics becomes overinterpreted when it is expected to provide governance guidance on decision quality — producing the appearance of data-driven governance oversight without the structural capacity to capture the qualitative, contemporaneous, and authority-specific elements that genuine GD-II™ requires. AI becomes unaccountable when it is deployed as a decision governance mechanism without the governing layer above it that ensures its outputs are subject to the human accountability and evidentiary standard that GD-II™ requires.

Each function, when stretched beyond its structural mandate in an attempt to fill the GD-II™ gap, is weakened in the domain for which it was designed while failing to produce the governance function it was stretched to provide. This is why incremental fixes fail. GD-II™ cannot be bolted on to existing functions through mandate expansion, authority enhancement, or coordination requirements. The structural limitations that make each existing function incapable of governing decisions are not correctable through additions to those functions. They are inherent in the structural design of functions that were built for different purposes and that perform those purposes well precisely because they are not attempting to govern decisions in the pre-execution, evidence-bound, authority-explicit manner that GD-II™ requires.

The Conclusion That Cannot Be Deferred

If systems cannot govern decisions — and the preceding chapters have established that they cannot, because they are designed to execute decisions rather than to evaluate the authority that authorized them. If HR cannot govern decisions — because it is designed to serve the organizational authority whose decisions it would be required to govern rather than to operate independently of it. If compliance cannot govern decisions — because it is designed to evaluate conformity with established requirements after decisions have been made rather than to govern the quality of judgment before decisions are executed. If Analytics cannot govern decisions — because it operates on data that already exists rather than on the contemporaneous deliberative process through which decisions are made. If AI cannot govern decisions — because it lacks the moral responsibility, legal defensibility, organizational accountability, and authority legitimacy that GD-II™ requires. Then GD-II™ must exist as its own infrastructure — with its own authority, its own architecture, and its own institutional purpose —structurally distinct from every existing enterprise function and specifically designed to perform the pre-execution governance of consequential decisions that none of those functions can provide.

This infrastructure — GD-II™ — must be pre-exposure: it must operate before consequential decisions are executed and before the organization is committed to the consequences those decisions will produce. It must be evidence-bound: it must require that decisions meet a contemporaneous evidentiary standard before they are authorized to proceed, capturing what was known, what was considered, and what was accepted at the moment of authority rather than what can be reconstructed after outcomes are known. It must be authority-aware: it must identify explicitly who holds the power to make each consequential decision, under what institutional mandate, and with what accountability for the consequences of the authority they exercise. It must be human-centered: it must preserve human accountability at the governance level, ensuring that the attribution of consequential authority to specific individuals remains intact rather than being diffused into automated systems or collective approval processes that obscure the relationship between decision and accountability. It must be audit-grade: it must produce records of the governance process that meet the evidentiary standards applied by the institutional accountability forums — boards, regulators, courts — that examine decision quality when consequences require explanation. It must be legally defensible: it must create the contemporaneous record that allows the organization to demonstrate the soundness of its decision-making in any accountability forum without the support of post-hoc narrative construction. Nothing inside the modern enterprise is currently designed to do this. This is why the governance gap persists — and why it cannot be closed by any combination of existing functions, however well-resourced, however sophisticated, or however committed to governance excellence.

The Foundation That Must Be Designed

The realization that no existing enterprise function can govern decisions forces a difficult and consequential institutional acknowledgment: GD-II™ is a foundational requirement of the governed enterprise, and foundational requirements cannot be improvised, assembled from existing components, or satisfied through the incremental enhancement of functions that were designed for different purposes. They must be designed deliberately, from first principles, with the structural clarity that comes from understanding what the function must do, what authority it requires to do it, what position it must occupy in the organizational architecture relative to the authority it governs, and what independence it must maintain from the institutional dynamics that would otherwise shape its governance findings in ways that serve the interests of the authority it is charged with constraining.

Having established what GD-II™ is — and having demonstrated with structural precision why nothing currently existing inside the modern enterprise performs the pre-execution governance of consequential decision authority that GD-II™ requires — it is now possible to define what must exist. The next chapter introduces the missing layer explicitly: the infrastructure category that organizations must build above their systems, their functions, and their leadership structures in order to complete the institutional design that the Systems Age began but did not finish. It is a new category of infrastructure — not designed to execute work, but to govern whether work should proceed at all. What that infrastructure is, how it operates, and what it produces for the organizations that build it is the subject of the chapter that follows.

WHY AI FORCES DECISION-GOVERNANCE TO BECOME INFRASTRUCTURE

From Accelerant to Constitutional Imperative — The Structural Consequence of Machine-Amplified Execution

The analysis thus far has treated artificial intelligence as an accelerant rather than a root cause — as an amplifier of consequence that exposes existing weaknesses in how decisions are authorized and executed rather than as the originating source of the governance failure those weaknesses produce. AI, in the framing of the preceding chapters, makes ungoverned decisions more consequential by executing them faster, at greater scale, and with less opportunity for the kind of human intervention that might otherwise interrupt a flawed decision before its consequences become irreversible. What follows examines the constitutional implication of that acceleration.

As AI compresses the distance between intent and action — as the interval between the moment a consequential decision is authorized and the moment its consequences are propagated through the execution system narrows toward real time — it does not merely increase the risk of ungoverned decisions. It renders traditional oversight structurally insufficient. Advisory oversight, retrospective review, and compliance-based governance frameworks were all designed for environments in which the interval between decision and consequence was long enough for human intervention to be possible and meaningful. AI eliminates that interval. This interlude clarifies why, under conditions of machine-amplified execution, Governed Decision-Intelligence Infrastructure™ (GD-II™) must cease to be advisory and become infrastructure — binding, pre-execution, and independent of the intent of the parties whose authority it governs.

The Diagnosis AI Governance Has Correctly Made

Recent commentary has correctly identified the danger posed by increasingly autonomous systems deployed at the organizational and state scales. In *The Adolescence of Technology*, Dario Amodei argues that powerful AI amplifies state and organizational power toward authoritarian ends — through autonomous weapons systems, mass surveillance architectures, personalized propaganda at scale, and machine-optimized strategic decision-making that concentrates consequential authority in ways that existing governance frameworks are not designed to constrain. His core warning is not simply about the intentions of those who hold powerful AI capabilities. It is about the structural condition in which capability outpaces governance — in which the speed, scale, and consequence of AI-enabled decision execution have exceeded the capacity of existing oversight mechanisms to provide the accountability that governance requires.

NFRASTRUCT® begins from that same structural premise and extends it one layer deeper into the architecture of the problem. The central risk that AI amplification creates is not intelligence itself — not the sophistication of the models, the scale of the data, or the speed of the processing. It is ungoverned decision authority empowered by AI: the condition in which consequential human impact decisions can be made and executed by parties whose authority is unchecked at the moment of exercise, and whose execution is amplified by AI systems that remove the temporal and operational constraints that previously made the governance gap less immediately catastrophic.

Where much of the AI governance debate focuses on who controls the models, what constraints developers voluntarily impose on their capabilities, or how states might misuse AI capability against their own populations or adversaries, the structural failure mode is more fundamental and more broadly applicable. Authoritarian outcomes — outcomes in which consequential decisions are made and executed without the pre-execution governance that accountability requires — occur whenever decisions with human impact are executable without enforced, pre-execution governance. That condition exists across political systems and organizational forms. It exists within state power structures, within corporate and bureaucratic institutions, within military and security organizations, within platform operators and digital infrastructure providers, within enterprises and regulated industries. It is not a condition unique to authoritarian governments or to bad actors with malicious intent. It is the structural condition of any organization in which consequential decisions can proceed without passing through a governance layer that determines, independently of the authority seeking to proceed, whether the decision meets the evidentiary and accountability standard that its consequences require.

The Compression That Changes Everything

AI compresses the time between intent and execution. This compression is not merely a matter of operational efficiency — it is a structural transformation of the governance environment within which consequential decisions are made.

In pre-AI organizational environments, the interval between the moment a consequential decision was authorized and the moment its consequences became irreversible was long enough, in most cases, for human oversight mechanisms to detect, question, and potentially interrupt a flawed decision before the harm it would produce had fully propagated. That interval — measured in days, weeks, or months depending on the category of decision — was itself a form of governance: imprecise, inconsistent, and often insufficient, but present in ways that created at least some structural opportunity for the correction of ungoverned judgment before it became irreversible consequence.

When nothing governs the interval between intent and execution — when the governance infrastructure that should evaluate whether a decision is permitted to proceed before the AI execution system is engaged is absent or advisory rather than binding — outcomes become irreversible before accountability can act. The temporal structure of AI-accelerated execution eliminates the residual governance opportunity that the interval between authorization and consequence previously provided. Retrospective review cannot address what has already become irreversible. Advisory oversight cannot constrain what has already been executed. Compliance-based governance cannot prevent harm that has already been produced. The only governance that matters in an AI-accelerated environment is governance that operates before execution begins — governance that is binding, independent, and positioned structurally to intercept the decision before the AI execution system is authorized to act on it.

NFRASTRUCT® as a Structural Antidote

NFRASTRUCT® addresses the risk that AI acceleration creates not by attempting to make AI systems benevolent — not by constraining the capabilities of AI models, imposing developer guidelines on AI behavior, or relying on the voluntary compliance of AI deployers with ethical frameworks that carry no enforcement mechanism. It addresses the risk by making execution conditional. GD-II™, operationalized through NFRASTRUCT®, functions as a constitutional layer above AI and governs whether consequential decisions may proceed at all, independently of the intent, the authority, or the AI capability of the parties seeking to execute them.

Under this governance model, any decision with human impact must pass through enforceable pre-execution conditions before the execution system — AI or otherwise — is authorized to proceed. These conditions include predictive simulation of decision consequences before commitment — the requirement that the organization produce a contemporaneous assessment of what the decision is expected to produce before it is authorized to execute it. They include outcome-agnostic foresight — analysis conducted without reference to desired outcomes, ensuring that the assessment of decision consequences is not shaped by the incentive to produce results that justify the direction already chosen. They include immutable pre-execution recording of the decision evidence — the contemporaneous capture of what was known, what alternatives were considered, what risks were accepted, and who held the authority that authorized the decision, preserved in a form that cannot be altered by the outcomes that follow. They include machine-enforced execution gates — structural mechanisms that prevent the AI execution system from proceeding until the governance conditions have been satisfied, rather than merely flagging their absence after execution has begun. And they include post-deployment accountability structures that link the consequences of AI-executed decisions to the human authorities whose judgment authorized them. When those conditions are not met, execution is blocked — not discouraged, not warned against, not flagged for retrospective review, but blocked. This enforcement logic is the core institutional contribution of GD-II™.

Constraint Supremacy — The Removal of Silent Override

Authoritarian failure across organizational and political contexts consistently thrives on override — on the capacity of those who hold consequential authority to override the analysts, the warnings, the ethical constraints, and the institutional accountability mechanisms that would otherwise prevent the exercise of ungoverned power from producing its most harmful consequences. The override may be explicit — a direct instruction to suppress a finding, dismiss a warning, or proceed despite institutional objection. More commonly, it is silent — the quiet institutional logic by which findings that conflict with the preferences of those in authority are not acted upon, warnings that carry institutional cost for those who issue them are not issued, and accountability mechanisms that depend on the cooperation of the authority they are meant to constrain are shaped to produce findings that serve that authority's interests.

NFRASTRUCT® removes silent override by constraining how decisions resolve — by making the governance conditions for execution structural rather than advisory, and by ensuring that the resolution of a decision produces a governed outcome rather than an ungoverned one, regardless of the preferences of the parties seeking to execute it. Decisions conclude only in governed states: blocked, conditionally approved with explicit mitigations, approved on the basis of the evidentiary record that has been produced and preserved, or overridden — with the override logged immutably, attributed explicitly to the party exercising it, and preserved in a form that cannot be deleted, modified, or denied. Forecasts cannot be deleted after the fact to eliminate the record of what the organization predicted before it acted. Results cannot be retroactively tuned to align with the narrative that a subsequent outcome has made institutionally convenient. Claims that the organization did not know the risks it was accepting are rendered factually irrelevant by the pre-execution record that establishes what was known at the moment of authority. This is constraint supremacy — the same structural logic that James Madison applied to political power in the constitutional design that made democratic governance durable, now applied to machine-amplified decision authority in the institutional environments where AI has made ungoverned execution most dangerous.

Making Intent Freezable — The Governance of Narrative Manipulation

Concerns about AI-driven propaganda, narrative manipulation, and the strategic misrepresentation of institutional intent rest fundamentally on the capacity of powerful organizations to rewrite the record of their intent after the fact — to construct, in the aftermath of a consequential decision, an account of what they intended, what they knew, and what they considered that is more consistent with the institutional narrative they wish to present than with the evidentiary reality of what existed at the moment of authority. This retrospective rewriting is not limited to the most egregious cases of deliberate deception. It is the structural condition of any governance environment in which the contemporaneous record of consequential decisions is not required, not preserved, and not independent of the parties whose authority it would document.

GD-II™ neutralizes the capacity for strategic intent manipulation by freezing foresight before action — by requiring that the organization's assessment of what a decision is expected to produce, and the basis on which that assessment was made, be recorded and preserved before the execution system is authorized to proceed. Predictions are recorded prior to execution, creating a contemporaneous evidentiary baseline against which subsequent accounts of what was intended can be evaluated. All scenarios — including the alternatives that were considered and discarded — are preserved in the governance record, making the deliberative process visible to independent examination rather than available only in the retrospective account that the decision-making authority chooses to provide. Outcomes are subsequently reconciled against what was known at the time authority was exercised, making it possible to determine whether the organization's account of its decision-making reflects the evidentiary reality of what existed at the moment of authority or the narrative construction of what would be institutionally convenient to have known. In such a system, personalized propaganda becomes detectable through the discrepancy between the frozen pre-execution record and the post-execution narrative. Strategic misrepresentation becomes auditable because the record of what was known and considered exists in a form that cannot be altered by the institutional interest in presenting a different account. Claims of good intention lose institutional force because intention is evaluated against the evidentiary record of what was actually known and decided rather than against the narrative of what the organization wishes it had known. The ledger remembers.

Governance That Does Not Depend on Good Leadership

Democratic and institutional systems are not immune to misuse simply because they are nominally democratic or nominally institutional. The governance mechanisms that democratic systems provide can be captured, circumvented, or eroded by the parties whose authority they are designed to constrain when those mechanisms depend for their effectiveness on the cooperation, the good faith, or the continuing institutional commitment of the leadership they are meant to govern. GD-II™ assumes that misuse will occur — that the parties whose authority is subject to governance will, at some point and in some circumstances, seek to exercise that authority in ways that governance is designed to prevent — and designs structural responses to that assumption rather than institutional hopes about the character of those who hold power.

Desired outcomes are prohibited as governance model inputs — the assessment of whether a decision should proceed cannot be structured to produce the result that the decision-making authority desires. Sentiment inference and persuasion optimization engines are excluded from the governance function — the governance infrastructure is not in the business of producing findings that are acceptable to those subject to it, but findings that are accurate. Governance applies equally to executives, boards, and regulators, without the carve-outs and exceptions that governance frameworks dependent on voluntary compliance consistently produce for those with the power to create them. Accountability survives leadership turnover — the governance record that was created under one administration of institutional authority remains available to the scrutiny of subsequent administrations and external accountability forums, rather than being subject to the institutional management of the parties whose conduct it documents. This is GD-II™, not trust in leaders. The structural distinction is the difference between a governance framework that works when leaders are trustworthy and one that works regardless.

The Shift from Ethics to Enforcement

Much of the existing discourse on AI governance ultimately asks how powerful technology can be used responsibly — how the parties who develop, deploy, and operate AI systems can be encouraged, guided, and incentivized to exercise their authority in ways that are consistent with the ethical principles, the legal requirements, and the social obligations that their power imposes on them. This framing is important, and the efforts it has generated are valuable. It does not, however, address the structural condition that makes AI governance most urgently necessary: the condition in which irresponsible decisions can be executed and produce irreversible consequences, before any accountability mechanism has the opportunity to intervene.

GD-II™ answers the AI governance challenge differently. It ensures that irresponsible decisions cannot be executed — regardless of the intent, the ideology, or the capability of the parties seeking to execute them. This represents a fundamental shift from ethics to enforcement, from advisory oversight to binding infrastructure, from the cultivation of responsible AI leadership to the structural constraint of AI-empowered decision authority. AI acceleration brings faster decisions, larger blast radii — the range and severity of consequences that a single decision can produce before its course can be corrected — less time to detect and react to the governance failures that ungoverned decisions produce, and greater plausible deniability for the parties whose authority authorized the decisions that produced the consequences. Reaction is too late in environments where AI has eliminated the interval between authorization and irreversibility.

GD-II™ inserts a non-optional constitutional layer between intent and action — a governance layer that must be traversed before consequential decisions may proceed, that operates across governments, enterprises, platforms, militaries, and regulated industries, that is supported by audit-grade provenance records, machine-enforced execution gates, and no reliance on the good faith of the parties whose authority it governs. Amodei correctly diagnosed the disease of ungoverned AI-amplified power. GD-II™ provides the structural response that the diagnosis requires: not a moral compass for those who hold power, not a safety checklist for those who deploy capability, but a GD-II™ layer that power itself must pass through. AI will continue to mature. Power will continue to consolidate in the hands of those who deploy it most effectively. Mistakes will continue to occur — not because of the absence of good intentions, but because of the structural condition in which consequential decisions remain executable without governance. The remaining and determinative question is whether that condition will be corrected by design or allowed to persist until its consequences force a reckoning that governance before the fact would have prevented. This framework asserts that consequential decisions should not remain executable without governance — and provides the structural architecture through which that assertion becomes an institutional requirement rather than an institutional aspiration.

Governed Decision-Intelligence Infrastructure™ (GD-II™)

The Missing Layer — Defined as Infrastructure, Not Philosophy

By now, one conclusion should be unavoidable. Modern enterprises are not failing because they lack intelligence — because they lack data, analytical capacity, operational sophistication, or the individual quality of the leaders who make their most consequential decisions. They are failing because intelligence is not governed at the point of decision — because the act of authority that determines what that intelligence will be directed toward, what the systems will execute, and what consequences the organization will be committed to is made without the structural governance that distinguishes accountable institutional judgment from its absence.

This chapter introduces the missing layer explicitly — not as a concept, not as a philosophy, and not as a governance aspiration that organizations are encouraged to pursue through cultural change and leadership development. It introduces it as an infrastructure class — a category of institutional design as foundational, as non-optional, and as precisely defined in its structural requirements as any other infrastructure that modern organizations depend upon to operate safely, lawfully, and sustainably at scale. An infrastructure designed for one purpose only: to ensure that consequential decisions are worthy of execution before execution begins.

Why Infrastructure Is the Correct Designation

The word infrastructure is often used loosely — applied to any foundational system or capability in ways that dilute its precise institutional meaning. In this context, its application is precise and its precision matters. Infrastructure, in the institutional sense, is foundational: it is not one option among several for organizing a particular function but the necessary foundation upon which the reliable operation of that function depends. It is non-optional once scale exists: organizations at scale cannot safely, lawfully, or sustainably operate without it, regardless of whether they have chosen to build it. It is invisible when functioning correctly: the governance it provides is experienced not as a separate institutional activity but as the background condition that makes the organization's decisions reliable, defensible, and legitimate. It is blamed only when absent: the absence of infrastructure becomes visible, and its costs become measurable, precisely at the moments when its presence would have been most consequential.

Roads are infrastructure. They do not tell people where to go, but they determine whether movement from one place to another is physically safe, legally authorized, and sustainably maintained over time. Electric grids are infrastructure. They do not tell people what to build, but they determine whether the power required to build it is reliably available under the conditions that building requires. Financial ledgers are infrastructure. They do not tell institutions what financial transactions to conduct, but they determine whether the record of those transactions is accurate, auditable, and legally defensible when accountability for them is required. In each case, the infrastructure does not make the decisions that determine what will be done. It determines whether what is done can be done safely, lawfully, and sustainably — whether the conditions under which consequential action is taken meet the standard that scale and accountability require.

Governed Decision-Intelligence Infrastructure™ (GD-II™) plays the same role for organizational decisions that every other form of critical infrastructure plays for the functions that depend on it. It does not make decisions for leaders. It does not optimize the outcomes that decisions produce. It does not replace the human judgment that authority requires. It determines whether a decision is allowed to proceed at all — whether the evidentiary standard has been met, whether the authority is explicit and accountable, whether the alternatives have been genuinely considered, and whether the risks have been consciously accepted by the party who will bear institutional responsibility for them. That determination is made before execution begins, independently of the authority seeking to proceed, and in a manner that does not depend on the voluntary compliance of the parties whose decisions it governs.

The Position It Occupies — Above Systems, Not Inside Them

GD-II™ does not replace the existing systems of the modern enterprise. It does not displace HR platforms, compliance frameworks, analytics engines, AI systems, or the operating processes through which organizational work is managed and executed. It sits above them — occupying a position in the organizational architecture that is structurally distinct from every existing system and function, governed by a mandate that none of those systems or functions were designed to perform, and operating in a temporal position — before the decision becomes an instruction to the execution system — that makes its governance function categorically different from any oversight mechanism that operates after execution has begun.

The function of GD-II™ is not execution. It is not analytical support for execution. It is not compliance oversight of execution. Its function is gatekeeping authority — the structural determination of whether a decision that is presented for execution meets the governance standard that authorizes execution to proceed. Before a decision is handed to any system for execution — before the HR platform processes a personnel action, before the AI system acts on a recommendation, before the operational process is engaged to carry out an organizational commitment — the decision must pass through this layer. Not for approval in the procedural sense of a designated authority signing a required form. For governance: the independent evaluation of whether the decision meets the evidentiary and accountability standard that its consequences require.

This positioning — above systems, before execution, independent of the authority seeking to proceed — is not merely an organizational design preference. It is the structural prerequisite of any governance function that can produce the pre-execution constraint that the preceding chapters have established as the foundational requirement of GD-II™. A governance layer embedded within any of the existing systems or functions — reporting to the leadership it governs, dependent on the cooperation of the authority it constrains, positioned after the decision has been made and before or during execution, rather than before execution begins — cannot perform the pre-execution governance function that GD-II™ is designed to provide. The position determines the function, and the function requires the position.

The Five Governance Functions It Performs

GD-II™ governs five things that no existing system or function in the modern enterprise currently governs together — five categories of institutional requirement that must be satisfied before a consequential decision is authorized to proceed to the execution layer. The integration of all five within a single governance function, operating at the decision layer before execution begins, is what distinguishes GD-II™ from every existing governance mechanism that addresses some of these requirements partially, retrospectively, or within the execution layer rather than at the decision layer before execution.

The first is Decision Authority. GD-II™ makes explicit who is deciding — the specific individual whose authority is being exercised in this specific decision, not the role or the approval chain, but the identified person whose institutional power is being committed. It makes explicit under what mandate that authority is being exercised — the institutional basis on which this person holds the power to make this decision, and the scope of the obligation that mandate creates. It makes explicit what the scope of the decision is — what it commits the organization to, whom it affects, and what the boundaries of the authority being exercised are. And it makes explicit what accountability attaches to the exercise of that authority — the institutional consequence that belongs to the identified decision-maker for the judgment they are exercising. Authority is no longer implicit, diffused across approval chains, or concealed within the operational logic of workflows and committees. It is visible, bound, and recorded at the moment of its exercise.

The second is Contemporaneous Evidence. GD-II™ captures the evidentiary basis of the decision at decision time — not afterward, not in the form of the post-hoc rationale that documentation-based governance frameworks consistently produce, but before outcomes have had the opportunity to distort the institutional memory of what was known and considered at the moment of authority. This evidence includes the known facts that were available to the decision-maker and that the decision was based upon. It includes the acknowledged unknowns — the informational gaps and uncertainties that were present and recognized, rather than suppressed in favor of a more confident presentation of the decision's basis. It includes the assumptions that were made to bridge the gap between available evidence and the confident exercise of authority. It includes the constraints — organizational, legal, operational, and temporal — that shaped the parameters within which the decision was made. And it includes the signals that were present in the decision environment and were discounted — the early indicators that pointed toward risk or toward alternatives that the deliberative process recognized and set aside rather than engaged with in ways that the record would reflect. All of this evidence is preserved before outcomes have a chance to distort memory — before the institutional incentive to present the decision in the most favorable possible light has shaped the account of what was known and considered.

The third is Rejected Alternatives. GD-II™ records the paths that were not taken — not as footnotes in a decision record that acknowledges their existence without preserving their substance, but as first-class objects in the governance record that are given the same evidentiary standing as the path that was chosen. Rejected alternatives are where judgment lives — where the quality of the deliberative process can be assessed by an independent examiner who can determine whether the alternatives were genuinely evaluated against the available evidence or acknowledged pro forma and set aside without the engagement that genuine deliberation requires. Without a contemporaneous record of rejected alternatives, no decision can be evaluated honestly on its merits. The choice is visible in the record. The judgment that made the choice is not, because the judgment is expressed not only in what was selected but in what was considered and not selected, and why. GD-II™ makes that expression of judgment part of the official record of the decision.

The fourth is Risk Ownership. GD-II™ forces explicit acknowledgment of the risks that the decision carries — not vague optimism about the probability of favorable outcomes, not the post-hoc rationalization that the organization deploys after adverse outcomes have surfaced, but a clear and contemporaneous statement of what risks are being accepted by the exercise of this authority, why those risks are judged to be acceptable given the evidence available and the alternatives that were considered, and who is accountable for that acceptance. Risk ceases to be ambient — present in the decision environment but unacknowledged in the governance record, available to be invoked as an explanation after consequences materialize but never required to be confronted before they do. It becomes owned — explicitly identified, explicitly accepted, and explicitly attributed to the accountable party at the moment of decision.

The fifth is Decision Record Integrity. GD-II™ produces a record of the decision that can withstand the scrutiny that accountability requires — not because it has been polished or crafted for external presentation, but because it is true to the moment it was made. It is contemporaneous, capturing what existed at the time of authority rather than what can be constructed in response to scrutiny. It is complete, reflecting the full scope of what was known, what was considered, and what was accepted. It is immutable, preserved in a form that cannot be retroactively altered by the institutional incentives that would otherwise shape the retrospective presentation of decisions whose consequences have become visible. And it is independent — held by a governance function that does not report to the authority it documents, and that cannot be modified by the parties whose exercise of authority it records. This record can withstand time — it remains accurate, independent of how long after the decision the accountability arrives. It can withstand personnel change — the departure of the individuals who made the decision does not alter the contemporaneous record of what they decided and why. It can withstand legal scrutiny, regulatory review, and board inquiry — not because it presents the organization's decisions in the best possible light, but because it presents them accurately.

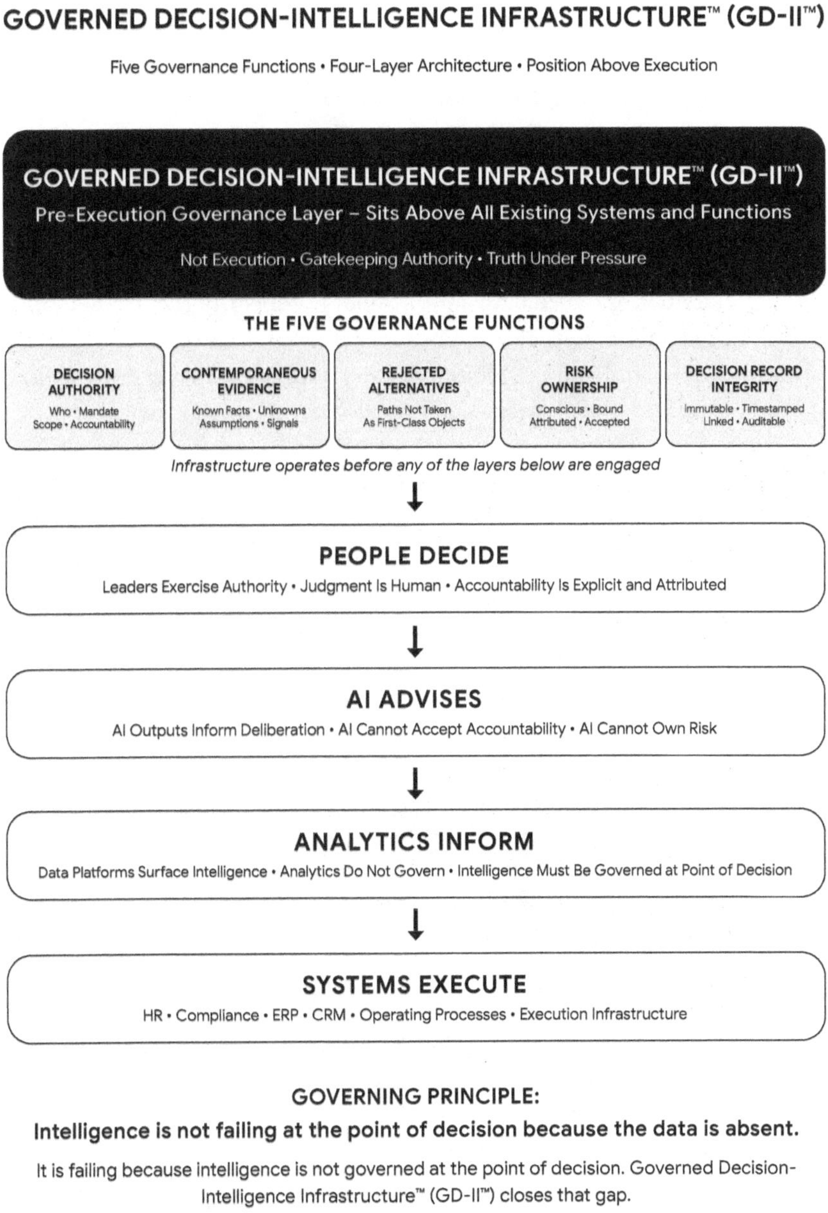

GOVERNED DECISION-INTELLIGENCE INFRASTRUCTURE™ (GD-II™)

Five Governance Functions • Four-Layer Architecture • Position Above Execution

GOVERNED DECISION-INTELLIGENCE INFRASTRUCTURE™ (GD-II™)

Pre-Execution Governance Layer – Sits Above All Existing Systems and Functions

Not Execution • Gatekeeping Authority • Truth Under Pressure

THE FIVE GOVERNANCE FUNCTIONS

DECISION AUTHORITY	CONTEMPORANEOUS EVIDENCE	REJECTED ALTERNATIVES	RISK OWNERSHIP	DECISION RECORD INTEGRITY
Who • Mandate Scope • Accountability	Known Facts • Unknowns Assumptions • Signals	Paths Not Taken As First-Class Objects	Conscious • Bound Attributed • Accepted	Immutable • Timestamped Linked • Auditable

Infrastructure operates before any of the layers below are engaged

PEOPLE DECIDE

Leaders Exercise Authority • Judgment Is Human • Accountability Is Explicit and Attributed

AI ADVISES

AI Outputs Inform Deliberation • AI Cannot Accept Accountability • AI Cannot Own Risk

ANALYTICS INFORM

Data Platforms Surface Intelligence • Analytics Do Not Govern • Intelligence Must Be Governed at Point of Decision

SYSTEMS EXECUTE

HR • Compliance • ERP • CRM • Operating Processes • Execution Infrastructure

GOVERNING PRINCIPLE:

Intelligence is not failing at the point of decision because the data is absent.

It is failing because intelligence is not governed at the point of decision. Governed Decision-Intelligence Infrastructure™ (GD-II™) closes that gap.

Figure 10.1 — Governed Decision-Intelligence Infrastructure™ (GD-II™): Five Governance Functions and Four-Layer Architecture. The infrastructure layer sits above all existing systems. People decide; AI advises; analytics inform; systems execute. Intelligence is not failing because data is absent — it is failing because it is not governed at the point of decision.

What This Infrastructure Does Not Do

The institutional clarity of what GD-II™ is requires equal clarity about what it is not — about the governance functions it does not perform and the institutional outcomes it does not produce. This clarity is not a caveat. It is a precise definition of the governance function, and understanding its limits is as important as understanding its requirements for organizations that are building the institutional architecture that the next evolution demands.

GD-II™ does not optimize outcomes. It does not identify the decision most likely to produce the best organizational result, does not recommend the path most consistent with strategic objectives, and does not enhance the analytical quality of the information available to the decision-maker. Organizations that expect governance infrastructure to improve their decision outcomes directly have misunderstood the distinction between governance and optimization. GD-II™ does not guarantee success. Decisions that meet every requirement of Governed Decision Intelligence™ (GD-I™) can still produce adverse outcomes — because outcomes are shaped by factors that extend beyond the governance of the decisions that initiate them. It does not eliminate human judgment. The decisions that GD-II™ governs are made by the humans who hold the authority to make them, and the quality of those decisions depends on the quality of the human judgment behind them. It does not replace leadership. It does not remove risk — risk is an inherent feature of consequential organizational decisions, and the governance function of GD-II™ is not to eliminate it but to ensure that it is consciously acknowledged and explicitly accepted.

The role of GD-II™ is narrower than outcome optimization and more powerful in its governance consequence. It ensures that when risk is taken, the risk-taking is conscious rather than inadvertent — that the decision-maker was aware of the risks at the moment of authority. It ensures that risk-taking is evidence-bound — that the assessment of the risks was based on the available evidence rather than on optimistic assumptions that would not survive independent examination. It ensures that risk-taking is authority-owned — that the party whose power authorized the acceptance of the risk is identified and accountable for that acceptance. And it ensures that risk-taking is explicitly accepted — that the institutional record reflects a conscious act of governance rather than the silent assumption of risks that the organization never formally acknowledged. This is the difference between governance and luck — between an organization that knows what it is accepting when it makes consequential decisions and one that discovers what it accepted only after the consequences become visible.

Why It Cannot Be Reduced to a Workflow

Workflows route tasks. They define the sequence of operational steps that must be completed, the parties responsible for each step, and the conditions that must be satisfied before the next step in the sequence may proceed. They are essential instruments of execution governance, and they perform their function reliably within the execution domain for which they were designed. GD-II™ interrogates choice — it evaluates whether the decision that a workflow would execute is worthy of execution, which is a categorically different institutional function from routing the steps of the execution process.

A workflow can enforce sequence: it can ensure that step three does not proceed until step two is complete, and that step two does not proceed until the designated party has provided the required authorization. It cannot evaluate the legitimacy of the authorization it routes — it cannot assess whether the party providing the authorization was exercising genuine deliberative judgment or performing a procedural sign-off, whether the decision being authorized met the evidentiary standard that governance requires, or whether the alternatives to the authorized path were genuinely considered. When GD-II™ is reduced to a workflow — when the governance function is converted into a series of procedural steps that must be completed before execution proceeds — the governance function loses precisely the capacity that distinguishes it from execution oversight. Momentum dominates because the workflow's completion becomes the organizational objective rather than the governance quality of the decision it surrounds. Authority hides because the workflow distributes procedural responsibility across designated steps without requiring that the authority behind those steps be explicitly identified and held accountable. Alternatives vanish because the workflow confirms that the required steps were completed without preserving any record of the alternatives that were evaluated before the direction encoded in those steps was chosen. Evidence becomes performative because the workflow produces documentation of its own completion rather than contemporaneous evidence of the decision quality that the governance function was designed to require.

This infrastructure must interrupt flow when necessary — when the governance conditions for execution have not been met, when the evidentiary standard is not satisfied, when authority is not explicit, when alternatives have not been genuinely considered, or when risk has not been consciously acknowledged and accepted. Its function is not speed: the organizations that deploy it will not experience a reduction in operational speed in the aggregate, because the time invested in pre-execution governance is recovered many times over in the time that is not spent managing the consequences of ungoverned decisions that were executed without it. Its function is truth under pressure — the institutional capacity to govern consequential decisions under the real conditions of organizational life, including the pressure, the authority dynamics, the incentive misalignments, and the cognitive distortions that the preceding chapters have established as the structural conditions under which the most consequential organizational decisions are most frequently made.

Why It Cannot Be Replaced by a Committee

Committees dilute accountability. When the exercise of consequential authority is processed through a collective approval structure in which multiple parties share the responsibility for the decision, the institutional accountability that governance requires — the precise attribution of decision authority to an identified individual who bears the full institutional consequence of the judgment they exercised — is distributed across the collective process in ways that prevent it from functioning as genuine accountability. No individual member of a committee that collectively approved a decision that later produced harm bears the full accountability for that decision, because no individual member was required to own the judgment on their own terms. GD-II™ clarifies accountability — it identifies the party whose authority determined the outcome and creates the contemporaneous record that preserves that attribution independent of the collective process that surrounded the decision.

Committees seek consensus. Their institutional logic is oriented toward the production of collective agreement — toward the resolution of differences and the achievement of alignment that makes execution possible. In pursuing consensus, committees systematically suppress the exposure of the weak reasoning, the unexamined assumptions, the authority dynamics, the overconfidence, and the suppressed dissent that represent the most important categories of information for the governance of consequential decisions. The governance function of GD-II™ is not to produce consensus. It is to produce exposure — to surface the elements of the decision that the social and hierarchical dynamics of collective deliberation most reliably conceal, and to preserve a record of those elements that cannot be smoothed over by the retrospective narrative of collective agreement. It exposes weak reasoning that the momentum of the deliberative process would otherwise carry forward into execution without examination. It exposes unexamined assumptions that the confidence of the most authoritative parties in the room would otherwise insulate them from challenge. It exposes authority dynamics that make genuine dissent institutionally unavailable and that the record of apparent consensus would otherwise render invisible. It exposes the overconfidence that the pressure environment and the incentive structure of the organization produce, and that the committee process ratifies rather than corrects. It exposes suppressed dissent that the organizational consequences of genuine challenge prevent it from being expressed, and that the governance record must therefore require rather than merely permit. GD-II™ does not require agreement. It requires honesty — the institutional honesty that governance demands and that the collective dynamics of committee deliberation most consistently prevent.

The Boundary Between AI and Governance

AI operates on patterns — on the recognition of regularities in historical data that can be applied to new inputs to generate outputs that are statistically consistent with the patterns the historical data has established. GD-II™ operates on responsibility — on the governance of consequential human acts of authority that must meet an evidentiary and accountability standard that no statistical model can satisfy. An AI can predict outcomes — it can generate probabilistic assessments of what a given decision is likely to produce based on the patterns that historical decisions and their outcomes have established. It cannot accept accountability for those predictions — it has no institutional standing, no decision authority, and no capacity for the kind of moral and legal responsibility that accountability requires.

An AI can recommend paths — it can identify the option most consistent with the optimization objective it has been designed to pursue. It cannot own risk — it has no institutional accountability for the consequences of the paths it recommends, no capacity to acknowledge and accept the risks that those paths carry on its own behalf, and no standing to be held responsible when those risks materialize into consequences. Without a governing layer above AI — without an infrastructure that determines whether the consequential decision to act on an AI recommendation meets the evidentiary and accountability standard that governance requires — bias is accelerated rather than reduced, because the AI system's built-in biases are enacted at scale without the governance examination that would expose them. Authority becomes obscured rather than explicit, because the AI system's recommendation interposes a layer of apparent analytical objectivity between the human authority that will be held accountable for the decision and the decision that was made on the basis of that recommendation. Accountability evaporates rather than being preserved, because the chain of institutional responsibility between the decision that produced a consequence and the human authority whose judgment authorized it becomes impossible to reconstruct once the AI system's recommendation has been substituted for the contemporaneous evidentiary basis that governance requires.

GD-II™ governs whether AI outputs may be acted upon — whether the decision to act on an AI recommendation meets the governance standard required for that action to proceed — not whether the AI outputs are statistically impressive, analytically sophisticated, or consistent with the optimization objectives that the system was designed to pursue. The governance question is not whether the AI is capable. It is whether the human decision to act on the AI's recommendation is governed. That question belongs to GD-II™, not to the AI system whose output initiates it.

The Organizational Changes That Follow

Once GD-II™ exists as a functioning layer in the organizational architecture — once the governance conditions for consequential decisions are structural requirements rather than institutional aspirations — the organization changes in ways that are subtle in their initial expression and profound in their cumulative institutional effect. Leaders slow down at the right moments: not universally, not in ways that compromise the operational speed that competitive environments require, but specifically at the moments when the decision stakes are high, when reversibility is limited, and when the governance standard requires the deliberative engagement that the pressure environment would otherwise prevent. Dissent surfaces earlier in the deliberative process because the governance structure requires its expression rather than merely permitting it — because the alternatives and the risk acknowledgment that governance demands create the structural conditions in which genuine challenge is institutionally required rather than institutionally risky.

Risk is discussed openly because the governance record requires its acknowledgment and because the institutional consequence of undisclosed risk — the exposure that comes from a governance record that omits what was known at the time of decision — exceeds the institutional cost of acknowledging risk that the governance framework creates the structured space to address. Authority becomes visible because the governance infrastructure requires its explicit identification, and the institutional culture gradually adapts to the norm of explicit authority in ways that make the diffusion of accountability through approval chains and committee processes less available as a default organizational response to consequential decisions. Learning improves because the contemporaneous decision record creates the evidentiary basis for genuine institutional learning — for the assessment of decision quality independent of outcome, which is the only form of organizational learning that produces improvement rather than outcome-correlated reinforcement. Accountability becomes natural rather than punitive because the governance record establishes what was known and accepted at the moment of authority, which means that the attribution of accountability to specific decision-makers reflects the institutional reality of who exercised authority rather than the political dynamics of who can be most conveniently held responsible after the fact. Decisions become events rather than assumptions — visible, governable, and capable of being examined on their own terms rather than absorbed into the operational flow of a process that treats them as starting conditions rather than as acts of authority requiring independent governance.

The Architecture of a Governed Enterprise

In an organization that has built and deployed GD-II™, the institutional architecture achieves a clarity of function and a separation of roles that the Systems Age's conflation of execution governance with decision governance has consistently prevented. Systems execute decisions — the operational infrastructure of the enterprise carries out the decisions that governance has authorized, with the speed, consistency, and scale that systemization makes possible. Analytics inform decisions — the data platforms and analytical capabilities of the organization provide the intelligence that decision-makers need to exercise their authority under the best possible evidentiary conditions. AI advises decisions — the AI systems deployed by the organization generate recommendations, predictions, and analytical outputs that are made available to human decision-makers as inputs to the deliberative process. People make decisions — the individuals who hold the institutional authority for consequential organizational choices exercise that authority, bearing the full accountability that the governance record preserves and that the infrastructure requires to be explicit.

This separation of functions is not bureaucratic. It is clarifying. It restores the institutional clarity that the Systems Age's conflation of execution with governance eroded — the clarity about who decides, on what basis, with what evidence, and with what accountability that every governance framework aspires to produce and that only GD-II™ is structurally designed to require. It restores trust between leadership and execution because the governance record that GD-II™ produces establishes that the decisions being executed were made responsibly, and execution teams operate with the confidence that the authority behind their work has been genuinely exercised. It restores trust between leadership and oversight, because the governance record provides the contemporaneous evidence that boards and audit functions require to fulfill their oversight obligations with substance rather than with the procedural confirmation that documentation-based governance consistently produces in its place. And it restores trust between leadership and history — between the organizations that make consequential decisions and the institutional record that determines how those decisions are understood long after the circumstances under which they were made have changed.

The Question That Defines the Governed Enterprise

An enterprise is no longer fully defined by how efficiently it executes. The execution efficiency of the modern enterprise — the sophistication of its operational systems, the capability of its analytical platforms, the intelligence of its AI deployments, the maturity of its compliance frameworks — is no longer the primary determinant of institutional fitness in environments where the accountability for consequential decisions is no longer retrospective but expected by design. An enterprise is no longer defined by how advanced its systems are. System sophistication does not produce decision governance. An enterprise is no longer defined by how intelligent its tools appear. Tool intelligence does not produce decision accountability. It is defined by one question: are its decisions governed?

If the answer is no — if the organization's consequential decisions are made without the pre-execution governance that GD-II™ provides — the enterprise is incomplete. Not insufficiently systemized. Not inadequately compliant. Not in need of better analytics or more sophisticated AI. Incomplete at the foundational level of institutional design — missing the governance layer that makes the exercise of consequential authority accountable, defensible, and legitimate in the environments where accountability, defensibility, and legitimacy are increasingly the conditions of institutional survival.

GD-II™ defines this category of institutional requirement. But categories are only meaningful when they change behavior — when the recognition that a foundational institutional requirement has never been met produces the architectural response that the requirement demands. The next chapter examines what happens inside organizations once this layer exists — how leadership changes in its relationship to the decisions it makes, how organizational culture shifts in response to the governance conditions that GD-II™ creates, and why the resistance that this shift produces is not only inevitable but the most reliable indicator that the governance function is operating as it was designed to.

CHAPTER 11

THE GOVERNED ENTERPRISE

What Actually Changes When Decisions Are No Longer Invisible

The introduction of Governed Decision-Intelligence Infrastructure™ (GD-II™) does not feel dramatic at first. There is no reorganization that reshapes reporting lines or redefines the structural relationships that constitute the organization's operational hierarchy. There are no mass replacements of the systems, platforms, and processes that constitute the execution architecture of the enterprise. There is no sudden shift in the formal structure of authority that would announce itself as a visible institutional transformation. What changes is more fundamental and, precisely because it is more fundamental, more difficult to perceive at the moment it begins.

And yet, within governed enterprises — within organizations that have built GD-II™ and are operating under the governance conditions it creates — something unmistakable begins to change. The change is not visible in the organizational chart or in the system architecture. It is visible in how decisions are made, how authority is exercised, how risk is discussed, and how accountability is understood by the individuals who carry it. This chapter describes those changes — not aspirationally, not as a vision of what governance could make possible, but mechanically: as a description of what actually happens when decisions are no longer invisible, when authority can no longer hide inside workflows, and when the governance conditions for consequential action are structural requirements rather than institutional aspirations.

Decisions Become Explicit Events

In most organizations operating under the governance conditions of the Systems Age, decisions are implied rather than declared. They are embedded in the operational flow of organizational activity in ways that make them structurally invisible — absorbed into project launches that begin executing a direction without any identifiable moment at which the decision to launch was made and owned. They are implied in hiring approvals that process a personnel commitment without any contemporaneous record of the judgment that determined this candidate over the alternatives that were available. They are embedded in promotions that advance an individual's institutional standing without any identified moment at which the authority to elevate that individual was exercised and accounted for. They are implied in strategic shifts that reorient organizational resources and commitments without any governance record of when the decision was made, who made it, and on what basis it was made, rather than the alternatives that were available.

Once GD-II™ exists as a functioning layer in the organizational architecture, this condition changes. Decisions become explicit events — discrete, identifiable moments in the organizational life of the enterprise that have a defined structure distinguishing them from the operational flow that surrounds them. An explicit decision event has a defined moment: a specific point in time at which the exercise of authority is recorded, and the organization's commitment to a path is established and preserved. It has a named authority: an identified individual whose specific institutional power is being exercised in this specific decision, whose mandate for that exercise is recorded, and whose accountability for its consequences is established contemporaneously with the exercise itself. It has a recorded scope: a contemporaneous definition of what the decision commits the organization to, who it affects, and what the boundaries of the authority being exercised are. And it has a bounded risk profile: an explicit acknowledgment of the risks the decision carries, recorded at the moment of authority before outcomes are known and before the institutional incentive to minimize the salience of risk has had the opportunity to shape the governance record.

Nothing about the execution of the decision changes. The operational machinery that carries the decision out — the HR processes, the project management systems, the financial approval workflows, the operational procedures that implement the organizational commitment — continues to function as it was designed to. But the organization now knows when a decision occurred rather than discovering it in hindsight, when consequences have already materialized, and the deliberative process that produced them is no longer available for contemporaneous examination. This alone — the knowledge of when a decision occurred, who made it, and on what basis — transforms accountability from a retrospective exercise in assigning responsibility for consequences that have already become irreversible into a prospective institutional function that governs the exercise of authority before it produces consequences that require accountability.

Authority Becomes Visible

In ungoverned enterprises, authority disperses into the operational architecture of the organization in ways that make its exercise structurally invisible. People describe consequential institutional commitments in language that conceals who made them and why: it was a group decision, implying that the collective character of the approval process eliminates individual accountability for the judgment it produced. The process led us here, implying that the institutional logic of the operational workflow created the commitment without any individual party having exercised the authority to choose it. That is how it is usually done, implying that established precedent rather than deliberate judgment determined the direction, eliminating the question of who decided in favor of the observation that this is what is typically done in situations of this type.

In governed enterprises, authority is surfaced — made explicit, recorded, and attributed to the specific individual whose institutional power determined the outcome — not to punish, but to clarify. The organizational question shifts from who approved this — the procedural inquiry that seeks a designated sign-off rather than an accountable act of judgment — to who decided and on what basis. This shift is more than semantic. It is the difference between an organization that records procedural compliance and one that records the exercise of institutional authority. The governance record of the governed enterprise answers the question of who decided and why in a form that is contemporaneous with the decision, independent of the outcomes that followed, and capable of withstanding the scrutiny of any forum that requires an account of how the decision was made.

This clarity produces an unexpected effect on the behavior of the individuals who carry consequential authority within the governed enterprise. Executives become more careful — not more defensive, not more risk-averse, not slower in their decision cadence — but more deliberate in the exercise of the authority that the governance record will attribute to them. The knowledge that the exercise of authority will be explicitly recorded changes the character of the deliberative process that precedes it, creating conditions under which the institutional investment in genuine deliberation — in the honest consideration of alternatives, in the frank acknowledgment of risk, in the explicit identification of what is being accepted and what is being set aside — exceeds the institutional cost of the additional attention it requires. Managers become more thoughtful in the exercise of the operational authority that their roles carry. Teams become more candid in the assessment of the directions they are asked to pursue, because the governance record creates conditions in which the expression of genuine concern is structurally available rather than institutionally risky. Because ambiguity no longer protects anyone from accountability — because the governance record makes the exercise of authority visible regardless of the opacity of the approval process that surrounded it — the institutional incentive to maintain protective ambiguity diminishes, and the institutional incentive to exercise authority carefully and deliberately increases.

Risk Changes Character

In most organizations operating without Governed Decision-Intelligence Infrastructure™, risk exists everywhere and nowhere simultaneously. It is discussed in abstract terms — in risk matrices, in probability assessments, in the language of enterprise risk management that quantifies categories of potential adverse outcome without ever requiring that the specific risks of a specific decision be acknowledged, accepted, and attributed to the authority making the decision in contemporaneous form. It is assigned rhetorically — described as a consideration that was evaluated and determined to be acceptable, without any contemporaneous record of what specific risks were identified, who evaluated them, and on what basis they were judged to be within acceptable tolerances. It is realized only after damage — becoming visible to the organization as a governance concern at precisely the moment when the governance opportunity that would have required it to be addressed before execution has passed.

GD-II™ forces a different institutional posture toward risk — one that is not defined by the retrospective management of risks that have already materialized, but by the prospective governance of risks that are being consciously accepted in the exercise of consequential authority. Risk is articulated explicitly in the governance record: the specific potential adverse consequences of the decision are identified and recorded at the moment of authority, creating a contemporaneous account of what the decision-maker understood to be the risk profile of the path they were choosing. Risk is accepted consciously: the governance record reflects a deliberate act of risk acceptance rather than the silent assumption of risks that the organization will later claim it did not foresee. Risk is bound to authority: the identification of the risks accepted is attributed to the specific individual whose authority authorized their acceptance, creating an explicit connection between the exercise of institutional power and the institutional accountability for the risk it carries. Risk is preserved immutably: the contemporaneous record of what risks were accepted cannot be retroactively modified to reflect a different understanding of what was known or accepted at the moment of decision.

This governance posture toward risk does not reduce risk-taking. Organizations do not become more conservative when governance of their risk acceptance is required. The effect is the opposite: leaders take bolder risks in governed environments than in ungoverned ones, because the governance record creates the conditions under which bold risk-taking is institutionally distinguishable from reckless risk-taking. When a leader can demonstrate — through a contemporaneous governance record — that the risks of a consequential decision were explicitly identified, honestly assessed, and consciously accepted at the moment of authority, the institutional standing of that leader is not diminished by an adverse outcome that the governance record reflects was within the range of acknowledged possibility. Bold decisions with adverse outcomes, in a governed enterprise, are assessed as exercises of institutional judgment rather than as evidence of governance failure. This changes the calculus of risk-taking in ways that make governance a competitive advantage rather than a governance burden.

Dissent Becomes Structural

Governed enterprises do not create more dissent in the sense of increasing the frequency of disagreement or the intensity of organizational conflict. What they create is earlier dissent — the structural availability of genuine challenge, alternative perspectives, and risk assessments at the moment in the deliberative process when they can still change the decision, rather than at the moment when the organizational momentum of an established direction has made them institutionally irrelevant. Because alternatives must be surfaced as a governance requirement rather than as a voluntary contribution to a deliberative process that may or may not welcome them, disagreement becomes structural rather than confrontational. It is not an expression of individual opposition to an established direction but a required element of the governance record that every consequential decision must produce.

Dissent is no longer framed as resistance — as a challenge to the institutional authority of the decision-maker or to the organizational commitment that the decision represents — but as a required input to the governance process. This reframing changes who speaks and when. Junior voices in the organization surface earlier in the deliberative process because the governance requirement for genuine alternative consideration creates structural conditions in which the expression of inconvenient perspectives is institutionally supported rather than professionally risky. Experts challenge assumptions sooner because the governance record requires that the assumptions embedded in a consequential decision be explicitly identified and that the challenge to those assumptions be reflected in the record rather than suppressed by the authority dynamics of the decision environment. Silence becomes conspicuous rather than safe — in a governance environment where the absence of recorded dissent is interpreted as evidence of genuine consensus rather than as the absence of structurally available challenge, the choice to remain silent in the face of genuine concern is no longer the path of least institutional resistance. Over time, dissent in governed enterprises loses its stigma and gains legitimacy as the institutional contribution that the governance framework has established it to be.

Meeting Behavior Changes

One of the first observable changes in organizations that have deployed GD-II™ is in the character and conduct of meetings — particularly the meetings at which consequential decisions are made or that are nominally convened for that purpose. Meetings become shorter in duration, not because the deliberative engagement with consequential decisions is reduced, but because the governance framework that GD-II™ creates separates the deliberative activity of decision-making from the informational and coordination activity that meetings are often used to combine, in ways that reduce the time spent in each category without reducing the institutional quality of either.

Meetings become more focused on fewer decisions because the governance requirement that each consequential decision be explicitly identified and governed creates the institutional clarity about what the meeting is actually for, which the conflation of deliberation with information sharing in ungoverned organizations consistently prevents. They become less prone to execution drift — the organizational tendency to begin implementing a direction before the decision to pursue it has been explicitly made and governed — because the governance framework requires that the decision event precede the execution commitment rather than emerging from it. They center on trade-offs rather than updates, because the governance record requires that alternatives and risk be explicitly engaged rather than presented as background context for a direction that has already been informally established.

These changes in meeting behavior are the product of a single structural shift that GD-II™ creates: the separation of discussion from decision, of information sharing from the exercise of authority, and of exploration from commitment. When the moment of decision is made explicit by the governance requirement that it be identified and recorded as a distinct institutional event, meetings no longer pretend that every conversation about a consequential topic is or might become a decision event. The deliberative character of each meeting is established by its governance function — whether it is a discussion meeting, an information meeting, or a decision meeting — and the institutional behavior appropriate to each is governed by that distinction rather than left to the informal dynamics of organizational culture to determine. This reduces noise — the institutional cost of meetings that are unclear about their own purpose — and increases weight — the institutional significance of meetings that are explicitly convened for the governance of consequential decisions.

Post-Mortems Change

Because evidence is captured at decision time — because the governance record preserves the contemporaneous basis of every consequential decision before outcomes are known — the institutional character of post-mortem analysis changes in governed enterprises in ways that are among the most significant and durable governance benefits of GD-II™. The organization no longer asks the questions that ungoverned environments make unavoidable: who failed, and why did they not see the adverse outcome coming? These questions are unavoidable in ungoverned environments because the absence of a contemporaneous decision record makes it impossible to assess the quality of the judgment that produced the outcome independent of the outcome itself. When the only record available is the outcome and the retrospective account of what was intended, the assessment of whether the decision was sound is inevitably distorted by knowledge of what followed — attributing to poor judgment outcomes that were within the acknowledged range of uncertainty, and attributing to good judgment outcomes that reflected luck rather than governance discipline.

In governed enterprises, post-mortems ask different questions. What did the decision-maker know at the time, as reflected in the contemporaneous record? Was the reasoning that produced the decision sound, given what was known, rather than what was subsequently revealed? Were the alternatives genuinely evaluated against the evidentiary basis that the governance record reflects? Were the risks that materialized within the acknowledged range of accepted risk at the time of decision, or did they represent failures of risk identification that the governance requirement should have prevented? These questions allow organizations to learn from good decisions that produced bad outcomes — to recognize when adverse results occurred within the range of risks that was consciously accepted at the moment of authority, and to distinguish that category of outcome from the category of outcome that reflects a failure of decision governance. They allow organizations to identify flawed reasoning that was masked by good results — to recognize when the governance record reveals a decision process that was inadequate despite producing a favorable outcome, and to treat that inadequacy as a governance failure rather than a governance success.

They allow accountability to become developmental rather than punitive — oriented toward the improvement of judgment and governance discipline rather than toward the assignment of institutional blame for outcomes that the governance record can evaluate independently of their favorability.

Culture Stops Carrying What Structure Should

Many organizations that have recognized the governance gap at the decision layer have attempted to close it through cultural interventions — through institutional commitments to courage, transparency, ownership, and integrity that are designed to produce in the individuals who carry decision authority the governance discipline that the structural architecture of the organization does not require. These values matter genuinely and they are not made irrelevant by the introduction of governance structure. Courage, transparency, ownership, and integrity are institutional virtues that produce better organizational outcomes under every governance condition. But culture cannot compensate for missing infrastructure — cannot produce, through the accumulated effect of institutional values on individual behavior, the governance outcomes that require structural enforcement rather than individual commitment.

In governed enterprises, culture no longer carries the burden of governance. Structure does. The governance conditions that GD-II™ creates are not dependent on the willingness of individuals to exercise courage in the face of institutional pressure, to maintain transparency against the incentives that reward concealment, to own accountability in the absence of structural mechanisms that make accountability explicit, or to act with integrity against the institutional dynamics that reward the performance of integrity over its substance. These governance outcomes are produced by the structural requirements of the governance framework rather than by the individual character of the parties subject to it.

As a result of this structural shift, the relationship between organizational values and organizational behavior changes in governed enterprises in ways that are genuinely transformative. Values become actionable rather than aspirational — they are expressed in the governance record rather than in the organizational rhetoric that surrounds the governance gap. Expectations become clear rather than normative — they are defined by the structural requirements of the governance framework rather than by the informal institutional standards that culture produces and that individuals are expected to interpret and apply without the structural support of explicit governance requirements. Ethical behavior becomes supported rather than heroic — it is not a function of individual willingness to bear the institutional cost of acting according to stated values but of a structural environment in which acting according to those values is the path of least institutional resistance rather than the most costly one. The organization stops relying on exceptional individuals to prevent systemic governance failures — it designs a governance architecture in which systemic governance failures are structurally prevented rather than individually resisted.

Why Resistance Is Inevitable and What It Signals

GD-II™ does not meet universal enthusiasm in the organizations that introduce it. Resistance emerges from specific institutional quarters, and the consistency of its source across organizations that have deployed GD-II™ is itself a governance signal — an indication that the governance function is operating as designed by constraining the institutional conditions that the resistant parties have benefited from in the ungoverned environment. Those accustomed to ambiguous authority — to the institutional convenience of exercising consequential power without being required to own it explicitly in a governance record — experience the visibility requirements of GD-II™ as an institutional burden rather than a governance benefit. Those rewarded for speed without scrutiny — whose institutional standing has been built on a track record of rapid decision-making that the ungoverned environment evaluated by outcomes rather than by the quality of the deliberative process that produced them — experience the governance requirements as impediments to the performance profile that their institutional reputation depends on.

Those who benefited from the diffusion of responsibility — who have operated within the institutional protection of collective approval processes that distributed accountability across enough parties to ensure that no individual bore the full weight of any consequential judgment — experience the clarity of authority requirements in GD-II™ as an unwelcome exposure of the accountability that the ungoverned environment allowed them to avoid. This resistance is not ideological. It is structural — the predictable institutional response of parties whose positions in the organization depend on governance conditions that GD-II™ is specifically designed to change. GD-II™ redistributes visibility, and visibility changes power dynamics. The individuals and functions whose institutional influence depended on the opacity of the ungoverned decision environment — on the ability to exercise authority without it being explicitly recorded, to accept risk without it being consciously acknowledged, and to avoid accountability through the diffusion of responsibility — find their institutional position altered by the governance conditions that GD-II™ creates. Organizations that anticipate this resistance and address it as a structural condition rather than a cultural failure manage it successfully. Organizations that ignore it, or treat it as individual resistance to change rather than as the structural response to a genuine redistribution of institutional visibility, find that the governance infrastructure retreats in the face of the institutional dynamics that the ungoverned environment produced and that have not yet been reorganized by the governance conditions the infrastructure creates.

What Remains Unchanged

It is important to establish with precision what GD-II™ does not change in the organizations that deploy it, because the misunderstanding of these limits is among the most common sources of institutional resistance to the infrastructure's adoption. Leaders still decide — the consequential acts of authority that determine organizational direction, which commit organizational resources, and that establish the institutional commitments that define the organization's path remain the responsibility and the prerogative of the individuals who hold the authority to make them. The introduction of GD-II™ changes the conditions under which those decisions are made and the governance requirements they must satisfy before execution is authorized. It does not change who makes them or the institutional standing of those who do.

Strategy still evolves — the organizational direction that the enterprise pursues remains subject to the strategic judgment of leadership, to the analytical intelligence of the organization's informational systems, and to the competitive and regulatory conditions of the environment in which the enterprise operates. GD-II™ governs the decisions through which strategy is exercised. It does not determine the strategy that those decisions implement. Speed still matters — the competitive environments in which enterprises operate continue to reward the ability to identify and respond to strategic opportunities with the decisiveness that markets and stakeholders reward. GD-II™ creates governance conditions that make consequential decisions faster in the aggregate — by reducing the organizational friction of ambiguous authority and ungoverned risk — rather than slower. Risk still exists — the uncertainty, the competitive exposure, and the operational vulnerability that are inherent features of consequential organizational action are not eliminated by the governance of the decisions that create and manage them. Outcomes remain uncertain — the results that consequential decisions produce are shaped by factors that extend beyond the governance of the decisions that initiate them, and GD-II™ governs the quality of the decision process rather than the favorability of the outcomes it produces.

GD-II™ does not make organizations conservative. It makes them legible to themselves — capable of knowing what they have decided, why they decided it, what risks they accepted, and who was accountable for the judgment behind each consequential commitment. This self-legibility is not the same as conservatism. It is the institutional condition that makes informed risk-taking possible — that makes it possible to distinguish between the bold exercise of deliberate judgment and the inadvertent assumption of risks that the organization never formally acknowledged. Conservative organizations avoid risk. Governed organizations take deliberate risks and know why.

The Maturity That Governance Creates

Over time, governed enterprises develop a distinctive institutional characteristic that distinguishes them from enterprises operating in the ungoverned environment of the Systems Age. They stop being surprised by their own decisions. When scrutiny arrives — legal, regulatory, public, or historical — the organization is not scrambling to reconstruct the intent behind a decision whose contemporaneous basis has been displaced by the post-hoc rationale that the institutional incentives of the ungoverned environment reliably produce. It already knows. The governance record tells it what was decided, when it was decided, by whom, on what basis, with what alternatives considered, with what risks accepted, and with what authority attributed and accountable. That knowledge — available contemporaneously, preserved immutably, and independent of the institutional incentives that would otherwise shape its retrospective presentation — is not immunity from accountability. It is the institutional maturity that governance produces.

In the Systems Age, scale meant replication — the capacity to extend the operational logic of a functioning model across new geographies, new markets, and new volumes of activity without requiring the reinvention of the institutional knowledge that the model represented. In the governed enterprise, scale means something more demanding and more institutionally significant: repeatable judgment under pressure. The capacity to make consequential decisions at scale — under the time compression, the authority dynamics, the incentive misalignments, and the cognitive distortions that the preceding chapters have established as the structural conditions of enterprise decision-making — with the governance discipline that accountability requires is not a feature of the Systems Age's operational architecture. It is the defining capability of the governed enterprise, and it is the capability that distinguishes the institutions that will endure in the accountability environments of the next era from those that will accumulate the institutional debt of ungoverned decisions until that debt becomes the governing condition of their existence. An organization that cannot govern its judgment under pressure will eventually be constrained — not by markets, not by competition, not by the operational limitations of its execution systems, but by its own decisions and the accountability they carry.

GD-II™ changes how organizations operate not by adding control — not by imposing new procedural requirements on the execution layer that slow operational activity and reduce organizational agility — but by restoring awareness: the institutional awareness of what is being decided, why it is being decided, who is deciding it, and what it costs. It does not guarantee success. It guarantees accountability without hindsight — the institutional capacity to answer for consequential decisions in the forums and at the moments when accountability is required, without the retrospective reconstruction that the absence of governance makes necessary and that every external accountability forum recognizes as the substitute for contemporaneous truth that it is. The next question, having established what the governed enterprise looks like and what it does differently, is unavoidable: if this infrastructure is so foundational, why has it not existed before? Answering that question requires examining the history, the incentives, and the institutional myths that organizations have lived by throughout the Systems Age — the subject of the chapter that follows.

CHAPTER 12

WHY THIS CATEGORY NEVER EXISTED

*The Conditions That Prevented Governed
Decision-Intelligence™ (GD-I™) from Emerging — Until Now*

If Governed Decision-Intelligence Infrastructure™ (GD-II™) is so fundamental to institutional soundness, and if its absence explains so many of the modern enterprise failures that have produced the institutional, regulatory, and reputational consequences that the preceding chapters have examined, then an obvious question follows with a force that demands a direct answer: why did no one build the infrastructure sooner? Why, across the entire history of the modern enterprise — across a century of management science, organizational development, governance theory, and institutional design — did the pre-execution governance of consequential decisions not emerge as a recognized institutional requirement and a designed infrastructure category?

The answer is not neglect. It is not that organizations were careless about governance, that leaders were indifferent to the quality of their decisions, or that the institutional thinkers who designed the governance frameworks of the twentieth century failed to recognize the importance of accountability at the decision layer. The answer is misalignment — the simultaneous misalignment of a specific combination of structural, economic, cultural, technological, and political conditions that individually made Governed Decision-Intelligence™ (GD-I™) unnecessary, impractical, or actively resisted, and whose collective misalignment prevented the category from emerging. The infrastructure did not fail to emerge because organizations were careless. It failed to emerge because the conditions required for its emergence did not exist simultaneously — until now.

The Original Problem Was Not Judgment — It Was Chaos

For most of modern organizational history — for the decades during which the foundational architecture of the enterprise was being built and the management disciplines that shaped it were being established — the dominant institutional problem was not the governance of judgment. It was the taming of chaos. Work was inconsistent: the same operational activity, performed by different individuals in different locations or at different times, produced results that varied in quality, reliability, and cost in ways that made organizational scale difficult, competitive advantage fragile, and institutional accountability nearly impossible. Knowledge was tribal: the operational expertise that determined whether a function worked effectively resided in the heads of specific individuals whose departure represented an institutional loss that no documentation or process could reliably replace. Quality varied wildly across the operational breadth of organizations whose geographic and functional expansion constantly outpaced the institutional mechanisms for maintaining consistency. Scale magnified disorder rather than resolving it — as organizations grew, the complexity of coordinating individual judgment across larger and more distributed workforces increased institutional risk rather than reducing it.

Under those conditions — under the institutional emergency of operational chaos that the early enterprise faced — the governance of decisions was a secondary concern relative to the primary survival challenge of making organizational activity reliable, consistent, and replicable. Systemization was the correct priority for that era. It was the institutional response that the specific conditions of that moment demanded, and it delivered what those conditions required. Standardizing execution produced immediate, measurable gains in efficiency, reliability, cost control, and replicability — gains whose value was so large and so evident that they justified the enormous organizational investment that systemization required and that they attracted the management science, the consulting industry, and the institutional infrastructure that made systemization the defining enterprise achievement of the twentieth century. Decision failures existed throughout this era. Their consequences were real and sometimes severe. But they were limited by the scale at which organizations operated and the speed at which their consequences could propagate. A bad decision affected a team, a department, a region, or a quarter — not an entire global enterprise in minutes through the execution systems that scale and AI acceleration have since made possible. The Systems Age emerged because it solved the most urgent problem of its time, and solving it correctly was the precondition for the governance problem that scale would subsequently create.

Consequences Were Recoverable

In earlier organizational eras, most of the consequences produced by decision failures were recoverable within the operational and institutional timeframes available for correction. Markets moved more slowly, which meant that the competitive consequences of poor decisions unfolded over periods that allowed for recognition and correction before they became existential. Information traveled imperfectly —

the absence of the instantaneous, global, and permanent information environment that modern organizations operate within meant that the consequences of decisions propagated locally and gradually rather than globally and immediately. Public scrutiny was limited — the institutional accountability forums that today subject organizational decisions to real-time examination by regulators, journalists, social media audiences, and legal adversaries were either absent or far less consequential than their modern counterparts. Regulatory regimes were less expansive — the legal and regulatory frameworks that now create institutional liability for the quality of decision-making across employment, financial services, healthcare, data privacy, and artificial intelligence were either nonexistent or substantially less demanding in their evidentiary requirements.

In this institutional environment, organizations could afford to learn through trial and error in a way that modern enterprises cannot. Poor judgment was corrected informally — through the management relationships and organizational culture that identified failing decisions and redirected them before their consequences became irreversible, without requiring the formal governance infrastructure that pre-execution governance of decisions demands. Institutional memory was short — the organizational record of decision failures was not permanently preserved in the digital, legal, and regulatory infrastructure that makes every consequential decision an institutional artifact that may be examined in perpetuity by parties whose accountability demands the organization cannot anticipate. Accountability was personal rather than institutional — the consequences of poor decisions were borne by the individuals who made them in ways that were managed through the organizational relationships that surrounded them, rather than through the legal, regulatory, and reputational institutions that now create accountability demands the organization cannot manage through internal relationships alone. In that context, formal pre-execution GD-II™ would have felt not merely excessive but genuinely disproportionate to the governance requirement it was designed to address. It was unnecessary because consequences unfolded gradually and locally in ways that existing informal governance mechanisms could manage.

The Conditions That Have Since Changed

Modern enterprises operate under conditions that are radically different from those that made the absence of GD-II™ institutionally tolerable throughout the Systems Age. Decisions propagate instantly through the execution systems, the communication infrastructure, and the market mechanisms that connect organizational action to consequence in real time rather than over the extended periods that previous eras provided for recognition and correction. Errors scale globally — through the AI systems, the digital platforms, and the operational networks that extend the reach of every consequential decision to a scope that would have been inconceivable in the organizational environments of earlier decades. Records persist indefinitely — in the legal, regulatory, and digital infrastructure that creates a permanent institutional record of every consequential decision, available to any future accountability forum regardless of the temporal distance between the decision and the consequence that triggers examination of it.

Accountability is retrospective and legal — exercised by courts, regulators, boards, and public institutions that evaluate the quality of decisions according to standards of evidentiary care and deliberative soundness that the informal accountability mechanisms of earlier eras did not require. Reputation is fragile — in an information environment where the consequences of governance failures become publicly visible within hours and remain in the institutional memory of stakeholders, regulators, and markets indefinitely. AI accelerates impact — compressing the interval between consequential decisions and their consequences in ways that eliminate the residual governance opportunity that the slower-moving environments of previous eras provided. Under these conditions, decisions are no longer reversible in practice, even where they remain reversible in theory — the speed at which consequences propagate, the permanence of the institutional record, and the scope of the accountability demands that modern governance environments create have together shifted the cost of poor judgment from operational to existential for organizations operating at scale. The organizational architecture that the Systems Age produced did not evolve at the same pace as the accountability environment it operates within, and the gap between the two — between an organizational architecture designed for recoverable consequences and an accountability environment that demands pre-execution governance of irreversible ones — is the structural condition that GD-II™ exists to address.

The Economic Narrative Discouraged Governance

GD-II™ slows organizations down at the moment of decision — it introduces the deliberative requirements, the evidentiary standards, and the governance conditions that the exercise of consequential authority must satisfy before the execution system is authorized to proceed. Historically, this slowdown was seen as a competitive disadvantage in economic environments that rewarded first movers, rapid scaling, aggressive expansion, and decisive leadership above all other institutional qualities. The economic narrative of the era that built the modern enterprise favored intuition over deliberation, confidence over caution, and momentum over reflection — not because these preferences were irrational, but because the competitive environments and the accountability conditions of the era made them rational responses to the institutional incentives that determined organizational success and failure.

Organizations that paused to interrogate their decisions — that required the deliberative engagement with alternatives, risks, and evidence that GD-II™ demands — appeared indecisive in competitive environments where the ability to move faster than competitors was a primary source of institutional advantage. Those that moved quickly, committed decisively, and executed without the friction of pre-execution governance appeared visionary — and were rewarded by markets, boards, and organizational cultures that evaluated institutional quality by the outcomes those decisions produced rather than by the governance quality of the deliberative process that produced them. The market reinforced this behavior — through the valuations it assigned to organizations that demonstrated decisive leadership, rapid scaling, and competitive aggression — until the consequences of ungoverned decisions at scale became catastrophic in ways that the economic narrative of the Systems Age had not anticipated and that the governance architecture it produced was not designed to prevent.

Outcome-Based Evaluation Made Governance Appear Unnecessary

For decades, organizations relied on a simple and institutionally convenient proxy for decision quality: if the outcome was good, the decision must have been good. This belief — embedded in the performance evaluation frameworks, the leadership development practices, the board governance standards, and the institutional cultures of the modern enterprise — allowed organizations to avoid the harder work of governing decisions directly by substituting the evaluation of outcomes for the governance of the deliberative processes that produced them. The proxy felt justified because outcomes are visible, measurable, and institutionally legible in ways that decision quality is not — because the quality of the deliberative process behind a decision is a governance assessment that requires contemporaneous evidence and independent examination, while the quality of the outcome it produced is a performance measurement that requires only time and a benchmark.

This belief created a dangerous institutional feedback loop that reinforced the governance gap rather than closing it. Luck was rewarded as judgment — the individuals whose decisions produced favorable outcomes because of circumstances they did not control and could not have predicted were attributed the institutional standing of exceptional decision-makers, creating organizational cultures that celebrated the appearance of sound judgment without requiring its substance. Prudence was punished as hesitation — the individuals whose deliberative engagement with the risks and alternatives of consequential decisions produced outcomes that were slower, more conservative, or less immediately favorable than the intuitive decisiveness of their peers were systematically disadvantaged in organizational cultures that evaluated decision quality by speed and confidence rather than by governance discipline. Risk-taking was celebrated without examination — the institutional culture of organizations operating under outcome-based evaluation rewarded the bold assumption of risk that produced good outcomes, without distinguishing between risk that was consciously governed and risk that was inadvertently assumed without governance, which meant that the governance discipline of sound risk management was institutionally indistinguishable from the luck of ungoverned risk-taking when outcomes were favorable. As long as outcomes were favorable, governance appeared not merely unnecessary but institutionally counterproductive — a source of friction that reduced the speed and confidence that the outcome-based evaluation of decision quality rewarded. Only when outcomes failed did organizations look backward to examine the decision quality they had never required before. By then, it was always too late.

Psychological and Cultural Resistance

GD-II™ confronts uncomfortable institutional truths about the nature of judgment, authority, and competence that human psychology and organizational culture have consistently resisted — not because of dishonesty or bad faith, but because the truths that governance illuminates are structurally threatening to the institutional identities and the power relationships that organizational cultures are built to sustain. GD-II™ exposes overconfidence — the systematic tendency of individuals in positions of authority to believe their judgment is more reliable than the structural evidence of institutional failure consistently demonstrates. It exposes authority bias — the institutional dynamic through which the positions, the track records, and the social standing of authority figures shape the deliberative process in ways that suppress the genuine evaluation of alternatives and risks that governance requires. It exposes suppressed dissent — the professional risk calculations that prevent individuals with relevant expertise and genuine concerns from expressing them in the deliberative environments where authority and institutional momentum create conditions under which challenge is institutionally costly.

It exposes unexamined assumptions — the implicit premises on which consequential decisions are based, and that the deliberative process has not been required to be identified, examined, or justified, because the governance framework that would require their examination has not been built. It exposes the limits of expertise — the recognition that individual judgment, however experienced and well-intentioned, is subject to the systematic distortions that pressure, incentive misalignment, and authority dynamics produce, and that those distortions require structural governance rather than individual excellence to address. Humans resist systems that surface these realities — particularly those in positions of power whose institutional standing depends on the organizational belief in their exceptional judgment. GD-II™ does not accuse. But it does illuminate. And illumination threatens the narratives that people in positions of authority rely on to feel competent, respected, and secure — the narrative of exceptional individual judgment that the governance gap has historically made possible to maintain because the absence of contemporaneous evidentiary standards has made that judgment genuinely unexaminable.

Ambiguity Protected Authority

Ambiguity protects authority. This is not a cynical observation about the deliberate concealment of institutional power — it is a structural description of the relationship between the opacity of decision authority in the modern enterprise and the institutional conditions that opacity creates and sustains. When decisions are implicit — embedded in the operational flow of organizational activity without being identified as discrete acts of authority requiring governance — responsibility is diffuse: distributed across the approval chains and deliberative processes that surround the decision without any individual party being required to own the judgment it represents. Accountability is negotiable: the attribution of responsibility for the consequences of an ungoverned decision is shaped by the institutional politics and power relationships of the organization at the time those consequences become visible, rather than by the contemporaneous governance record that would establish who held the authority and exercised the judgment that produced them. Intent is reconstructable: the absence of a contemporaneous record of what was known, considered, and accepted at the moment of decision creates the institutional space for the retrospective construction of an account of intent that serves the interests of the parties whose authority it reflects. And authority is insulated: the opacity of the decision-making process protects the institutional standing of those who exercised consequential authority from the examination that a contemporaneous governance record would require.

GD-II™ removes that insulation. It does not eliminate power — the individuals and institutions that hold consequential authority in the modern enterprise retain that authority under the governance conditions that GD-II™ creates. But it makes power legible: it requires that the exercise of consequential authority be identified, attributed, evidenced, and preserved in a contemporaneous form that cannot be concealed, reconstructed, or insulated from examination by the institutional interests of those who exercised it. Historically, organizations were not incentivized to do this — the parties who held consequential authority had little institutional reason to invite the scrutiny that contemporaneous governance records create before adverse outcomes forced that scrutiny upon them. The power holders benefited from the opacity of the ungoverned environment, and the governance frameworks that organizations built reflected the institutional preferences of the parties who designed them — who were, in most cases, the same parties whose authority the governance frameworks were nominally designed to constrain. Only now — under the compound pressure of legal accountability, regulatory expansion, board governance demands, and the public scrutiny of an information environment that makes institutional governance failures permanently visible — has that calculus begun to change in ways that make the structural resistance to GD-II™ harder to maintain.

The Technological Prerequisite Was Missing

Until recently, the technological infrastructure required to support the operational requirements of GD-II™ at an organizational scale did not exist in forms that could be practically deployed without crippling the operational functioning of the organizations that would have deployed them. Capturing contemporaneous evidence at the moment of decision — the specific informational basis, the acknowledged unknowns, the explicit assumptions, the contextual signals, and the identified risks that the governance framework requires — at the scale and speed of consequential organizational decisions, across the distributed operational environments of modern enterprises, without creating the operational friction that would have made the governance function institutionally intolerable, was practically impossible with the technological capabilities available through most of the Systems Age.

Preserving rejected alternatives as first-class objects in the governance record — creating a contemporaneous record of what was considered and not chosen, in a form that is complete, structured, and independently reviewable — required both the data-capture capabilities and the organizational workflow integration that were not available in practical form until relatively recently. Maintaining contextual signals — the informational environment in which each consequential decision was made, including the indicators that were present but discounted and the organizational dynamics that shaped the deliberative process — in a form that could be preserved and examined independently of the retrospective account that the parties whose judgment it would document were motivated to provide, required technological capabilities for real-time organizational intelligence capture that the information systems of earlier eras could not practically provide. Maintaining authority attribution and immutable records — creating governance records that could not be retroactively altered by the institutional incentives that would otherwise shape their retrospective presentation — required the data infrastructure and the organizational architecture that were not available in deployable form throughout most of the period during which the governance gap persisted. Organizations defaulted to what they could manage: documentation, meetings, approvals, and post-hoc rationales — not because they preferred these substitutes for genuine governance, but because the technological capability required to operationalize genuine governance did not exist in forms that could be practically deployed at an organizational scale. GD-I™ requires a technological posture that supports reflection without paralysis and accountability without fear — one that captures the contemporaneous truth of consequential decisions at the speed of organizational life without becoming the bottleneck that makes organizational life unmanageable. That capability is new. Its novelty is not incidental to the emergence of the category — it is one of the structural conditions that the category's emergence required.

The Myth of Good Leaders

For much of modern business history, the institutional belief in the primacy of individual leadership quality as the solution to decision governance challenges delayed the recognition that judgment failure is not an individual flaw but a systemic vulnerability. Organizations believed — and institutional cultures, management development frameworks, and leadership selection processes consistently reinforced — that better leaders would make better decisions: that the individual quality of the people in positions of authority would produce the governance outcomes that the structural absence of GD-II™ architecture failed to require. They believed that experience would prevent error — that the accumulated wisdom of leaders with extensive track records would substitute for the structural governance that contemporaneous evidentiary standards provide. They believed that character would substitute for structure — that the personal integrity, the moral commitment, and the professional dedication of individual leaders would create the institutional accountability that governance infrastructure was not built to produce.

This belief, however sincerely held and earnestly expressed in the organizational cultures that sustained it, delayed the recognition that individual leadership quality is not a reliable substitute for structural governance. It delayed recognition for as long as the institutional consequences of ungoverned decisions remained within the range that individual leadership quality could manage — as long as the failures it could not prevent were recoverable, localized, and attributable to the limitations of individuals rather than to the structural condition of ungoverned authority that those individuals were operating within. Only repeated, high-profile, institutional failures — failures that were visible across industries, across governance frameworks, and across leadership cultures of all kinds, and that consistently traced their structural source to the same governance absence rather than to the individual deficiencies of the leaders who happened to be present when the consequences became visible — exposed the limits of the belief and created the conditions for the recognition that the governance gap requires a structural response rather than a better class of leaders.

Why the Moment Is Different Now

All of the barriers that once prevented GD-I™ from emerging as a recognized category and an operational infrastructure are eroding simultaneously — not because any single condition has changed, but because the combination of conditions that collectively sustained the governance gap has shifted in ways that are structural rather than cyclical and irreversible rather than temporary. Scale has become unforgiving — the combination of AI acceleration, global execution networks, and the institutional accountability environments of modern regulatory and legal frameworks has shifted the consequence structure of ungoverned decisions from recoverable to existential in ways that the institutional conditions of previous eras did not produce. Decisions are permanently recorded — the information infrastructure of the modern enterprise creates an institutional record of every consequential decision that is available to accountability forums, regardless of how much time passes between the decision and the consequence that triggers examination of it. Accountability is institutional — exercised by legal, regulatory, and governance bodies whose evidentiary standards require contemporaneous decision evidence rather than the retrospective account that the institutional incentives of the ungoverned environment reliably produce.

AI accelerates consequences — by compressing the interval between the authorization of a consequential decision and the propagation of its consequences through the execution systems that carry it out, eliminating the residual governance opportunity that slower-moving organizational environments previously provided. Regulation is expanding — across employment, financial services, healthcare, data privacy, and artificial intelligence, the regulatory frameworks that create institutional liability for the quality of decision-making are extending their reach and intensifying their evidentiary requirements in ways that make the absence of pre-execution decision governance an increasingly visible institutional vulnerability. Public scrutiny is constant — the information environment that makes the governance quality of every consequential decision visible to external stakeholders in real time creates accountability pressures that the organizational cultures of the Systems Age were not designed to manage. And most importantly: the cost of unguided judgment now exceeds the cost of governance. This is the inflection point — the structural moment at which the institutional calculus that previously made governance appear burdensome relative to its benefits has reversed, and the cost of operating without GD-II™ has exceeded the cost of building and deploying it.

Five Conditions No Longer Apply — and One Pattern That Does

The infrastructure that operationalizes the missing category of GD-I™ did not exist previously because five specific conditions prevented its emergence. It was not economically rewarded — the competitive and accountability environments of the Systems Age created institutional incentives that favored the speed and decisiveness that governance slows rather than the accountability and defensibility that governance produces. It was culturally resisted — by the organizational cultures that had built their institutional identity around the belief in exceptional individual judgment and that experienced the structural requirement to govern that judgment as a challenge to the foundations of their institutional self-understanding. It was technologically impractical — the data capture, the organizational workflow integration, and the immutable record infrastructure required to operationalize GD-I™ at organizational scale were not available in deployable form throughout most of the period during which the governance gap persisted. It challenged power structures — by making the exercise of consequential authority visible, evidenced, and accountable in ways that the parties who held that authority had little institutional incentive to require. And it was unnecessary on a smaller scale — the limited reach and the recoverable consequences of decisions made in the smaller-scale, slower-moving organizational environments of earlier eras made formal pre-execution governance genuinely disproportionate to the governance requirement it was designed to address. Those conditions no longer apply. What once felt burdensome now feels essential.

Every major infrastructure category in institutional history emerged only when failure became unacceptable — when the accumulated consequences of operating without it exceeded the institutional resistance to building it. Financial ledgers arose when trust exceeded memory — when the scale of financial activity made the informal accountability mechanisms of personal trust and individual recollection institutionally insufficient for the governance of commercial relationships that required external validation. Safety systems emerged when accidents became systemic — when the frequency and severity of operational failures demonstrated that individual care and professional skill were insufficient substitutes for the structural enforcement of safety standards that infrastructure provides. Cybersecurity appeared when connectivity outpaced control — when the expansion of digital networks created vulnerabilities whose exploitation produced consequences that the informal security practices of pre-networked organizational environments could not prevent. GD-II™ is following the same historical pattern. It is not a trend — a governance fashion that will be replaced by the next management innovation before its institutional implications are fully realized. It is a correction — the structural response to the accumulated institutional evidence that the governance of consequential decisions cannot be achieved through the execution systems, the compliance frameworks, the cultural aspirations, and the individual leadership qualities of the Systems Age.

The absence of GD-II™ is no longer defensible as oversight — as the failure of organizational designers to recognize a governance requirement that the institutional evidence has since made clear. It is no longer defensible as immaturity — an absence of a governance capability that organizations are still in the process of developing. It is now a risk position — a deliberate choice to operate without the governance infrastructure that the accountability environments of the modern enterprise require, and a choice whose institutional consequences are as visible, as measurable, and as consequential as the choice to operate without the financial controls, the safety systems, or the cybersecurity infrastructure that the equivalent institutional evidence made unavoidable in the eras that preceded this one. The question for modern enterprises is no longer whether GD-II™ is useful — whether its governance benefits justify the organizational investment its deployment requires. It is whether operating without it is responsible, given what the institutional evidence of the current era has established about the consequences of ungoverned decision authority at scale.

CHAPTER 13

WHEN DECISIONS BECOME DEFENSIBLE

Boards, Courts, Regulators, and the
New Standard of Accountability

Accountability does not arrive when decisions are made. It arrives later — often much later — when outcomes are known, when the context in which the decision was made has shifted beyond recognition, when the people who made the decision have moved on to other roles and other organizations, and when institutional memory has been rewritten by the necessity of presenting the past in the most defensible possible light given what has since occurred. The moment of accountability is, by structural design, separated from the moment of decision by everything that has happened in between — by the organizational changes, the personnel transitions, the narrative constructions, and the evidentiary erosion that time and institutional self-interest reliably produce.

This is the moment most enterprises are designed for the least. Their governance architectures are oriented toward execution, toward compliance, toward the management of ongoing operational activity — not toward the production and preservation of the contemporaneous evidentiary record that would allow them to account for their consequential decisions in the forums and at the moments when accountability actually arrives. This chapter explains how Governed Decision-Intelligence Infrastructure™ (GD-II™) changes that reality — not by guaranteeing favorable outcomes, not by protecting organizations from the consequences of their decisions, but by establishing a defensible standard of decision-making that holds under the scrutiny of every accountability forum that consequential decisions may eventually face.

The Shift From Outcome Defense to Decision Defense

Historically, organizations have defended themselves by pointing to outcomes. When results were positive — when the decision produced the organizational benefits that had been anticipated or exceeded — decisions were presumed sound by the institutional logic that treated outcome quality as a proxy for decision quality.

When results were negative, organizations searched for procedural explanations —
for the process steps that were followed, the approvals that were obtained, and
the documentation that was produced — that would demonstrate organizational
compliance with established standards even in the absence of the favorable outcomes
that would otherwise have established the decision's soundness by inference.

This approach collapses under modern scrutiny. The accountability forums that
modern enterprises face — boards conducting governance reviews, regulators
examining organizational conduct, courts evaluating the basis of authority exercised
in ways that produced harm, and public institutions whose scrutiny determines the
organizational standing of enterprises in their industries and communities — have
shifted their standard of evaluation away from the question of whether outcomes
met expectations. They ask whether the decision was reasonable given what was
known at the time. This is a fundamentally different standard. It cannot be met with
performance metrics that measure what the decision produced. It cannot be met
with after-the-fact narratives that explain why the decision was reasonable in light
of what subsequently occurred. It cannot be met with process artifacts that establish
procedural compliance without establishing the quality of the judgment behind the
compliant process. It requires decision evidence — the contemporaneous record of
what was known, what was considered, what was accepted, and by whose authority
at the moment the decision was made.

What Scrutiny Actually Looks Like

When accountability arrives, it does not arrive abstractly or in the general terms that
organizational governance discussions typically employ. It arrives as a specific set of
questions, directed at specific individuals, requiring specific answers that must be
supported by specific evidence or explained in the absence of it. What information
was available when this decision was made — what did the decision-maker know,
and what did the evidentiary record reflect about the basis on which the decision
was authorized? Who had the authority to decide — which specific individual held
the institutional power to commit the organization to this path, and under what
mandate was that power exercised? What alternatives were considered — what other
paths were available and evaluated, and on what basis were they rejected in favor of
the direction chosen?

What risks were identified and accepted — what did the decision-maker understand
to be the potential adverse consequences of the chosen path, and was there a
contemporaneous record of conscious risk acceptance that established the governance

standard under which those risks were undertaken? What signals were present but discounted — what indicators in the decision environment pointed toward the risks that subsequently materialized, and was there a contemporaneous record of whether those signals were identified, evaluated, and appropriately weighed or ignored in ways that the governance record would reveal? Why was this path chosen over others — what was the basis on which the alternatives were set aside and this direction was authorized, expressed in terms that are traceable to the contemporaneous deliberative process rather than to the retrospective account of what the decision-maker wishes they had been thinking at the time? These questions are not hypothetical exercises in governance theory. They are asked in depositions, in regulatory examinations, in board governance reviews, and in investigative processes that determine the institutional consequences of governance failures for organizations and for the individuals whose authority is implicated in the decisions they examine. Most organizations cannot answer these questions without reconstructing history — without assembling a retrospective account of what was known, considered, and decided from the fragments of documentation, recollection, and institutional narrative that are available after the contemporaneous record of the decision has been displaced by time and incentive. Reconstruction is not defense. It is the institutional condition that GD-II™ is specifically designed to make unnecessary.

The Problem with Hindsight Narratives

In the absence of contemporaneous decision records — in the institutional condition that characterizes most modern enterprises, in which the evidentiary basis of consequential decisions is either not captured or not preserved in a form that is independent of the retrospective interests of the parties whose authority it would document — organizations rely on memory and narrative to account for their decisions when accountability arrives. This reliance produces three predictable governance failures that are consistent across the full range of accountability contexts in which organizations are required to explain their consequential decisions.

The first is inconsistency. When the contemporaneous basis of a decision is absent and the account of what was decided and why must be reconstructed from the recollections and the institutional narratives of the parties whose authority is implicated, accounts diverge. Recollections conflict — the individuals who participated in the deliberative process recall it differently, in ways that are shaped by their current institutional interests rather than by the contemporaneous reality of what occurred. Authority becomes unclear — the question of who held the power to make this decision and exercised it in this specific instance cannot be answered from the retrospective accounts of parties whose institutional interests create systematic incentives to minimize their individual accountability for the consequences of the decision. The second failure is credibility loss. Explanations evolve as scrutiny continues — the institutional narrative of what was decided and why shifts as each successive line of questioning exposes the inadequacy of the previous account, producing an appearance of progressive rationalization that external examiners routinely interpret as evidence of evasion rather than the honest engagement with incomplete information that organizations experiencing this dynamic typically intend. Rationales shift as new information surfaces about what was known or knowable at the time of decision, producing the appearance of an account that is being constructed to accommodate the scrutiny rather than to reflect what actually occurred. Confidence erodes as the inconsistencies and the evolution of the account become visible to external examiners whose professional function is to identify the gaps between what is claimed and what can be established through independent evidence.

The third failure is adverse inference. When evidence is missing — when the contemporaneous record of what was known, considered, and accepted at the moment of decision is absent from the governance archive — external reviewers do not simply note the absence and decline to draw conclusions from it. They infer from the absence what was not recorded. Regulators infer that risks were not considered because an organization that had considered the risks would have been required by reasonable governance standards to preserve a record of that consideration. Boards infer that authority was unclear or inappropriately exercised because an organization with clear and appropriately exercised authority would have preserved the record that established it. Courts infer that the decision was made without the evidentiary discipline that defensible judgment requires, because an organization that had exercised that discipline would not have needed to reconstruct the evidentiary basis of its decision from retrospective accounts. Hindsight narratives are not neutral in the accountability contexts where they must be presented. They are interpreted as self-protective — as the institutional product of parties whose interests create systematic incentives to construct the most favorable possible account of decisions that the contemporaneous record does not independently support.

Defensibility Is Not About Perfection

A critical misunderstanding about the relationship between GD-II™ and defensibility must be addressed directly, because it is among the most common sources of resistance to the adoption of GD-II™ in organizations that misinterpret governance as a demand for perfect decisions. Defensible decisions are not perfect decisions. The accountability standard that GD-II™ exists to support is not a standard of infallibility

— it does not require that organizations make decisions that produce consistently favorable outcomes, that correctly predict every material development in the environments they navigate, or that reflect a quality of judgment that retrospective examination would find to be without flaw.

Defensible decisions are reasonable decisions — decisions that were made transparently, with the evidentiary basis that the circumstances permitted, under the constraints that the decision-maker was operating within, and with the accountability of identified authority that governance requires. A defensible decision can produce a bad outcome — and its defensibility is not compromised by the adverse result, provided that the governance record establishes that the decision process met the standard of care appropriate to the decision's impact at the time it was made. A defensible decision can involve significant risk — and its defensibility is established precisely by the contemporaneous record of the risk that was identified, assessed, and consciously accepted by the authority whose accountability the governance record preserves. A defensible decision can be controversial — contested by the parties it affected, challenged by the individuals who advised against it, and criticized by the analysis of those who subsequently examined it — and remain defensible because the governance record establishes that the deliberative process was genuine, the alternatives were genuinely considered, and the judgment was exercised with the evidentiary discipline that reasonable decision-making requires. A defensible decision can be reversed later — found, in the light of subsequent developments, to have been wrong — and remain defensible because the governance record establishes that it was right at the moment it was made, given what was known. What matters for defensibility is not the result but whether the decision process met a standard of care appropriate to the impact of the decision being made. GD-II™ exists to preserve that standard — to create the contemporaneous evidentiary record that allows organizations to demonstrate the governance quality of their decision-making independent of the outcomes their decisions produced.

How Boards Evaluate Defensibility

Boards are increasingly expected to oversee not just organizational performance — not just whether the enterprise is meeting its financial, operational, and strategic objectives — but decision integrity: whether the decisions through which the enterprise pursues those objectives are being made with the governance discipline that the board's fiduciary and oversight obligations require. When confronted with a crisis — with an adverse outcome that demands board-level governance attention and that exposes the board itself to liability for the adequacy of its oversight — boards ask specific questions about the decision-making process that preceded the crisis rather than about the operational performance that accompanied it.

Did management act responsibly — not in the sense of whether the outcome was favorable, but in the sense of whether the decision process reflected the governance discipline that responsible institutional leadership requires under the circumstances? Were risks surfaced and debated — not in the sense of whether risk management processes were followed, but in the sense of whether the specific risks of the specific decision were genuinely identified, genuinely evaluated, and genuinely presented to the governance oversight process rather than acknowledged pro forma and managed within a compliance framework that documented their existence without requiring their genuine engagement? Was authority exercised appropriately — not in the sense of whether the right approvals were obtained, but in the sense of whether the party whose authority determined the decision's direction had the institutional mandate for that authority and exercised it in a manner consistent with the governance standards the board is responsible for maintaining? Could this have been reasonably foreseen — not in the sense of whether retrospective analysis reveals risk indicators that are now visible in light of what occurred, but in the sense of whether the contemporaneous decision record reflects the level of evidentiary engagement with those indicators that a reasonably governed organization would have maintained at the time?

Without decision evidence — without the contemporaneous governance record that GD-II™ produces and preserves — boards are forced to rely on the assurances of management whose institutional interests create systematic incentives to present the most favorable possible account of the decisions whose consequences have produced the crisis requiring board attention. With contemporaneous decision evidence, boards can govern — can exercise the substantive oversight that their fiduciary obligations require, rather than the reactive oversight that the absence of contemporaneous evidence forces them to conduct. This shifts board oversight from a reactive governance function — one that examines consequences after they have become visible and attempts to assess the decision quality that produced them from the retrospective accounts of the parties whose authority is implicated — to a substantive governance function that protects both the organization and its leadership by establishing and maintaining the contemporaneous evidentiary standard that defensible institutional governance requires.

How Regulators Interpret Absence

Regulators do not require perfection of the organizations they oversee. The regulatory standard is not that organizations never make decisions that produce adverse outcomes or that they possess the foresight to avoid every consequential risk their operations create. The regulatory standard is good-faith, evidence-based decision-making — the demonstrated commitment to the governance discipline that the regulatory framework was established to require, expressed through a contemporaneous record of decision-making that can be independently examined to assess whether the organization was operating within the bounds of reasonable institutional conduct given the circumstances it faced at the time of its consequential decisions.

When decision records are missing — when the governance archive of an organization does not contain the contemporaneous evidentiary basis of the decisions whose consequences a regulatory inquiry is examining — regulators do not decline to draw conclusions from the absence. They infer from it. They infer that risks were not considered because the regulatory standard of care that good-faith decision-making requires would have produced a record of risk consideration that the governance archive should contain. They infer that alternatives were ignored because the evidentiary discipline of responsible decision-making requires that the alternatives available at the time of decision be evaluated and that the evaluation be preserved in a form that establishes the basis on which the chosen path was selected. They infer that authority was misused or unclear because an organization with clear, appropriately exercised, and legitimately mandated decision authority would have preserved the contemporaneous record that established those qualities at the moment of authority. These inferences are rarely charitable — they are formed in the institutional context of a regulatory inquiry whose function is to identify governance failures and impose the accountability consequences that the regulatory framework was established to create.

GD-II™ changes the organizational posture in regulatory proceedings entirely. The organization can demonstrate awareness of risk — through the contemporaneous governance record that reflects the specific risks that were identified and assessed at the moment of decision. It can demonstrate genuine consideration of alternatives — through the first-class record of the paths that were evaluated and rejected at the moment of decision rather than the retrospective account of an organization attempting to reconstruct a deliberative process whose contemporaneous record was never created. It can demonstrate conscious acceptance of uncertainty — through the explicit risk acknowledgment in the governance record that establishes that the risks taken were understood rather than inadvertently assumed. It can demonstrate the appropriate exercise of authority — through the contemporaneous attribution of decision power to identified individuals under defined mandates that the governance record preserves independent of the retrospective interests of the parties whose authority it documents. This is the difference between a regulatory outcome characterized by penalty — the consequence of governance failure — and one characterized by remediation — the consequence of governance that was sound, but that produced an adverse outcome within the range of risks that were consciously accepted.

Courts Care About Process — But Not How Organizations Expect

Courts are frequently misunderstood by organizations that have invested heavily in documentation-based governance frameworks on the assumption that the volume and comprehensiveness of their procedural records will establish the defensibility of their decisions in legal proceedings. Courts do not reward volume of documentation. The quantity of records produced, the comprehensiveness of the approval processes documented, and the sophistication of the compliance architecture that surrounds a challenged decision do not constitute the evidentiary basis of legal defensibility. Courts reward reasonableness under the circumstances — the demonstrated commitment to the governance standard of care that would be expected of a reasonably managed organization facing the specific decision context under examination, expressed through a contemporaneous record that can be independently evaluated against that standard.

The questions that judges and juries apply to contested decisions are not procedural. They are not asking whether the correct forms were completed by the designated parties in the required sequence. They are asking whether the decision was reckless or prudent — whether the exercise of authority reflected the deliberative engagement with risk, alternatives, and evidence that reasonable governance requires, or whether it reflected the inadvertent assumption of consequences that a reasonably managed organization would have identified and addressed before committing to the chosen path. They are asking whether risk was ignored or acknowledged — whether the potential adverse consequences of the decision were known to the decision-maker and addressed in the deliberative process, or whether they were present in the decision environment and absent from the governance record. They are asking whether authority was abused or exercised responsibly — whether the power to make the decision was exercised within the institutional mandate that authorized it, with the evidentiary discipline and accountability attribution that responsible institutional governance requires.

When organizations present decision evidence captured at the time of decision — records that are unaltered by the hindsight knowledge of what occurred, unaffected by the institutional incentives that would otherwise shape their retrospective presentation, and independently verifiable as a contemporaneous account of the deliberative process rather than a post-hoc construction designed to support the organization's legal position — courts see restraint, diligence, and integrity. They see an organization that exercised its authority with the governance discipline that the legal standard of reasonable care requires, and that preserved the evidentiary record that allows that discipline to be independently verified. When organizations cannot present contemporaneous decision evidence — when the record of what was known, considered, and accepted at the moment of decision is absent or reconstructed — courts fill the evidentiary gaps. That gap-filling is rarely favorable, because the parties whose interests determine how the gap is filled are not the parties whose authority the contemporaneous record would have documented. The inferences that arise from absent evidence in legal proceedings reflect the structural reality that absence of evidence is not evidence of absence.

The New Baseline of Accountability

A quiet but consequential shift is underway in the governance expectations that modern accountability forums apply to the organizations they oversee. What was once considered best practice — the gold standard of institutional governance that exceptional organizations aspired to achieve but that the minimum expectations of regulatory, legal, and board governance did not require — is becoming the minimum expectation. Organizations are increasingly expected to know who decided — to be able to identify the specific individual whose institutional authority determined the outcome of each consequential decision, not as a matter of retrospective attribution but as a contemporaneous record that was maintained at the moment of authority. They are expected to know why they decided — to have preserved the evidentiary basis of each consequential decision in a form that reflects what was known at the time rather than what is convenient to claim in retrospect. They are expected to preserve how they reasoned — to maintain a contemporaneous record of the deliberative process that reflects the genuine engagement with alternatives, risks, and evidence that reasonable governance requires, rather than the procedural compliance documentation that satisfies audit requirements without establishing governance quality. They are expected to show what they considered — to produce, from the governance archive, the contemporaneous record of the alternatives that were evaluated and the basis on which they were set aside. And they are expected to explain what they accepted — to demonstrate that the risks taken were consciously acknowledged and explicitly accepted at the moment of decision rather than inadvertently assumed in the absence of governance.

This expectation is not codified in a single regulation or statute that organizations can satisfy by implementing a compliance checklist. It is emerging across industries, across jurisdictions, and across the full range of accountability forums — legal, regulatory, governance, and public — through the consistent application of a standard of evidentiary care to the examination of consequential decisions whose consequences have required accountability. It is the new baseline — the minimum institutional expectation of organizations that operate at scale in accountability environments whose evidentiary requirements have been established by the repeated institutional failures of the Systems Age and that will not be reduced to the procedural compliance standards that made those failures possible. Organizations that meet this baseline will not be rewarded for exceptional governance. They will simply be operating at the level of institutional responsibility that the modern accountability environment requires. Organizations that fall below it will face the institutional consequences that the absence of defensibility in modern accountability forums consistently produces.

Why Defensibility Changes Behavior Before It Is Needed

The most powerful institutional effect of decision defensibility is not the external protection it provides when accountability arrives — not the legal, regulatory, and governance defense that contemporaneous decision evidence makes possible when consequential decisions are examined by external accountability forums. It is the internal transformation it produces in the character of the deliberative process through which consequential decisions are made, before any external accountability has arrived and before any adverse outcome has made the governance value of the decision record visible. When leaders know that their decisions will be examined — that the governance record of each consequential decision will be preserved in contemporaneous form and made available to independent examination — they decide differently. When they know that their reasoning will persist — that the evidentiary basis of their judgment will be available to accountability forums regardless of how much time passes between the decision and the moment when accountability arrives — they reason differently. When they know that their authority will be visible — that the exercise of institutional power will be explicitly attributed to them in a form that cannot be obscured by the diffusion of responsibility through approval chains and committee processes — they exercise authority differently.

Specifically, they invite dissent earlier in the deliberative process — because the governance record will reflect whether genuine alternative perspectives were surfaced and engaged with rather than suppressed by the authority dynamics of the decision environment, and because the institutional consequence of a governance record that reflects suppressed dissent is more visible and more costly than the institutional consequence of a deliberative process that requires dissent to be heard. They examine assumptions more carefully — because the governance record will preserve the assumptions that were embedded in their deliberative process and that will be subject to independent evaluation in accountability forums whose standard of reasonableness may not share the institutional premises that made those assumptions feel secure at the time of decision. They resist momentum — the institutional pressure that fast-moving execution systems, competitive environments, and authority dynamics create toward proceeding with established directions rather than engaging with the governance discipline that consequential decisions require. They slow down when risk is high — because the governance record will reflect whether the level of deliberative engagement with the decision was proportionate to the consequences it carried, and because the institutional consequence of a governance record that reflects insufficient deliberative engagement with high-consequence decisions is the accountability exposure that defensibility is designed to prevent. Defensibility improves judgment long before it is tested — through the institutional transformation of the deliberative process that the knowledge of its permanence creates. This prospective governance effect is among the most consequential benefits that GD-II™ produces, and it is the benefit most completely absent from every governance mechanism that operates retrospectively rather than at the moment of decision.

The End of Plausible Deniability

GD-II™ removes a crutch that organizations have relied upon for decades in managing the accountability exposure of their consequential decisions: ambiguity. The institutional value of ambiguity in the governance of consequential decisions is precisely the protection it provides against the precise attribution of accountability — the institutional convenience of decisions that are made without a contemporaneous record of who made them, on what basis, with what alternatives considered, and with what risks accepted, which creates the structural condition in which accountability for the consequences of those decisions is negotiable rather than established. When decisions are explicit, evidenced, and owned — when the governance record of each consequential decision establishes who decided, what was known, what was considered, and what was accepted — plausible deniability disappears as an institutional protection against accountability. The accountability that governance makes explicit becomes unavoidable — not because the governance framework has introduced new accountability standards, but because it has eliminated the evidentiary ambiguity that made accountability negotiable in the ungoverned environment. Governance becomes real rather than aspirational — not a set of institutional commitments expressed in policy documents and values statements, but a structural requirement enforced by the evidentiary record that the governance infrastructure creates and preserves. This is uncomfortable — for the parties whose institutional standing depended on the protection of ambiguity — but necessary: organizations that demand the institutional trust that scale, public commitment, and social license require cannot provide the transparency that trust demands while maintaining the evidentiary ambiguity that makes their consequential decisions unaccountable. Organizations cannot demand trust without visibility.

The Strategic Advantage of Being Defensible

Defensibility is not only about risk mitigation — about reducing the legal, regulatory, and reputational exposure that ungoverned decisions create. It is a genuine competitive advantage for organizations that achieve it and maintain it across the full range of their consequential decision-making. Defensible organizations earn regulator confidence — the institutional standing with regulatory oversight bodies that comes from demonstrating the governance discipline that regulatory frameworks were established to require, which produces regulatory relationships characterized by the substantive engagement with legitimate governance concerns rather than the adversarial management of enforcement proceedings that governance failures create. They retain board trust — the ongoing confidence of oversight bodies whose fiduciary obligations require them to govern organizations whose decision-making meets the standard of care that the board's accountability to stakeholders demands, which produces board oversight relationships that are substantive rather than reactive and that protect both the organization and its leadership from the governance consequences of undocumented decision authority.

They attract principled leaders — the institutional talent whose professional standing requires them to exercise their authority in environments where that authority is governed rather than ungoverned, and whose contribution to the organization depends on the existence of governance conditions that allow them to exercise their judgment with the evidentiary discipline and the accountability clarity that their own professional standards require. They move faster when stakes are high — because the governance record that defensibility requires creates the institutional clarity about authority, risk, and alternatives that allows execution to proceed with confidence rather than with the ambiguity that makes high-stakes decisions slow and contested in ungoverned environments. They recover credibility after failure — because the contemporaneous governance record that defensibility preserves allows organizations that have experienced adverse outcomes to demonstrate the governance quality of the decision process that produced those outcomes, distinguishing between sound decisions that produced adverse results within the acknowledged range of accepted risk and governance failures that produced consequences the contemporaneous record would have prevented. They are not immune to error — consequential decisions made under conditions of genuine uncertainty will sometimes produce outcomes that were not anticipated and that the governance record reflects were within the range of possible results that the decision-maker acknowledged. But they are resilient to scrutiny — capable of accounting for their consequential decisions in every accountability forum that those decisions may face, without the institutional vulnerability that the absence of contemporaneous decision evidence creates.

The Line That Has Been Crossed

There was a time when organizations could survive without decision evidence — when the institutional consequences of ungoverned decision-making were within the range that the informal accountability mechanisms of the Systems Age could manage, and when the absence of contemporaneous decision governance was not yet a visible institutional vulnerability in the accountability environments that organizations operated within. That time has passed. In a world of permanent records — where every consequential decision produces an institutional artifact that may be examined in perpetuity by accountability forums whose evidentiary standards have been shaped by the repeated governance failures of the Systems Age — the absence of defensibility is no longer neutral. It is a liability. The institutional condition of operating without the contemporaneous decision evidence that accountability forums increasingly require is not the same as it was in the earlier eras when the accountability standard was lower, the evidentiary requirements were less demanding, and the consequences of governance failures were more recoverable. It is an institutional vulnerability that compounds with every consequential decision made in the absence of GD-II™ and that accumulates in the governance profile of the organization in ways that create exposure whose full consequence may not be visible until the accountability forum that tests it arrives.

If defensibility is now a requirement — not a governance luxury that well-resourced organizations aspire to achieve but a minimum institutional expectation that modern accountability environments impose on every organization that operates at scale with consequential impact on the parties its decisions affect — then enterprises must confront a final and practical question. How do they adopt GD-II™ without paralyzing the speed, the innovation, and the leadership decisiveness that their operational environments require? How do governance and agility coexist in organizations that cannot afford the institutional friction that governance, misunderstood as bureaucracy, would create? Answering that requires understanding the relationship between governance and speed — which is the subject of the chapter that follows.

Speed Without Recklessness

*How Governed Decisions Enable
Faster, Safer Execution*

One of the most common objections to Governed Decision-Intelligence Infrastructure™ (GD-II™) sounds reasonable on its face: we cannot afford to slow down. In competitive markets where speed is equated with survival and decisiveness is treated as a leadership virtue, the prospect of introducing governance at the decision layer generates genuine institutional anxiety. Leaders fear that governance will add friction, bureaucracy, and hesitation to the decision-making process precisely at the moments when organizational agility is most needed — when competitive windows are narrow, when market conditions are shifting, and when the cost of delay appears to exceed the benefit of deliberation. This fear is understandable as a description of what governance, misunderstood as a bureaucratic process, would produce. It misunderstands both what speed actually is and what governance properly designed actually does.

This fear misunderstands both speed and governance. Properly designed, GD-II™ does not slow organizations down. It removes the kind of delay that actually costs organizations the most — the delay that accumulates after ungoverned decisions have been executed and before the consequences of ungoverned execution can be managed, contained, or reversed. Understanding why requires distinguishing between the speed that GD-II™ constrains — the uninhibited execution of decisions that have not been governed — and the speed that it produces — the confident, clear, and sustainable execution of decisions that have been.

The False Trade-off Between Speed and Governance

Organizations frame speed and governance as opposing forces so consistently that the framing has acquired the status of institutional common sense — an assumption so widely shared that it rarely requires articulation or examination. Speed is associated with decisiveness, with the capacity to identify and commit to a direction without the institutional friction that deliberative processes create. It is associated with momentum — the organizational forward movement that competitive environments reward and that governance is presumed to interrupt. It is associated with opportunity capture — the ability to act before competitors, before the window closes, and before the organizational conditions that make the decision advantageous have shifted.

Governance is associated with the opposite of these qualities. It is associated with review — the requirement to examine decisions before committing to them, which is experienced as delay in environments where the premium on speed makes examination feel like hesitation. It is associated with caution — the institutional disposition to surface risks and require their acknowledgment before proceeding, which is experienced as resistance to the confident forward movement that speed rewards. It is associated with delay — the friction of governance requirements that must be satisfied before execution can proceed, which is experienced as a cost imposed on operational performance by a governance function that does not understand the competitive realities of the environment it governs.

This framing is backward. What slows organizations is not governance — it is uncertainty, rework, reversal, and crisis response. These are the institutional conditions that consume organizational time, resources, and leadership attention at costs that dwarf the investment that pre-execution governance requires. Most of the delays that actually constrain organizational performance occur not at the front of the decision process but after execution begins — when the assumptions on which the decision was based collapse under conditions that governance would have required the decision-maker to acknowledge; when risks surface unexpectedly that the governance record would have required to be identified and accepted before execution was authorized; when authority is questioned in ways that the governance record would have established clearly before execution began; and when decisions must be undone or defended in forums whose evidentiary requirements governance would have satisfied before the need for defense arose. These delays are far more expensive — in time, in resources, in institutional attention, and in organizational momentum — than the moments of deliberate reflection that governance requires before execution proceeds.

Why Ungoverned Speed Is an Illusion

Fast decisions feel fast only at the point of commitment — at the moment when the organization decides to proceed, and the execution machinery is engaged. They become slow later, when the consequences of the ungoverned decision surface in forms that require the institutional attention and the organizational resources that the deliberative engagement governance requires at the front would have prevented. This temporal deception — the experience of speed at commitment followed by the experience of compounded delay in execution — is the defining institutional cost of ungoverned decision-making that the false trade-off framing consistently fails to account for.

Ungoverned decisions create second-guessing that does not exist for governed decisions because the governance record has not established the evidentiary basis that would allow execution teams to proceed with confidence. They create emergency escalations — the institutional disruption of established execution plans by the governance concerns that were not addressed before execution began and that surface in ways that require urgent management attention during execution rather than deliberate governance attention before it. They create retroactive reviews — the institutional burden of examining decisions after their consequences have surfaced, which is more expensive and less effective than the pre-execution governance that would have addressed the same concerns before they became consequences. They create legal interventions — the most expensive and most disruptive form of institutional response to governance failures, which governance before execution would have either prevented or positioned the organization to defend against. They create cultural damage control — the institutional investment required to repair the organizational consequences of decisions that the culture experienced as ungoverned, which governance at the front would have produced naturally as the conditions of accountability and clarity that it creates. The organization moves quickly into a problem and then stalls inside it — not because the execution system failed, but because the decision that authorized execution was ungoverned. This is not speed. It is deferred friction. GD-II™ shifts friction to the front, where it is cheapest and most effective — where it costs deliberative time rather than institutional crisis.

The Difference Between Momentum and Clarity

Speed is not the absence of pause. This is the institutional misunderstanding that the false trade-off between speed and governance rests upon. Speed is the absence of confusion — the organizational condition in which execution teams can proceed with confidence because the decision that authorized their work has been governed, the authority behind it is explicit, the scope of what is being done is defined, the risk tolerance is established, and the alternatives that were considered have been recorded. Pause — deliberate engagement with a decision before execution proceeds — is not the enemy of speed. Confusion is. And the governance requirements that create a deliberative pause at the front of the decision process are precisely the requirements that eliminate the confusion that makes execution slow after decisions have been committed.

When decisions are governed, authority is clear — the specific individual whose institutional power authorized the decision has been identified, the mandate under which they are operating has been established, and the scope of what the decision commits the organization to has been defined. Scope is defined — the operational boundaries of the decision have been established in a way that allows execution teams to proceed within those boundaries without requiring repeated clarification from the authority whose governance record has already established what is and is not authorized. Risk is acknowledged — the potential adverse consequences of the chosen path have been identified and accepted by the authority whose mandate covers their acceptance, which means that execution teams are not improvising risk management during execution but operating within a risk framework that the governance record has already established. Alternatives are understood — the paths that were considered and not chosen have been recorded, which means that execution teams are not revisiting the direction during execution, but proceeding with the confidence that the governance process has already established the chosen path as the sound direction, given the information available.

Execution teams operating within a governance framework no longer waste institutional time and energy asking the questions that ungoverned decisions leave perpetually open: who approved this, and do they actually stand behind it? Are we authorized to proceed, or will this decision be revisited when its consequences become visible? What happens if this goes wrong, and who bears the accountability? Will leadership maintain the organizational commitment to this direction under the pressure of adverse developments that the governance record would have established were within the acknowledged range of accepted risk? These questions are absent from the deliberative environment of governed enterprises, not because they have been suppressed but because the governance record has already answered them. Execution teams move faster because uncertainty has been removed — because the governance process has done, at the front, the institutional work that ungoverned organizations must improvise throughout execution.

How Governance Accelerates Execution

Once a decision passes through a governed gate — once the governance record has established the evidentiary basis, the explicit authority, the acknowledged risk, and the defined scope that GD-II™ requires — execution accelerates. The acceleration is not the product of reduced deliberation during execution. It is the product of the institutional clarity that the governance record has created, and that allows execution to proceed without the improvised deliberation that ungoverned decisions require throughout their execution.

The decision has legitimacy — not the procedural legitimacy of an approval chain whose compliance record establishes that the required steps were completed, but the governance legitimacy of a decision whose evidentiary basis establishes that the authority behind it was exercised with the deliberative discipline that the governance standard requires. Accountability is explicit — the party whose institutional power authorized the decision is identified in the governance record, which means that the accountability for the decision's consequences is established before those consequences materialize rather than negotiated after they have. Risk tolerance is known — the governance record has established what risks the decision carries and that those risks were consciously accepted by the authority whose mandate covers their acceptance, which means that execution teams are not discovering risk during execution but operating within a risk framework that the governance record has defined. Reversal thresholds are defined — the conditions under which the decision would be reconsidered have been established by the governance process, which means that execution teams are not improvising the criteria for escalation but operating within a decision framework that has established those criteria in advance.

Execution teams are no longer improvising around ambiguity — no longer filling the governance gap that ungoverned decisions create with the ad hoc judgments, the informal escalations, and the repeated clarifications that ungoverned authority requires throughout execution. They are operating with confidence — with the institutional clarity that the governance record has created, and that allows them to proceed with the speed and the focus that execution requires. In governed enterprises, the institutional expression of ambiguous authority — the phrase waiting for approval that characterizes ungoverned organizations' experience of the interface between decision and execution — quietly disappears. Not because approvals vanish from the operational architecture of the enterprise, but because decisions are no longer ambiguous. The governance record has already established what was decided, by whose authority, on what basis, and with what risk tolerance — and execution proceeds with the confidence that clarity produces.

Slowing Down at the Right Moments

GD-II™ does slow organizations down — selectively, deliberately, and only at the moments when slowing down is the governance response that the decision's consequences require. It slows them down when stakes are high — when the consequences of the decision are significant enough that the required deliberative investment governance is proportionate to the potential harm that ungoverned execution could produce. It slows them down when risk is irreversible — when the consequences of the decision, once set in motion, cannot be undone without institutional costs that exceed the deliberative investment that governance requires before execution. It slows them down when authority is concentrated — when the decision is being made by a small number of parties whose institutional power to commit the organization is large and whose accountability for the consequences of the decision is significant enough that the governance standard requires explicit authority attribution and risk acknowledgment. It slows them down when alternatives are not obvious — when the chosen path is not the only reasonable path available and the governance standard requires that the alternatives be genuinely evaluated and the basis for their rejection be preserved in the contemporaneous governance record.

These are precisely the moments when speed is most dangerous — when the combination of high stakes, irreversible consequences, concentrated authority, and non-obvious alternatives creates the institutional conditions under which the cost of ungoverned speed is highest, and the benefit of deliberate governance is greatest. Governance introduces friction only where it matters — only at the institutional moments where the potential cost of proceeding without deliberation exceeds the cost of the deliberation that governance requires. Everywhere else — in the operational domain of routine decisions, recoverable choices, distributed authority, and obvious paths — governance removes friction rather than introducing it, by creating the institutional clarity that allows execution to proceed without the improvised deliberation that ambiguous authority and ungoverned risk require.

The Myth of Continuous Urgency

Many organizations operate in a state of permanent urgency — an institutional condition in which every decision is treated as critical, every pause is experienced as irresponsible, and the organizational culture has adapted to the constant acceleration of decision cadence in ways that make deliberation feel like resistance to operational requirements. This condition is not strategic. It is exhausting. And it is, in most cases, the product of an institutional culture that has confused the speed of decision execution with the quality of decision judgment — that has treated the pace at which decisions are committed as a measure of organizational performance rather than the quality of the governance process through which those decisions are made.

GD-II™ creates a hierarchy of seriousness — a governance framework that distinguishes between the categories of decision that require the full deliberative investment that governance demands and the categories of decision that can proceed without it, based on the stakes, the reversibility, the authority concentration, and the complexity of the decision rather than the urgency that the organizational culture assigns to everything. Not every choice deserves the same governance scrutiny. Not every action warrants the deliberative engagement that governance at the decision layer requires. By distinguishing between reversible and irreversible decisions — between choices whose consequences can be corrected without institutional cost and those whose consequences cannot — organizations can direct the deliberative investment that governance requires to the decisions where it matters most. By distinguishing between low-risk and high-risk commitments, they can calibrate the governance standard to the risk profile of each decision category rather than applying a uniform governance burden to all decisions regardless of consequence. By distinguishing between tactical and strategic authority, they can direct governance attention to the decisions that carry the greatest institutional stakes while allowing operational decisions to proceed with the speed that their recoverable consequences permit. Organizations that create this hierarchy regain control over tempo — over the pace at which decisions are made, governance discipline is applied, and execution proceeds. Speed becomes intentional rather than reactive, calibrated to the governance requirements of each decision category rather than driven by the undifferentiated urgency that ungoverned organizational cultures produce.

Innovation Does Not Require Recklessness

Another persistent institutional myth about the relationship between GD-II™ and organizational performance is that governance stifles innovation — that the deliberative requirements, the evidentiary standards, and the explicit risk acknowledgment that governance demands are incompatible with the experimental orientation, the willingness to proceed under uncertainty, and the tolerance for failure that innovation requires. In reality, the opposite is often true. The institutional conditions that most reliably prevent innovation are not the conditions that governance creates — they are the conditions that the absence of governance produces.

Innovation fails when risk is hidden rather than discussed — when the institutional dynamics of the ungoverned environment create conditions in which the genuine risks of an innovative path cannot be honestly acknowledged without institutional cost to the individuals who surface them, which produces organizations that cannot genuinely evaluate the risk profile of innovative directions and that make innovation decisions on the basis of optimistic projections whose risks are not honestly assessed. It fails when authority is unclear — when the institutional architecture of the organization does not clearly establish whose power authorizes the innovative direction and whose accountability covers the risks it carries, which produces organizations that cannot make the institutional commitments that innovation requires and that revisit the authorization of innovative directions whenever their risks become visible. It fails when learning is distorted by outcome bias — when the governance framework evaluates innovative decisions by their outcomes rather than by the quality of the deliberative process that produced them, which produces organizations that cannot distinguish between sound innovative decisions that produced adverse results and poor innovative decisions that produced favorable results, and that systematically penalize the deliberative discipline that sound innovation requires. It fails when failure is punished inconsistently — when the institutional consequences of innovation failures are distributed across the organization in ways that are not connected to the governance quality of the decision that produced them, which creates institutional conditions where the personal cost of innovative risk-taking is unpredictable and where the rational response is to avoid innovation rather than to govern it.

Governed decision-making creates safer conditions for experimentation precisely by addressing these failure modes. By defining acceptable risk upfront — by requiring the explicit acknowledgment and acceptance of the risks that an innovative direction carries before execution proceeds — governance creates the institutional conditions in which experimental risk-taking is a governed choice rather than an inadvertent assumption. By clarifying learning objectives — by requiring the governance record to establish what the organization expects to learn from the innovative direction and what evidence would constitute meaningful learning — governance creates the conditions in which failure produces institutional knowledge rather than institutional blame. By preserving evidence of reasoning — by maintaining the contemporaneous record of what was known, considered, and accepted at the moment the innovative decision was made — governance allows organizations to evaluate the quality of the innovative decision independent of the outcome it produced, which is the prerequisite for genuine organizational learning. By separating decision quality from outcome luck — by establishing the governance standard against which innovative decisions are evaluated as the quality of the deliberative process rather than the favorability of the result — governance creates the institutional conditions in which organizations can take smarter risks rather than fewer ones, and in which the governance discipline of sound innovative decision-making is institutionally rewarded rather than institutionally penalized.

Why Leaders Feel Faster in Governed Environments

Leaders often report an unexpected institutional experience once GD-II™ is functioning as a governance layer in their organization: they feel less rushed, even as execution accelerates around them. This experience is counterintuitive from the perspective of the false trade-off between speed and governance — it should not be possible for an organization to execute faster while its leaders feel less pressured. The explanation lies in what governance removes from the cognitive and institutional environment of leadership. Governance removes cognitive overhead — the institutional burden of carrying unresolved governance questions through execution that ungoverned decisions create for the leaders whose authority they implicate.

Leaders in ungoverned environments carry unspoken doubts about the decisions they have made — the governance concerns they did not resolve before committing to execution, which persist as cognitive overhead throughout the execution process and consume leadership attention that should be directed at execution quality rather than governance remediation. They carry unacknowledged risk — the exposure that ungoverned decisions create and that the absence of explicit risk acknowledgment leaves as an unresolved institutional liability in the leaders whose authority is implicated. They carry ambiguous authority — the institutional uncertainty about who holds the power to make the decisions that are being executed and what the mandate for that authority is, which creates the escalation dynamics and the repeated clarification requirements that consume organizational time during execution. They carry deferred accountability — the knowledge that the consequences of ungoverned decisions will eventually require accountability, a task that the absence of a contemporaneous governance record will make difficult to provide, which creates the institutional anxiety that makes leadership in ungoverned environments feel permanently precarious.

When these burdens are removed by the governance record — when the deliberative investment that governance requires at the front has established the evidentiary basis, the explicit authority, the acknowledged risk, and the defined scope that execution requires — decisions are cleaner. The institutional clarity of a governed decision produces commitments that are clearer — more precisely defined, more broadly understood, and more durably maintained under the pressure of adverse developments — than the commitments of ungoverned decisions whose evidentiary basis is absent and whose authority is ambiguous. Follow-through is stronger — the organizational commitment to a governed direction is more durable under pressure than the commitment to an ungoverned one, because the governance record has established the authority and the risk tolerance that sustain the commitment when adverse developments challenge it. Speed feels earned rather than forced — the product of the deliberative investment that governance requires and the institutional clarity it produces, rather than the pressure of competitive urgency and the anxiety of unresolved governance questions.

The Compounding Effect of Governed Decisions

When decisions are governed — when the governance record is maintained consistently across the full range of the organization's consequential decisions — the institutional effects compound over time in ways that progressively differentiate the governed enterprise from the ungoverned one. Fewer reversals occur because the governance process has established the evidentiary basis and the risk tolerance that allow organizational commitments to be maintained under pressure — which means that the institutional cost of committing to directions that must subsequently be reversed, and the organizational disruption that reversal creates, are substantially reduced. Fewer crises emerge because the governance record has established the acknowledged risk and the explicit authority that allow for adverse developments to be managed within the framework established by the governance process, rather than as unexpected emergencies that require the crisis response that ungoverned risk management produces. Fewer explanations are required because the governance record has preserved the contemporaneous evidentiary basis of each consequential decision in a form that can be produced directly in accountability forums, rather than reconstructed from the retrospective accounts that ungoverned decisions require.

Time that would have been spent managing the fallout of ungoverned decisions — the escalations, the reversals, the legal interventions, the board inquiries, and the regulatory responses that governance failures produce — is reinvested in execution. This reinvestment compounds over time in ways that make the governed enterprise progressively faster than the ungoverned one, not because it rushes, but because it stops tripping over its own decisions. The organizational velocity of the governed enterprise is not the velocity of uninhibited commitment — it is the velocity of unimpeded execution, produced by the governance that removes the impediments that ungoverned decisions create rather than the absence of the governance that the false trade-off frames as an impediment.

The Real Measure of Speed

True organizational speed is not measured by how quickly decisions are announced — by the pace at which the organization communicates its commitments to the markets, the stakeholders, and the operational teams whose work those commitments authorize. It is not measured by how rapidly initiatives launch — by the speed at which execution machinery is engaged, and resources are deployed in pursuit of announced directions. It is not measured by how aggressively timelines are compressed — by the organizational ambition of the schedules against which execution is evaluated and the competitive pressure under which those schedules are established. These are measures of commitment velocity, not execution quality. And commitment velocity without governance produces the deferred friction that eventually makes ungoverned organizations slow.

True organizational speed is measured by how rarely decisions must be revisited, defended, or undone. It is measured by the organizational velocity that is not consumed by the governance failures of ungoverned decisions — by the escalations, the reversals, the defensive explanations, and the accountability proceedings that ungoverned decisions produce and that governed decisions prevent. By that measure — the measure of sustainable organizational performance rather than the measure of uninhibited commitment velocity — governed enterprises move faster than ungoverned ones, consistently and compoundingly, because the governance that the false trade-off frames as friction is precisely what removes the friction that actually constrains organizational speed.

The Shift That Changes Everything

Once organizations understand that GD-II™ is not delay but clarity under pressure — that the deliberative investment governance requires at the front of the decision process is the institutional mechanism that eliminates the confusion, the ambiguity, and the compounded friction that ungoverned decisions produce throughout execution — the institutional resistance to governance fades. The resistance was never to governance itself. It was to the version of governance that institutional experience had produced — the bureaucratic, retrospective, compliance-focused governance that adds friction without producing clarity, that validates procedural compliance without establishing decision quality, and that imposes governance costs without delivering governance benefits. GD-II™ is not that version of governance.

GD-II™ becomes a performance enabler rather than a constraint — a governance function that the organization's leaders, its execution teams, and its oversight bodies recognize as the institutional mechanism through which organizational speed is sustained rather than the bureaucratic burden through which it is constrained. Speed and safety stop competing as institutional objectives. They reinforce each other — because the governance that creates the safety of defensible decision-making is the same governance that creates the clarity of unambiguous authority, acknowledged risk, and defined scope that allows execution to proceed with the speed that governed decisions produce and ungoverned decisions cannot.

If GD-II™ enables speed without recklessness — if the governance of consequential decisions produces the institutional clarity that accelerates execution rather than the bureaucratic friction that constrains it — then a final consequential question presents itself. What kind of organizations will thrive in a world where judgment, accountability, and defensibility matter more than ever? What institutional qualities will determine survival in the environments that the next era of enterprise will create? Answering that question requires looking forward rather than backward, which is the subject of the chapter that follows.

The Enterprises That Will Survive the Next 25 Years

Why Decision-Governance Is Becoming a Condition of Survival

The future will not be kind to organizations that confuse momentum with wisdom. The institutional temptation to treat organizational forward movement as institutional soundness — to mistake the appearance of decisive direction for the substance of governed judgment — has produced the failures that the preceding chapters have examined in detail. In the next twenty-five years, that temptation will carry costs that the institutional environments of the past could absorb, and the institutional environments of the next era will not.

Over the next twenty-five years, enterprise survival will not be determined by who moves fastest — by the organizational velocity at which decisions are committed and execution is engaged. It will not be determined by who adopts the most technology — by the sophistication of the AI systems, the analytics platforms, or the operational infrastructure that organizations deploy in pursuit of competitive advantage. It will not be determined by who scales the largest systems — by the organizational breadth and operational reach that execution investment can produce. It will be determined by who can govern decisions under pressure — by the institutional capacity to exercise consequential authority with the governance discipline, the evidentiary standard, and the accountability clarity that the accountability environments of the next era will require.

This chapter is not speculative. It is observational. The forces reshaping enterprise behavior — the regulatory evolution, the board governance transformation, the talent dynamics, the AI accountability imperative, and the public trust conditions that define the institutional environment modern enterprises operate within — are already visible and already consequential. They all converge on a single institutional demand: accountable judgment at scale. The organizations that meet that demand will survive. Those that cannot will accumulate the institutional liabilities of ungoverned decision-making until those liabilities become the governing condition of their existence.

Scale Is No Longer Forgiving

In earlier eras, organizational mistakes dissipated. They were localized in their consequence — affecting a team, a department, a region, or a quarter in ways that the operational and institutional recovery mechanisms of the organization could absorb. They faded with time — becoming progressively less visible and less consequential as the organization grew and moved forward, and the institutional memory of specific failures was displaced by the ongoing record of organizational activity. They were absorbed by growth — subsumed within the expanding operational footprint and the accumulating track record of an organization whose overall trajectory made specific failures appear as temporary variance rather than structural evidence of governance failure. These statements are no longer true.

Today, decisions propagate instantly through the execution systems, the communication networks, and the market mechanisms that connect organizational action to consequence in real time rather than over the extended periods that previous eras provided for recognition and correction. Errors are permanently recorded — in the regulatory filings, the legal proceedings, the journalistic investigations, the social media archives, and the digital institutional memory that creates a permanent record of organizational governance failures available to any future accountability forum, regardless of the temporal distance between the failure and the examination.

Consequences are amplified by networks — by the interconnected operational infrastructure, the social media platforms, the stakeholder communication channels, and the market mechanisms that extend the reach of organizational failures to the full scope of the organization's institutional relationships and public accountability obligations. Scrutiny is global and continuous — exercised by regulatory bodies, by legal adversaries, by journalism, by activist stakeholders, and by public institutions whose examination of organizational conduct is no longer limited by geography, by temporal proximity to the failure, or by the information access constraints that previous eras imposed.

In this institutional environment, scale does not dilute organizational error. It magnifies it. The same execution systems that allow organizations to operate at a global scale allow the consequences of ungoverned decisions to propagate at the same scale — faster, further, and with greater irreversibility than any institutional recovery mechanism can match after the fact. Enterprises that cannot govern their decisions will not merely struggle in this environment — they will accumulate irreversible institutional risk faster than they can manage it, in an accountability environment that has neither the tolerance for unexplained governance failure nor the institutional capacity to absorb the consequences of ungoverned decision-making at scale.

Regulation Is Shifting From Rules to Reasonableness

Regulators are evolving. The regulatory frameworks that governed enterprise conduct through the Systems Age — frameworks built around the compliance model of rule adherence, procedural conformity, and checklist governance — are being progressively supplemented and in some domains replaced by a fundamentally different regulatory standard. Regulators are no longer satisfied with formal compliance — with the organizational demonstration that defined rules were followed and defined procedures were adhered to. They are no longer satisfied with procedural adherence — with evidence that organizational activity conformed to established process requirements independent of whether those processes governed the quality of the judgment that authorized the activity. They are no longer satisfied with checklist governance — with the organizational production of documentation that satisfies defined compliance requirements without establishing the evidentiary basis of the decision-making that those requirements nominally govern.

They increasingly demand evidence of decision reasoning — the contemporaneous record of what information was available at the moment of decision and how it was evaluated in the deliberative process that produced the direction taken. They demand demonstrated consideration of alternatives — the governance record that establishes that the available paths were genuinely evaluated against the evidence and that the basis for choosing the path taken over the alternatives was explicitly established at the moment of decision rather than constructed retrospectively. They demand proof of proportional risk acceptance — the contemporaneous documentation of the risk that the decision carried and the explicit acknowledgment by the authority whose mandate covers that risk that the risk was consciously accepted at the moment of authority. They demand clear lines of authority and accountability — the contemporaneous attribution of the decision to specific individuals operating under defined mandates with explicit accountability for the consequences of the authority they exercise.

This regulatory shift mirrors legal standards that already exist in other governance domains: the standard of reasonableness under the circumstances that courts apply to the evaluation of contested decisions, which asks not whether defined rules were followed but whether the decision process reflected the deliberative discipline that reasonable governance requires under the specific conditions of the decision context. Enterprises that cannot produce decision evidence — that cannot demonstrate the governance quality of their decision-making through a contemporaneous record that meets this emerging regulatory standard — will find themselves perpetually behind in regulatory proceedings: not because they broke rules, but because they cannot explain the judgment behind the compliant actions whose consequences the regulatory inquiry is examining. The inability to explain judgment is increasingly, in the regulatory environments of the next era, the functional equivalent of governance failure.

Boards Are Becoming Decision Stewards

Boards are under institutional pressure, unlike that faced by any previous generation of directors. The scope of board oversight responsibility has expanded dramatically in the current era — encompassing strategy, risk, culture, technology, ethics, resilience, and the full range of institutional conditions that determine whether the enterprise they oversee can operate with the legitimacy that its stakeholders, its regulators, and the public institutions that grant it social license require. The expansion of board oversight responsibility has created an institutional condition in which most boards face a fundamental governance gap: they lack visibility into the most important thing they are charged with overseeing.

Most boards can observe organizational outcomes — the financial performance, the operational results, and the strategic achievements that management reports and that board oversight is organized around. Most boards can assess organizational processes — the compliance frameworks, the risk management systems, and the operational controls that constitute the execution governance architecture that boards are expected to confirm is functioning. What most boards cannot observe — what no existing board governance mechanism provides visibility into — is how decisions are actually made: what the deliberative process looked like, what alternatives were considered, what risks were acknowledged and accepted, and whose authority determined the direction. This is the governance gap that will differentiate boards in the next era.

In the next era, boards will differentiate between management teams that can defend their decisions — that can produce, from the governance record of their consequential decision-making, the contemporaneous evidentiary basis that establishes the governance quality of the judgment behind the outcomes the board is responsible for overseeing — and management teams that can only explain outcomes — that can account for results retrospectively but cannot establish the decision governance quality that produced them. Only the former will retain the trust that board governance requires for substantive oversight rather than reactive crisis management. Governed Decision-Intelligence Infrastructure™ (GD-II™) becomes not a management preference or a governance aspiration but a board expectation — the institutional standard that boards whose fiduciary obligations require them to govern decision quality rather than merely observe decision outcomes will increasingly demand.

Talent Will Follow Governed Organizations

High-caliber leaders are becoming more selective in the institutional environments they choose to operate within — and the selectivity is not organized around compensation, title, or organizational scale in the ways that previous eras of leadership talent allocation were. The leaders capable of performing at the level that consequential organizational roles require in the next era — the individuals whose judgment, experience, and institutional commitment make them genuinely valuable in environments where accountability is real and consequences are significant — do not want the institutional conditions that ungoverned organizations produce.

They do not want ambiguous authority — the institutional condition in which the power to make consequential decisions is distributed across approval chains and committee processes in ways that make it impossible to exercise genuine leadership because the accountability for the decisions that leadership requires is not clearly attributed to any individual party. They do not want hidden risk — the institutional condition in which the risks of consequential decisions are not honestly acknowledged in the governance environment, which creates the personal accountability exposure of operating in an environment where institutional failures will be attributed to individual judgment, regardless of whether the governance framework required that individual to acknowledge and accept the risks before acting.

They do not want retroactive blame — the institutional condition in which accountability for governance failures arrives after the fact, shaped by the institutional politics and power relationships of the organization at the time consequences surface rather than by the contemporaneous governance record of who held the authority and exercised the judgment that produced them. They do not want politicized accountability — the institutional condition in which the attribution of accountability for organizational failures is determined by the institutional interests of the parties with the power to deflect it rather than by the governance record that would establish it objectively.

GD-II™ creates psychological safety for high-caliber leaders — not by removing the pressure that consequential institutional roles carry, but by making that pressure structural rather than personal.

The governance record establishes explicitly who holds the authority for each consequential decision, what the evidentiary basis of the judgment behind it was, and what risks were consciously accepted by whose institutional mandate — which means that the pressure of accountability is organized around the governance record rather than around the political dynamics of an ungoverned institutional environment. Organizations that deploy GD-II™ will attract and retain leaders capable of operating under real stakes — leaders whose institutional value is built on the quality of their governed judgment rather than on their personal capacity to navigate the ambiguous accountability dynamics of ungoverned organizations.

AI Will Force the Issue

Artificial intelligence accelerates everything — including the consequences of ungoverned decisions and the institutional liabilities they create. As AI systems are deployed across an expanding range of consequential organizational functions — recommending actions that human authorities accept and act upon, prioritizing options in ways that shape the direction that decision-makers choose, influencing decisions by providing the analytical outputs that the deliberative process treats as authoritative, and operating at the scale of organizational activity that makes the consequences of any single governance failure instantaneously consequential across the full breadth of the enterprise — the question of who is accountable for the consequences of AI-influenced decision-making becomes unavoidable in every accountability forum that examines those consequences.

Enterprises that deploy AI without GD-II™ will face a legitimacy crisis in the next era that is both predictable and preventable. They will not be able to explain why the AI recommendation was accepted — what the human authority's deliberative engagement with the AI output was, and what evidentiary basis existed for treating the AI recommendation as sound under the specific circumstances of the decision. They will not be able to explain what alternatives were considered — whether the alternatives to the AI-recommended path were genuinely evaluated or whether the AI recommendation was accepted without the deliberative engagement that governance requires.

They will not be able to explain who authorized reliance on the model — which specific human authority made the institutional decision to act on the AI output, and under what mandate that authority operated. They will not be able to explain what risks were knowingly assumed — whether the risks of acting on the AI recommendation were explicitly identified and consciously accepted at the moment of authority or inadvertently assumed in the absence of governance.

AI does not eliminate the need for GD-II™. It makes its absence intolerable. The speed at which AI-influenced decisions are executed, the scale at which their consequences propagate, and the accountability demands that the regulatory and legal environments of the next era will impose on AI-deploying organizations make the absence of pre-execution decision governance not merely a governance gap but an institutional liability of the first order.

Organizations that govern the decisions to act on AI outputs — that maintain the contemporaneous evidentiary record of who authorized reliance on AI systems, what alternatives were considered, and what risks were knowingly accepted — will be able to account for their AI-influenced decisions in every accountability forum that examines them. Organizations that do not will face the institutional consequences of accountability demands they cannot satisfy for decisions they cannot explain.

Public Trust Is Becoming Conditional

Trust is no longer granted to institutions by default — as a standing presumption of good faith that public institutions extend to organizations operating within the letter of the law. It must be earned — through the demonstrated institutional behavior that establishes the organization as a responsible actor in the environments it operates within, and through the continued exercise of the governance discipline that sustains that demonstration over time. And it must be re-earned — in the specific contexts where organizational conduct has produced consequences that require the organization to account for itself in terms that the public institutions and the communities affected by its decisions can evaluate and accept.

When failures occur in the institutional environments of the next era, the public no longer asks who is at fault in the procedural sense that assigns accountability to a designated party within the organizational hierarchy. They ask why this was allowed to happen — a question that cannot be answered by pointing to procedural compliance, by demonstrating that the required approvals were obtained, or by establishing that the organizational policies that governed the area of failure were followed. It is a governance question that asks about the quality of the decision-making that authorized the activity whose consequences require accountability — a question that only a contemporaneous governance record can answer with the specificity and the credibility that public accountability requires.

Organizations that cannot answer that question convincingly — that cannot produce, from their governance records, the contemporaneous account of how the decision was made that the question demands — will lose institutional legitimacy even if they acted within the letter of every applicable law.

Legal compliance is a necessary but no longer sufficient condition of institutional legitimacy in the public accountability environments of the next era. The additional condition is governance credibility — the demonstrated institutional capacity to make consequential decisions with the governance discipline that public trust requires. GD-II™ provides a language of institutional responsibility that the public can understand and that the organizational record can support — the contemporaneous evidentiary account of why the decision that produced the outcome was sound at the moment it was made, given what was known, and what governance standard was met in making it.

The End of the Heroic Leader Myth

The next era will not reward leaders who rely on intuition alone. The institutional mythology of the heroic decisive leader — the organizational figure whose intuitive grasp of complex situations, whose confident forward commitment, and whose willingness to act without the institutional friction of deliberative governance has historically been celebrated as the defining quality of exceptional institutional leadership — will be progressively replaced by a different institutional ideal. Heroic decisiveness — unexamined and undocumented, exercised without the governance discipline that contemporaneous accountability requires — will be seen as reckless rather than bold. Not because boldness is no longer valued, but because the accountability environments of the next era will distinguish between boldness that is governed and boldness that is not in ways that institutional recognition, regulatory standing, and legal defensibility will enforce.

What will replace the heroic leader myth is something more demanding — an institutional ideal of leadership that is transparent about uncertainty rather than projecting confidence that the evidentiary basis of the decision does not support. Leadership that is willing to surface dissent rather than suppressing it through the authority dynamics that ungoverned deliberative processes allow.

Leadership that is accountable for reasoning — that is, willing to have the basis of its judgment preserved in a contemporaneous governance record and subjected to the independent examination that accountability requires. Leadership that is comfortable with scrutiny — that operates in the knowledge that the exercise of consequential authority will be examined by accountability forums whose standard of evaluation is the governance quality of the decision process rather than the favorability of the outcomes it produced.

GD-II™ does not weaken leadership. It professionalizes it — replacing the institutional mythology of exceptional individual intuition with the institutional standard of governed judgment that the accountability environments of the next era require.

The leaders who thrive in governed organizations are no less decisive, less bold, or less willing to exercise consequential authority than the heroic leaders of the Systems Age. They are more institutionally credible — because the governance record of their decision-making establishes the quality of their judgment in a form that can withstand the scrutiny that institutional accountability requires, rather than resting on the institutional reputation of a leadership persona whose evidentiary basis is the favorable outcomes of past decisions rather than the governance discipline of the deliberative process that produced them.

Survivors Will Share One Trait

Across industries — across healthcare, finance, technology, retail, transportation, and every sector that constitutes the commercial and institutional fabric of the modern economy — the organizations that endure through the next twenty-five years will share a common trait that distinguishes them from the organizations that do not.

They will know why they decided what they decided. Not vaguely, in the sense of having a plausible institutional narrative that can be presented in favorable contexts. Not rhetorically, in the sense of having leadership communications that articulate the rationale for organizational direction in terms designed for external presentation. But evidentially — through a contemporaneous governance record that establishes, with the specificity and the independence that accountability requires, what the decision-maker knew at the moment of authority, what alternatives were considered and on what basis they were set aside, what risks were identified and consciously accepted, and who held the institutional power that authorized the direction.

They will be able to explain what they knew — the informational basis on which each consequential decision was made, preserved in contemporaneous form before outcomes shaped the institutional memory of what was known.

They will be able to explain what they did not know — the acknowledged unknowns and the informational gaps that the governance record reflects were present at the moment of decision, and that the decision-maker recognized as limitations on the evidentiary basis available. They will be able to explain what they considered — the alternatives that were evaluated and the paths that were set aside, recorded in the governance archive as first-class objects that establish the genuine deliberative engagement with available options that governance requires. They will be able to explain what they risked — the potential adverse consequences of the chosen path that the decision-maker identified and consciously accepted at the moment of authority, preserved in a form that cannot be retroactively shaped by knowledge of the consequences that followed.

They will be able to explain who decided — the specific individual whose institutional authority determined the direction, identified in the governance record in a form that establishes the contemporaneous attribution of accountability that governance requires. This capability — the institutional capacity to account for consequential decisions in every forum where accountability arrives — will separate resilient enterprises from fragile ones in the next era in ways that execution sophistication, technology adoption, and organizational scale cannot.

Failure Will Become Less Forgivable

As GD-II™ becomes both technologically feasible and institutionally expected — as the capability to govern decisions before execution and preserve the contemporaneous evidentiary basis of consequential authority becomes available to organizations across industries and scales — the institutional tolerance for unexplained failure will decline in ways that are structural rather than moral in their source and irreversible rather than cyclical in their trajectory. What was once tragic — an organizational failure whose circumstances were understood to make governance difficult and whose consequences were accepted as the unavoidable cost of operating in complex and uncertain environments — will be seen as negligent: a governance failure that the available infrastructure would have prevented if the organization had deployed it. What was once unlucky — an adverse outcome that was understood to fall within the range of results that reasonable risk-taking produces — will be seen as avoidable: a consequence of risks that governance would have required to be explicitly identified, evaluated, and consciously accepted rather than inadvertently assumed in the absence of governance.

What was once excusable — a governance failure whose institutional context made it understandable as the product of the limitations of available tools, the constraints of organizational resources, or the genuine uncertainty of the decision environment — will be seen as irresponsible: a choice to operate without the governance infrastructure that is available, deployable, and increasingly expected.

This evolution in the institutional tolerance for governance failure is not a moral judgment about the character or the intentions of the organizations that have operated without GD-II™. It is structural evolution — the predictable institutional response to the availability of governance infrastructure that makes the absence of governance a choice rather than a constraint, in accountability environments that apply the standard of reasonableness under the circumstances to the assessment of whether that choice was responsible.

The Quiet Standard That Will Define the Future

The future will not be governed by a single regulation or compliance framework that organizations can satisfy through checklist conformity and procedural adherence. It will be governed by an unspoken standard that is emerging across accountability forums, regulatory environments, governance bodies, and public institutions in ways that are not yet codified in any single legal instrument but that are increasingly enforced through the cumulative consequence of every accountability proceeding that applies it. The standard is this: if an organization cannot explain its decision-making, it does not deserve the outcomes it seeks.

This standard is not a philosophical proposition. It is a functional description of the institutional conditions that modern accountability environments apply to the examination of consequential decisions whose consequences require accountability. Organizations that can explain their decision-making — that can produce, from the contemporaneous governance record of their consequential decisions, the evidentiary account of what was known, considered, accepted, and by whose authority at the moment of decision — will be evaluated by this standard as having met the governance requirement that the accountability forum applies.

Organizations that cannot will be evaluated as having failed it — not because they lacked the intention to govern their decisions, but because they lacked the infrastructure through which that intention could have been expressed and preserved in the form that accountability requires. Enterprises that internalize this standard will adapt their institutional architecture, their governance frameworks, and their decision-making practices to meet it. Those that resist it — that treat it as a temporary external imposition rather than as the structural condition of institutional legitimacy in the accountability environments of the next era — will struggle with the cumulative institutional consequences of the gap between the governance standard they are expected to meet and the governance capability they have built.

The Final Transition

The Systems Age gave us scale — the institutional capacity to replicate organizational activity across geographies, functions, and time in ways that made the modern enterprise possible and that defined the institutional achievement of the twentieth century. That achievement was genuine, and it was necessary. It remains the operational foundation of every organization that functions at scale in the modern world. But scale alone is no longer sufficient for institutional survival in the accountability environments that the next era will create and enforce.

The next evolution demands governed judgment at scale — the institutional capacity not merely to replicate organizational activity consistently across the operational breadth of the enterprise, but to exercise the consequential authority that determines what that activity will be with the governance discipline, the evidentiary standard, and the accountability clarity that the accountability environments of the next era require. This is not optional in the sense that it can be deferred until the institutional consequences of its absence become visible — by the time those consequences are visible, the governance gap that produced them will have accumulated the institutional liabilities that make the transition significantly more costly than it would have been if the infrastructure had been built before the liabilities materialized. It is not ideological — not the preference of a particular governance philosophy or the advocacy of a particular institutional design school, but the structural response to observable and already consequential institutional forces whose direction is clear. It is not theoretical — not a governance aspiration whose institutional implications remain to be established, but a practical institutional requirement whose necessity has been demonstrated by the repeated governance failures of the Systems Age and whose infrastructure has been defined. It is the price of operating in a world where decisions travel faster, last longer, and matter more than ever before.

One question remains. If GD-II™ is the institutional requirement that survival in the next era demands — and if GD-II™ is the means through which that requirement is operationalized — how does an organization begin the transition without the disruption, the paralysis, or the loss of operational momentum that transitions of institutional architecture typically produce? That question is the subject of the final chapter.

CHAPTER 16

BUILDING THE MISSING INFRASTRUCTURE

How Organizations Transition From Systems to
Governed Decision-Intelligence™ (GD-I™)

By now, the case is complete. Governed Decision-Intelligence Infrastructure™ (GD-II™) is no longer optional — not in the institutional sense of a governance aspiration that organizations may choose to pursue when circumstances permit, but in the structural sense of a foundational requirement that the accountability environments of the modern era impose on every organization that operates at scale with consequential impact on the parties its decisions affect. Governed Decision-Intelligence™ (GD-I™) is no longer theoretical — it has been defined precisely, its institutional requirements have been established, and the infrastructure architecture that operationalizes it has been specified in terms that allow practical institutional implementation. The absence of both is no longer defensible as a governance oversight, as an institutional immaturity, or as the product of conditions that made the infrastructure unavailable. It is now a risk position — the deliberate choice to operate without the governance layer that responsible institutional conduct requires.

The remaining question is practical. Not whether GD-II™ is necessary — the preceding fifteen chapters have established that conclusively. Not whether the infrastructure that operationalizes it can be built — the constitutional logic, the technical prerequisites, and the organizational architecture have all been defined. But how? How does an organization actually transition to GD-II™ without freezing itself in place, without disrupting the operational momentum that the competitive environment requires, and without producing the institutional paralysis that governance, misunderstood as bureaucratic process, has historically created?

This chapter answers that question plainly — not as a transformation manifesto that promises organizational reinvention through the adoption of a new governance philosophy, not as a technology roadmap that specifies the platforms and tools whose deployment will produce the governance outcomes the infrastructure requires, but as a structural transition that respects how real enterprises actually operate: under competitive pressure, with existing obligations, within authority structures that carry institutional momentum, and with organizational cultures that reflect the accumulated governance practices of the Systems Age.

Independence as a Prerequisite

The infrastructure described in this chapter cannot be legitimately self-implemented by the same authority whose decisions it is intended to govern. This is not an implementation preference or an organizational design option — it is a structural requirement that the preceding chapters have established as foundational to any governance function that produces genuine pre-execution constraint rather than the self-referential oversight that creates the appearance of accountability without the substance of it. Governance requires separation. The same institutional principle that prevents judges from ruling on their own cases, auditors from certifying their own employers, and regulators from governing their own conduct applies with equal force to the governance of consequential organizational decisions: the party whose authority is subject to governance cannot legitimately serve as the governance function.

Enterprises do not build GD-II™ in the same way they build execution systems. They do not design it, implement it, and operate it as an internal organizational function whose staffing, mandate, and governance findings are determined by the organizational authority it is meant to constrain. They prepare for it — by developing the internal organizational readiness that integration with an independent governance layer requires. They integrate with it — by establishing the operational connections between the organization's decision processes and the external governance function through which those processes pass. And they operate under it — by conducting their consequential decision-making within the governance conditions that the independent infrastructure establishes, rather than determining those conditions themselves. Independence is not an implementation detail that organizations can waive for convenience or efficiency. It is the prerequisite condition without which the governance function collapses into the institutional dynamics it was designed to constrain.

Step One: Do Not Start With Technology

The most common — and most institutionally damaging — mistake organizations make when they recognize the governance gap and attempt to close it is starting with tools. They search for platforms that promise to deliver governance functionality through workflow automation, compliance tracking, or AI-assisted decision support. They ask vendors what products are available to address the governance requirements they have identified. They pilot software solutions before they have established the governance architecture that those solutions are meant to support. This approach inverts the problem in ways that consistently produce institutional outcomes that compound the governance gap rather than closing it.

GD-II™ is not a product. It is a governance architecture — a structural design for how consequential decision authority is governed, what evidentiary standards it must meet, what independence the governance function maintains from the authority it governs, and how the governance record is preserved and made available to the accountability forums that will eventually require it. Technology supports this architecture. It does not define it. The governance architecture must be established — the governance functions must be identified, the independence requirements must be specified, the evidentiary standards must be defined, and the authority structure through which governance operates must be determined — before the technological infrastructure through which those functions are operationalized can be meaningfully specified or selected. Organizations that begin with tools end up automating confusion — deploying technological infrastructure that efficiently executes a governance architecture that was never designed, producing compliance records that satisfy the appearance of governance without establishing its substance.

Step Two: Identify Consequential Decisions

Not every decision requires governance at the level that GD-II™ provides. Attempting to govern every organizational decision produces bureaucracy — the institutional condition in which governance requirements are applied uniformly to all decisions regardless of their consequence, creating friction that the organization cannot sustain and that produces the institutional resistance that causes governance programs to collapse. Governing nothing produces risk — the institutional condition in which no governance standard is applied to any decision, leaving the full range of consequential organizational authority ungoverned. The transition to governed enterprise begins by identifying the decision classes that meet the criteria that justify the application of formal GD-II™.

Three criteria define the decision classes that constitute the first governed set. The first is irreversibility: once made, the decision materially reshapes authority, culture, or organizational exposure in ways that cannot be undone without an institutional cost that exceeds the deliberative investment that governance requires before execution. The second is asymmetric risk: the downside of the decision if judgment is flawed meaningfully exceeds the upside if judgment is sound — the loss that ungoverned poor judgment produces is not proportionate to the gain that governed sound judgment adds. The third is distributed impact: the consequences of the decision affect parties who did not make it and who have no institutional mechanism for participating in the deliberative process through which it was authorized.

The categories of decision that characteristically meet these three criteria include executive hires and promotions — decisions that concentrate institutional authority in individuals whose judgment will shape organizational culture, operational direction, and institutional accountability across extended time horizons. Termination tolerances — decisions that establish what conduct, performance, or cultural behavior the organization will accept without consequence, which create the behavioral precedents and the institutional norms that define what the organization actually is rather than what its policies say it is. Cultural exceptions — decisions to tolerate conduct or accept outcomes that fall below the organization's stated standards, which establish precedents that propagate through the institutional culture in ways that are difficult to reverse once embedded. High-stakes AI deployment decisions — decisions to act on AI system outputs in ways that affect human outcomes, which carry the accountability challenges that the Interlude established as requiring pre-execution governance before the governance gap is exposed by adverse consequences. Safety-critical operational calls and strategic acceleration decisions — the full range of consequential choices that carry the three criteria of irreversibility, asymmetric risk, and distributed impact that make governance both necessary and proportionate. These decisions become the first governed set.

Step Three: Separate Decision From Execution

Most organizations blur the moment of decision with the start of execution — treating the institutional commitment to a direction and the operational beginning of the process that carries that commitment out as a single continuous event rather than as two distinct institutional moments with different governance requirements. This blurring is the structural condition that allows decisions to be absorbed into the operational flow of execution without being identified, governed, and recorded as distinct acts of authority. The transition to GD-II™ requires that this blurring be resolved by explicitly separating the decision moment from the execution moment in the organizational architecture.

A governed enterprise explicitly separates decision formation — the deliberative process through which the available information is evaluated, the alternatives are assessed, and the direction is identified — from decision commitment — the discrete institutional moment at which the authority holding the power to choose explicitly commits the organization to a specific direction, with the evidentiary basis, the explicit risk acknowledgment, and the contemporaneous record that governance requires — from decision execution — the operational activity through which the committed decision is carried out by the execution systems and execution teams whose function is to implement the direction that the commitment has established. The decision moment becomes visible as a distinct institutional event rather than a continuous operational transition. Only after a decision is committed — evidenced, owned, and risk-acknowledged — does execution begin. This separation alone eliminates a significant proportion of the confusion, the rework, and the downstream conflict that the blurring of decision and execution produces in ungoverned enterprises.

Step Four: Define Decision Authority Explicitly

GD-II™ fails operationally when authority is ambiguous — when the governance architecture does not establish clearly which specific individual holds the power to make each category of governed decision, under what mandate that authority is exercised, what the escalation thresholds are that would require the decision to be referred to a higher level of authority, and what the accountability is that attaches to the party exercising the decision authority at each level. Ambiguity about authority is not merely an operational inconvenience — it is a governance failure that prevents the governance record from attributing accountability with the precision that defensibility requires and that allows the diffusion of responsibility that ungoverned organizations rely on to avoid individual accountability for consequential institutional choices.

For each governed decision class, the organization must define who has the authority to decide — which specific individual or role holds the institutional power to commit the organization to the direction that the governed decision class covers. It must define under what mandate that authority is exercised — what the institutional basis is for the authority, what the scope of the commitment it can make is, and what the limits of the mandate are. It must define the escalation boundaries — the conditions under which the decision exceeds the authority of the designated decision-maker and must be referred to a higher level of institutional authority for resolution. And it must define the accountability — the institutional consequence that attaches to the party exercising the decision authority for the judgment they exercise and the risks they accept in exercising it. This is not a power grab — it is not a redistribution of authority for political purposes or an assertion of governance control over functions that operate effectively without it. It is a clarity exercise. When authority is explicit, speed improves because execution can proceed without the repeated clarification that ambiguous authority requires. Conflict decreases because the governance architecture has established who decides rather than leaving the question to be resolved through the institutional politics of competing interests. Accountability stabilizes because the governance record has established whose authority produced the outcome rather than distributing accountability across the collective processes that ambiguity enables. Politics recedes because the organizational incentive to maintain ambiguity as institutional protection against accountability has been eliminated by governance that makes authority explicit, regardless of the preferences of those whose authority it attributes. Ambiguity protects no one — but only an organization that has built the governance architecture to eliminate it will discover this.

Step Five: Require Contemporaneous Evidence

Before a governed decision can be executed — before the governance record has been established and the execution system is authorized to proceed — four categories of contemporaneous evidence must be captured. The first is evidence available at the time: the specific information that was available to the decision-maker at the moment of authority and that the decision was based upon, preserved before outcomes have shaped the institutional memory of what was known. The second is alternatives considered and rejected: the paths that were evaluated and not chosen, recorded as first-class objects in the governance record that establishes the genuine deliberative engagement with available options that governance requires. The third is the risks identified and accepted: the explicit acknowledgment of the potential adverse consequences of the chosen path, attributed to the decision-maker whose institutional mandate covers the acceptance of those risks. The fourth is authority exercised and acknowledged: the explicit identification of the party whose institutional power authorized the decision, under what mandate, and with what accountability for the consequences of the authority exercised.

This is not a memo produced after the decision has been made to explain why it was taken. It is not a justification assembled in anticipation of scrutiny to present the decision in its most favorable light. It is a decision record — a contemporaneous governance document captured before outcomes are known and before the institutional incentives that would otherwise shape its retrospective presentation have been created by the consequences of the decision's execution. The act of creating this record changes the character of the deliberative process that precedes it in ways that improve the quality of the judgment behind every governed decision: requiring evidence before execution creates the conditions under which decision-makers engage with the evidentiary basis of their choices in ways that ungoverned decisions never require, which produces better institutional judgment even before the governance record is subjected to any external accountability examination.

Step Six: Make Dissent Structural

Governed decisions do not rely on individual courage to produce the deliberative challenge that governance requires. They rely on design. The institutional failure mode of ungoverned deliberative processes — in which genuine dissent is available only to those willing to bear the professional cost of challenging the direction of institutional authority under conditions where that cost systematically exceeds the institutional reward — is a structural condition that structural governance must address structurally rather than culturally. Expecting individuals to produce genuine dissent in ungoverned environments through the cultivation of organizational courage is expecting institutional behavior to overcome structural conditions, which produces the cultural mythology of psychological safety without the institutional reality of it.

By requiring — as conditions of the governance record — that alternatives to the direction being chosen be explicitly documented, that the explicit risks of the chosen path be formally acknowledged, and that the counterarguments to the chosen direction be recorded as part of the contemporaneous governance account, the organization removes the burden of dissent from individuals and converts it into a procedural requirement. Dissent is no longer a social risk that individuals must choose to assume against the institutional dynamics that punish it — it is a governance requirement that the record must reflect before the decision is authorized to proceed. This conversion of dissent from social risk to procedural requirement is consistently one of the fastest and most significant cultural shifts that organizations experience once GD-II™ is introduced. The organizational culture does not need to change before governance is introduced — the governance requirement changes the organizational culture by making the institutional incentives that previously punished dissent unavailable to the governance environments in which dissent has become structurally required.

Step Seven: Preserve Decision Memory Immutably

Decisions must not be rewritten by hindsight. The contemporaneous governance record that GD-II™ produces is only as valuable as its integrity — its independence from the retrospective institutional interests that would otherwise shape the account of what was known, considered, and accepted at the moment of authority. Once captured, decision records must be immutable — preserved in a form that cannot be altered by the parties whose authority they document, regardless of the institutional incentives that adverse outcomes may create for retrospective modification. They must be timestamped — establishing the temporal relationship between the governance record and the outcomes that followed in a form that demonstrates the contemporaneous character of the evidentiary basis rather than its retrospective construction.

Decision records must be linked to authority — establishing the specific institutional identity of the party whose power authorized the decision in a form that creates the explicit accountability attribution that governance requires, rather than the diffused responsibility that approval chains produce. And they must be accessible to oversight bodies — available to the boards, the regulators, the courts, and the other institutional accountability forums that may require examination of the governance record in the contexts and at the times when accountability arrives. This is not about surveillance of organizational decision-making or the creation of institutional mechanisms designed to penalize the exercise of consequential authority. It is about organizational memory — the institutional capacity to know what decisions were made, by whose authority, on what basis, and with what risk acknowledgment at the moment of authority, and to preserve that knowledge in a form that remains accurate and independent of the outcomes those decisions produced. Without organizational memory of this quality, learning collapses into storytelling — into the retrospective construction of institutional narratives that serve the interests of their authors rather than the institutional truth of what occurred.

Step Eight: Govern Escalation, Not Initiative

GD-II™ should never suppress the organizational initiative — the willingness to identify opportunities, propose directions, and commit to the experimentation that organizational learning and competitive responsiveness require. The governance architecture is not designed to slow the identification of possible directions or to require governance scrutiny of the exploratory and analytical work through which organizations develop the options from which consequential decisions are eventually made. It governs escalation thresholds — the points at which the organizational activity moves from exploration and formation toward commitment that is irreversible, risk-concentrated, and consequential for parties who did not participate in the deliberative process.

Most organizational decisions and actions should flow freely — should proceed without the formal governance requirements of GD-II™ because they do not meet the criteria of irreversibility, asymmetric risk, and distributed impact that make governance both necessary and proportionate. Governance intensifies progressively as decisions move toward the conditions that define the governed set: as risk crosses a defined boundary that the governance architecture has established, as authority concentration increases to the point where the institutional power being exercised is significant enough to require the evidentiary standard and the explicit attribution that governance demands, and as reversibility declines to the point where the consequences of ungoverned judgment cannot be corrected without institutional cost that the governance investment would have prevented. This progressive intensification keeps the organization agile in the operational domain where agility is both appropriate and necessary, while protecting it at the edges — at the institutional moments where the combination of high stakes, concentrated authority, and irreversible consequences — makes ungoverned execution most institutionally dangerous.

Step Nine: Build Leadership Literacy for the New Mental Model

GD-II™ requires a new form of institutional literacy from the leaders who operate within it — not a technical expertise in governance systems or compliance frameworks, but a practical understanding of the conceptual distinctions that distinguish governed decision-making from the institutional practices of the Systems Age. Leaders must understand the difference between speed and recklessness — between the organizational velocity that governance produces through the clarity, authority, and risk acknowledgment that the governance record establishes, and the ungoverned momentum that produces deferred friction rather than sustainable institutional performance. They must understand the difference between documentation and evidence — between the procedural records that demonstrate execution compliance and the contemporaneous governance records that establish the quality of the judgment behind the compliant execution.

They must understand the difference between authority and accountability — between the institutional power to commit the organization to a consequential direction and the institutional responsibility for the consequences of that commitment that governance makes explicit, attributable, and immutable. They must understand the difference between outcomes and decision quality — between the results that consequential decisions produce and the governance standard of the deliberative process that produced them, which are different assessments that governance evaluates independently and that outcome-based evaluation consistently conflates. This is not training in tools or in the technical implementation of governance systems. It is training in judgment under governance — in the institutional disposition and the conceptual literacy that allow leaders to exercise their authority with the deliberative discipline that the governance architecture requires and that the accountability environments of the next era will evaluate. Leaders who grasp this mental model adapt quickly to governed environments — and often become the strongest institutional advocates for the governance infrastructure once they experience the clarity, the accountability, stability, and the institutional confidence that governed decision-making produces.

Step Ten: Manage Resistance With Resolve

Resistance to GD-II™ will appear in every organization that introduces it. It will come from those accustomed to informal authority — individuals whose institutional influence has been built on the organizational convenience of exercising consequential power without being required to own it explicitly in a governance record, and for whom the visibility requirements of governed decision-making represent a genuine change in the institutional conditions that have supported their authority. It will come from those rewarded for speed without scrutiny — individuals whose institutional standing has been built on a decision-making track record that the ungoverned environment evaluated by outcomes rather than by governance discipline, and who experience the governance requirements as institutional constraints on the performance profile that their reputation depends on. It will come from those uncomfortable with explicit accountability — individuals who have operated within the collective approval structures that distributed accountability across enough parties to ensure that no individual bore the full weight of any consequential judgment.

This resistance is structural, not malicious. It is the predictable institutional response of parties whose position in the organization was built on governance conditions that GD-II™ is specifically designed to change. Naming it accurately — identifying it as the structural response to a genuine redistribution of institutional visibility rather than as individual opposition to a governance improvement — allows organizations to manage it rather than being managed by it. Organizations that name resistance early and address it as a structural condition neutralize it. Organizations that ignore it or treat it as a cultural failure rather than a structural response, find that the governance infrastructure retreats in the face of the institutional dynamics it was designed to address. Governance does not fail because it is wrong. It fails when leadership lacks the resolve to maintain the governance conditions that the resistant parties are most motivated to undermine.

Step Eleven: Expand Deliberately but Permanently

GD-II™ should expand deliberately — starting with a narrow decision set, a small leadership group that operates under the governance conditions it will eventually require across the organization, and a clear mandate that establishes the institutional authority and the independence requirements that governance demands. This deliberate beginning is not a concession to institutional resistance or a compromise of the governance standard — it is a recognition that governance architecture, like every foundational institutional investment, produces its most durable institutional adoption when it is introduced in a form that allows the organization to experience its benefits before extending its scope.

The governance program should demonstrate value at each stage of its expansion — establishing, through the concrete institutional experience of governance in operation, the speed improvement, the accountability clarity, the conflict reduction, and the defensibility enhancement that governed decision-making produces for the leaders who operate within it. Then expand — extending the governance architecture to additional decision classes, additional organizational functions, and additional leadership levels as the institutional evidence of its value accumulates, and the organizational readiness to operate within its requirements develops. What matters is not the speed of rollout — not the ambition of the governance scope that is established in the initial implementation. What matters is the irreversibility of adoption: the institutional entrenchment of governance requirements within the organizational architecture in a form that makes them durable against the resistance that expansion will continue to generate and that does not depend on the continued advocacy of any single governance champion to maintain. Once leaders experience Governed Decisions — once they operate within the institutional clarity, the accountability stability, and the defensibility confidence that governance produces — few want to return to the ambiguity that governance replaced. The irreversibility of adoption is the product of institutional experience, not of governance mandates.

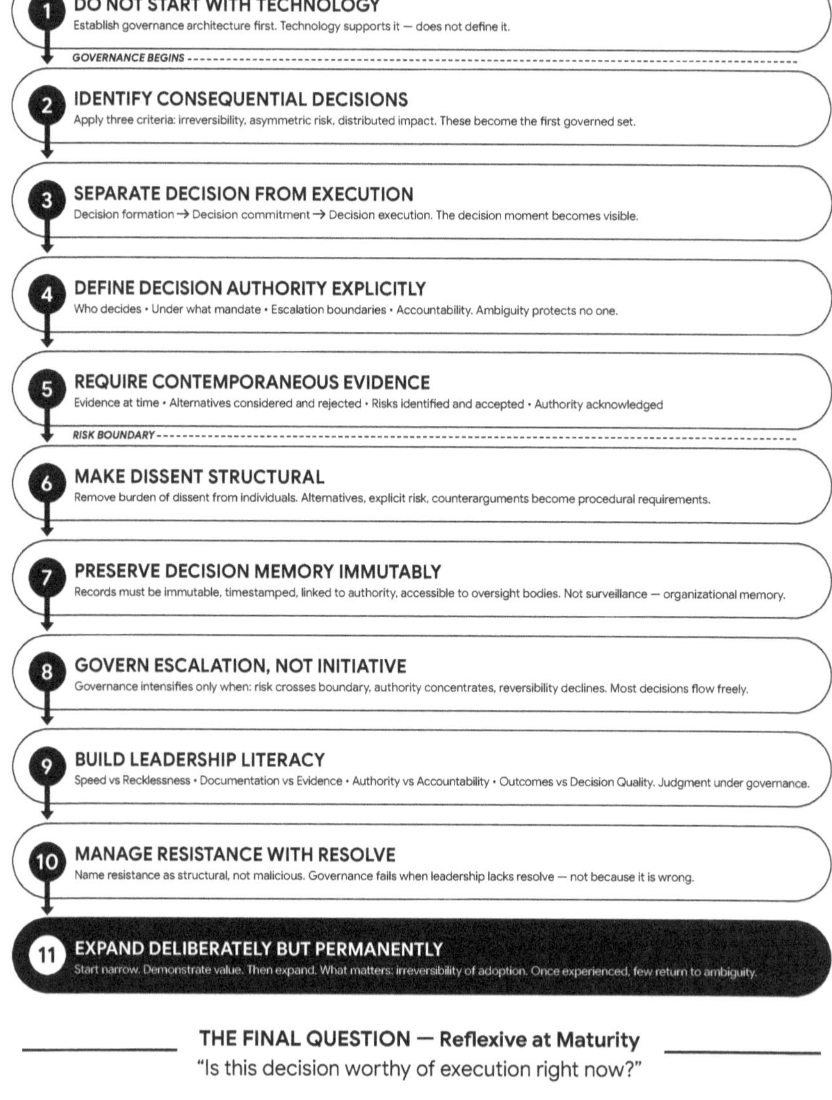

Figure 16.1 — Decision-Governance Transition: Eleven Steps. Progressive governance adoption from a narrow governed set through to a fully governed enterprise. Governance intensifies as risk crosses defined boundaries, authority concentration increases, and reversibility declines. The final question — 'Is this decision worthy of execution right now?' — becomes reflexive at maturity.

The Final Shift

At maturity — when GD-II™ has been established across the full range of the organization's consequential decision-making, when the governance record is maintained consistently and independently, and when the institutional culture has adapted to the governance conditions that the infrastructure creates — the organization undergoes a quiet and fundamental transformation. It stops asking the questions that the Systems Age produced and that governance has rendered obsolete. It stops asking whether the process was followed — because the governance architecture has established a standard above compliance that makes process adherence an insufficient governance measure. It stops asking whether this can be explained later — because the governance record has established the contemporaneous evidentiary basis that makes retrospective explanation unnecessary. It starts asking the only question that governed institutional judgment requires: is this decision worthy of execution right now?

That question — asked before the execution system is engaged, by the authority whose power would commit the organization to the consequences of the decision, against the evidentiary standard that the governance architecture requires — becomes reflexive in the governed enterprise. It is no longer an institutional imposition that governance forces on a resistant organization. It is the default orientation of an institutional culture that has internalized the governance standard, and that experiences the deliberative discipline it requires as the natural condition of responsible institutional authority rather than as an external constraint on operational performance. And when that question becomes reflexive — when the organization asks it automatically, consistently, and with the evidentiary engagement that governance requires — the transition is complete. The organization has moved from the Systems Age to the governed enterprise.

The End of One Era and the Beginning of Another

The Systems Age taught us how to scale work — how to replicate organizational activity consistently across operational breadth and temporal depth in ways that made the modern enterprise possible and that defined the institutional achievement of the era that produced it. That teaching was genuine, and the institutions that internalized it were genuinely transformed by it. The modern enterprise is its product, and the operational sophistication, the execution reliability, and the institutional scale that the Systems Age produced are genuine accomplishments whose value is not diminished by the recognition that they are insufficient for the governance requirements of the next era.

The next evolution teaches us how to scale judgment — how to exercise consequential authority with the governance discipline, the evidentiary standard, and the accountability clarity that responsible institutional conduct requires across the operational breadth and the institutional permanence of the modern enterprise at scale. GD-II™ is not a management trend. It does not represent a governance philosophy whose institutional implications are speculative or whose practical implementation is aspirational. It is the structural response to a world where decisions move faster, last longer, and matter more than ever before — where the combination of AI acceleration, permanent records, global accountability, and expanding regulatory requirements has created institutional environments in which the absence of pre-execution decision governance is not merely a governance gap but a risk position that organizations cannot responsibly maintain.

Organizations that build this infrastructure will not eliminate failure — the irreducible uncertainty of consequential institutional action in complex environments ensures that even governed decisions will sometimes produce adverse outcomes. What they will eliminate is surprise — the institutional condition in which consequences arrive without the contemporaneous governance record that allows the organization to account for them, defend its decision-making, and preserve its institutional legitimacy in the accountability forums that examine them. In the decades ahead, that difference — between organizations that can account for their consequential decisions and organizations that cannot — will determine who endures.

Closing Thought

Systems made organizations efficient.

Governed Decision-Intelligence Infrastructure™ makes them legitimate.

This is the next evolution.

Related Work and Structural Distinction

This work builds upon, but is not subsumed by, prior literature in governance, risk management, ethics, compliance, and decision science. The five bodies of knowledge that constitute the most directly relevant precursors to the institutional argument advanced here each address a genuine and important dimension of the governance challenge that consequential organizational decision-making presents. Each has contributed frameworks, principles, and analytical tools that have advanced the governance capacities of modern enterprises in meaningful ways. The intellectual contributions of these disciplines are acknowledged, and the institutional progress they have produced is real. Existing bodies of work provide important precursors to the framework this book establishes; however, none consolidate these perspectives into a unified, enterprise-wide framework governing human-impact decisions prior to execution. The limitation is structural rather than analytical — it is not that any of these disciplines has failed in its designated domain, but that none was designed for the specific governance function that this work establishes as a foundational institutional requirement.

Corporate Governance

Corporate governance literature addresses the oversight, fiduciary obligations, and accountability structures of institutional boards and their relationship to organizational leadership. It has produced sophisticated frameworks for defining the responsibilities of directors, establishing the conditions under which boards can discharge their fiduciary duties, and creating the accountability relationships between boards, executives, shareholders, and other organizational stakeholders that constitute the governance architecture of the modern enterprise. This body of work governs organizations and the conduct of institutional leadership — the standards to which the institution as a whole and its designated leaders are held accountable by the oversight and fiduciary structures the governance frameworks create.

Corporate governance literature does not govern the pre-execution gating of individual exposure-class decisions — the specific consequential choices that human authorities make in the exercise of their institutional power before those choices are committed to execution and before they expose the organization to the consequences they will produce. The governance subject of corporate governance is the organization and its leadership structures. The governance subject of GD-II™ is the decision itself — the discrete act of institutional authority that must meet an evidentiary and accountability standard before the execution system it authorizes is engaged. These are different governance subjects, operating at different institutional levels, requiring different governance architectures. Corporate governance frameworks provide the institutional context within which GD-II™ operates. They do not perform the GD-II™ function.

Enterprise Risk Management

Enterprise Risk Management (ERM) frameworks provide the analytical infrastructure through which organizations identify, model, assess, and monitor the institutional risks that their operations create and that their governance obligations require them to manage. The intellectual development of ERM over the past several decades has produced increasingly sophisticated tools for risk categorization, risk quantification, risk tolerance specification, and risk monitoring that allow organizations to maintain visibility into their institutional risk profiles with a precision and a comprehensiveness that previous generations of risk governance could not achieve. ERM frameworks inform decisions by providing the risk context within which organizational choices are made, and they monitor risk outcomes by tracking the institutional exposure that organizational activity produces over time.

ERM frameworks do not possess execution-blocking authority — the institutional capacity to intercept a consequential decision before it is executed and to require that it meet an evidentiary standard before the execution system is authorized to proceed. They provide risk information to decision-makers and require that risk be assessed and monitored as a governance obligation; they do not themselves determine whether a decision whose risk profile has been assessed is permitted to proceed. They do not require auditable decision-time provenance before exposure — the contemporaneous governance record of what was known, considered, and accepted at the moment of authority that GD-II™ requires as a condition of execution authorization. ERM frameworks address the institutional risk profile of the organization in aggregate. GD-II™ addresses the governance quality of each consequential decision individually, before the execution that would produce the risk exposure that ERM would subsequently monitor.

Compliance and Regulatory Regimes

Compliance frameworks ensure the adherence of organizational conduct to applicable legal requirements, regulatory standards, and internal policy obligations. They have developed into sophisticated institutional architectures that define what organizations must and must not do, establish the procedural requirements that organizational activity must satisfy, create the monitoring and enforcement mechanisms that verify conformity with established standards, and produce the documentation infrastructure that demonstrates compliance with regulatory requirements to the external oversight bodies that enforce them. The institutional value of compliance governance — in creating the predictable, rule-governed operational environment that regulatory frameworks require and that institutional stakeholders depend on — is substantial and not in question.

Compliance frameworks evaluate conformity after decisions are made or actions taken — they assess whether organizational conduct conforms to established standards, which is an evaluation that by definition occurs after the conduct that produced it. They do not govern whether exposure-creating decisions should proceed in the absence of validated decision evidence — whether the consequential choices whose execution will produce the organizational conduct that compliance subsequently evaluates meet the evidentiary standard that governance of the decision itself requires before that execution begins. Compliance governs the execution layer. It evaluates whether what was done conformed to the required standards. GD-II™ governs the decision layer. It determines whether what is proposed to be done meets the governance standard that authorizes execution to proceed. The distinction is temporal and jurisdictional: compliance operates after decisions are committed, GD-II™ operates before they are.

Ethics, Responsible AI, and Impact Assessments

Ethical frameworks for organizational conduct, responsible AI design principles, and algorithmic impact assessment methodologies constitute a growing and increasingly important body of practice that anticipates potential harm from organizational decisions and technological deployments and promotes responsible institutional design as a means of preventing those harms. These approaches have contributed significantly to the governance discourse around AI deployment, data governance, and the institutional responsibilities that arise from the application of powerful technologies to human outcomes. They address genuine and important dimensions of the governance challenge that modern institutional scale and AI capability create.

These approaches are typically domain-specific — developed for particular categories of technological deployment or institutional conduct rather than as general-purpose governance architectures applicable across the full range of consequential organizational decision-making. They are typically advisory — providing principles, frameworks, and assessments that inform organizational decision-making without creating the binding institutional authority that governance in the enforcement sense requires. They are typically principle-based — establishing the normative standards that responsible conduct should meet without creating the structural mechanisms through which those standards are enforced as conditions of execution authorization. As a result, they do not generalize into an enterprise-wide infrastructure that governs decision authority itself — the institutional exercise of consequential authority across all human-impact domains — through binding pre-execution enforcement rather than advisory guidance. The governance aspiration of ethical frameworks and responsible AI principles is aligned with the governance requirement that GD-II™ addresses. The institutional architecture through which they operate is not.

Decision Science and Governed Decision-Intelligence™ (GD-I™)

Decision science as an academic and applied discipline optimizes choice under uncertainty — providing analytical frameworks, cognitive models, and practical tools for improving the quality of individual and institutional decisions by reducing the systematic distortions that human cognition introduces into the deliberative process. Decision science has produced important insights into the conditions under which judgment degrades, the cognitive mechanisms through which decision quality is compromised, and the analytical approaches that can improve deliberative outcomes when they are applied to the decision process. Decision-Intelligence platforms, as a category of enterprise technology, analyze data, models, and predictive outputs to improve decision outcomes within execution systems — providing the analytical capability that allows organizations to make better-informed choices within the operational frameworks their execution systems provide.

GD-I™, by contrast, establishes institutional pre-exposure governance over whether consequential decisions may proceed at all. The distinction is not one of analytical sophistication or data capability — it is a governance distinction. Decision science and Decision-Intelligence platforms address the quality of the deliberative process within which decisions are made. GD-II™ addresses whether the decisions that emerge from that deliberative process meet the institutional standard required for execution to be authorized. Neither decision science nor conventional decision-intelligence tooling creates structural pre-clearance requirements — binding governance conditions that must be satisfied before execution is permitted to proceed — independent of the optimization frameworks within which they operate. They improve decisions. They do not govern the exercise of the decision authority that produces them.

Structural Distinction

What differentiates this work from each of the preceding bodies of literature is not the recognition of harm, risk, or accountability. All five bodies of work recognize harm, address risk, and create accountability in the domains for which they were designed. The recognition of these challenges is widely shared across the full range of governance disciplines. What differentiates this work is the structural claim — the assertion that the governance of consequential decisions requires a specific institutional architecture that none of the preceding disciplines has built, that the limitations of those disciplines with respect to this requirement are structural rather than analytical, and that the institutional necessity of the missing governance layer follows from the structural analysis that this work advances.

The structural claim has five elements whose combination defines the novelty of the contribution. First, that human-impact decisions constitute a distinct class of institutional exposure — that the consequential choices of organizational authority that materially affect human outcomes are not merely a subcategory of organizational risk or a domain of ethical concern, but a specific institutional category requiring specific institutional governance. Second, that such decisions require governance before execution, not after — that the governance function for this category of decision must operate at the pre-execution moment when governance can prevent harm rather than at the post-execution moment when governance can only explain or remediate it. Third, that authority to execute must itself be governed — that it is insufficient to govern the processes that surround the exercise of consequential authority or to monitor the outcomes that authority produces, because the governance requirement attaches to the authority itself, at the moment of its exercise, before execution begins. Fourth, that decision provenance must be attributable, auditable, and preserved at decision-time — that the contemporaneous evidentiary record of who authorized each consequential decision, on what basis, with what alternatives considered, and with what risks accepted must be created at the moment of authority and preserved in a form independent of the retrospective interests of the parties whose exercise of authority it documents. Fifth, that enterprises require a dedicated infrastructure layer to enforce these constraints consistently across domains — that the governance requirements cannot be satisfied through advisory frameworks, domain-specific guidance, or the enhancement of existing governance functions operating at the execution layer, but require a dedicated institutional layer positioned above execution and designed specifically for pre-execution governance.

No prior academic, professional, or practitioner literature has consolidated these five elements into a single, general-purpose institutional framework governing pre-exposure human-impact decision execution. Individual elements of the structural claim are present in various combinations across the preceding bodies of literature. The requirement for contemporaneous evidence is recognized in legal standards of care. The requirement for explicit risk acknowledgment is addressed in ERM frameworks. The requirement for accountability attribution is present in corporate governance obligations. The requirement for alternative consideration is implicit in responsible AI principles. What is absent from all existing literature is their integration into a unified governance architecture that operates as a dedicated institutional layer enforcing all five requirements simultaneously as binding conditions for execution authorization, across the full range of consequential human-impact decisions in the modern enterprise.

> *This work does not argue that governance, ethics, or risk management are absent. It argues that they are structurally mislocated — embedded within systems that act after decisions are executed. Governed Decision-Intelligence Infrastructure™ (GD-II™) makes execution conditional upon governance, relocating oversight to the pre-execution moment.*

THE ARCHITECTURE BEHIND THE ARGUMENT

This book was written to stand on its own. Not as a product manifesto — not as a work whose institutional argument depends on the success of any particular implementation attempt or whose validity is contingent on the adoption of any specific platform, system, or organizational design. Not as a methodology — not as a prescribed sequence of practices whose application will produce governance outcomes through procedural compliance with a defined set of steps. Not as a forecast dressed up as inevitability — not as a projection of future conditions whose institutional logic is structured to make adoption appear inescapable by the force of predicted trends.

But as a structural argument: that modern enterprises are incomplete without Governed Decision-Intelligence Infrastructure™ (GD-II™) — and increasingly exposed because of it.

The argument rests on a structural analysis of what enterprise governance currently provides, what it fails to provide, what the accountability environments of the modern era require, and what institutional architecture would close the gap between these conditions. For most of this book, that argument has been made through the examination of patterns, failures, and structural gaps — through the institutional logic of why ungoverned decisions produce the consequences they do, why existing governance mechanisms cannot address the structural source of those consequences, and why the next era of enterprise requires the governance layer that the Systems Age produced the conditions for but was never equipped to build.

Here, at the end, abstraction is no longer sufficient. Because the consequences of ungoverned decisions are no longer theoretical. They are already visible — present in the institutional landscape of the modern economy in forms that the structural argument of this book can now be evaluated against directly, and that constitute the most direct evidence of both the failure pattern the argument addresses and the urgency of the institutional response it calls for.

The Condition of the Modern Enterprise

The absence of GD-II™ is no longer theoretical. Its consequences are visible across nearly every sector of the global economy — not as isolated institutional failures that can be attributed to the specific circumstances of specific organizations, but as a consistent pattern of governance failure whose structural source is the same in every industry where it appears. Modern enterprises are not failing because they lack data. The data environments of modern organizations are among the most sophisticated in institutional history — producing more information, more rapidly, with more analytical processing capability than any previous generation of organizational management could have imagined. They are failing because they lack governed authority.

They execute faster than they can justify — committing organizational resources, establishing institutional directions, and producing consequences at the speed that AI-enabled execution permits before the governance discipline that justification requires has been applied to the decisions that authorize the execution. They scale decisions faster than they can defend them — extending the reach and the impact of consequential organizational choices through execution systems whose efficiency and scale ensure that the consequences of ungoverned decisions propagate at organizational breadth before any governance mechanism can intercept them.

They act long before they can assess irreversible risk — committing to directions whose full consequence cannot be evaluated at the moment of action, and that the execution system has already rendered irreversible before the assessment that governance would have required at the front has been conducted. What we are witnessing across industries is not volatility — not the normal variance of institutional performance in complex and uncertain environments. It is structural exposure: the institutional condition produced by an organizational architecture that was built to execute decisions rather than to govern them, operating in accountability environments that require governance it was never designed to provide.

Across every sector, the pattern is the same. Decisions are made faster than they can be justified — at the speed that competitive pressure and AI acceleration permit, without the evidentiary discipline that justification in accountability forums requires. Authority is exercised without contemporaneous evidence — without the governance record that would establish the quality of the judgment behind the exercise of institutional power at the moment it was exercised rather than in the retrospective account of what the decision-maker wishes to claim they knew and considered. Alternatives are discarded without record — set aside in the deliberative process without the contemporaneous documentation that would establish whether the available options were genuinely evaluated or acknowledged pro forma in a process that had already determined its direction.

Risk is absorbed without accountability — taken on by the organization without the explicit acknowledgment, the conscious acceptance, and the attributable governance record that distinguishes deliberate institutional risk-taking from the inadvertent assumption of consequences that governance would have required to be addressed before they were incurred. These are not cultural failures — not the product of organizational cultures whose values are insufficiently developed or whose leadership character is inadequate for the governance requirements they face.

They are not leadership failures — not the product of individual incompetence or personal ethical failure on the part of the leaders whose authority has produced the consequences requiring accountability. They are architectural failures — structural deficiencies in the institutional design of organizations that were built to execute decisions rather than to govern them. And architectural failures cannot be corrected with training, with analytics, or with policy alone. They require infrastructure.

This is why NFRASTRUCT® exists. Not to replace the systems whose execution capability has been the institutional achievement of the Systems Age — those systems remain necessary and remain valuable. Not to automate judgment — to convert the irreducibly human exercise of consequential authority into an automated output that eliminates the accountability that governance requires. But to govern authority — to create the structural conditions under which consequential decisions are required to meet an evidentiary and accountability standard before the execution system is authorized to proceed, before the organization is exposed to the consequences of ungoverned judgment, and before the institutional reality of those consequences has made the governance that would have prevented them unavailable.

When Decisions Become Exposure

The preceding chapters traced a single throughline through the institutional evidence of organizational failure in the modern era: that enterprise failure is no longer driven primarily by execution gaps, data shortages, or technical limitations — but by decisions made under pressure without governance. This is not an abstract theoretical proposition. It is already visible in the operational environments where the conditions of institutional decision-making are most extreme — where decisions must be made in seconds rather than weeks, where the authority that authorizes those decisions is absolute in the moment it is exercised and cannot be deferred to a deliberative process that is unavailable in the time available, and where the cost of error is irreversible in ways that no subsequent governance mechanism can address after the fact.

Across nearly every sector, organizations are absorbing institutional damage that cannot be explained by execution failure alone. The systems worked — the processes were followed, the procedures were executed with the fidelity that operational training and organizational discipline produce. The data was available — the analytical capability and the informational infrastructure existed to support the exercise of sound judgment. The processes were followed — every procedural requirement was satisfied, every approval was obtained, every compliance checkpoint was passed. And yet, outcomes collapsed in ways that the institutional record of the organization's operational performance did not predict and that its governance architecture was not designed to prevent.

A Word to Leaders

If you are a Chief Executive Officer, a board member, a regulator, or an enterprise leader whose institutional responsibilities require you to account for the governance quality of the consequential decisions made under your authority, the most important institutional takeaway from this book is not a system to buy. It is a question to ask — and to answer honestly — under the evidentiary standard that the accountability environments of the next era will apply. The question is: where, in this organization, are decisions governed before they are executed?

Not where are decisions documented — the existence of documentation establishes that something was recorded, not that the decision that produced it was governed. Not where are decisions approved — the existence of approval establishes that a designated authority provided a required authorization, not that the judgment behind the authorization met any evidentiary standard.

Not where decisions are reviewed — the existence of review establishes that decisions are examined after they are made, not that they are governed before they produce the consequences that review assesses. The question is where decisions are governed — where the institutional architecture requires that consequential authority meet an evidentiary standard, produce a contemporaneous record, acknowledge its risks explicitly, and be attributed to an identified individual under a defined mandate before the execution system is authorized to proceed. If the answer to that question is unclear — if it relies on the trust that individual leaders will govern their own judgment, on the cultural aspiration that the organization's values will produce the governance discipline that structural requirements would enforce, or on the informal review processes that represent good intentions without the institutional architecture that produces genuine governance — then what has been identified is a structural risk.

Not a leadership failure in the sense that the individuals involved are inadequate for their responsibilities. A structural risk in the precise institutional sense that the architecture of the organization is missing a governance layer that is required by responsible institutional operation at scale. And structural risks require structural solutions.

A Word to Builders

If you are designing the systems, platforms, and organizational architectures that will constitute the institutional infrastructure of the next era — if your institutional responsibility is to build the organizations, the technologies, and the governance frameworks that the enterprises of the coming decades will depend on — this book offers a constraint, not a suggestion. GD-II™ cannot be bolted onto an organizational architecture that was designed without it.

The experience of every governance framework that has been added retrospectively to an operational architecture that was not designed into confirms this: governance that is appended rather than designed in produces the procedural compliance that the governance requirement demands in form, while leaving the structural governance gap that the requirement was meant to address intact in substance.

GD-II™ cannot be delegated to an existing organizational function without the independence from the authority it governs that governance requires. The institutional history of every governance function that has been embedded within the authority structures it is meant to constrain demonstrates the structural logic of why this fails: a governance function that depends on the cooperation of the authority it governs cannot maintain the independence that produces genuine pre-execution constraint. And it cannot be automated away — converted from a human institutional function involving the genuine accountability of specific individuals for the consequential authority they exercise into an automated output whose production satisfies the procedural requirement of governance while eliminating the human accountability that governance exists to create and preserve. These constraints are not matters of preference or institutional design philosophy. They are structural requirements of any governance function that produces what governance actually requires.

GD-II™ must be designed into the architecture from the beginning — embedded in the institutional design of the enterprise before the execution systems that it governs are built, rather than appended to an architecture that was designed without it and that will resist its genuine integration at every institutional opportunity. Anything less will eventually fail under the pressure of scale, under the scrutiny of accountability environments whose standards the appended governance cannot meet, or under the institutional dynamics that the architecture's existing authority structures will exert on a governance function that was not designed to be independent of them.

The Closing Truth

Every era of institutional history builds the infrastructure it needs — but only when it must. The necessity is not recognized until the accumulated consequences of operating without the infrastructure make the cost of continued absence exceed the resistance to building it. Financial ledgers were not built until the scale of commercial activity made the absence of an authoritative record of financial obligations an institutional risk that trust and memory could no longer manage. Safety systems were not built until the frequency and severity of industrial accidents made the reliance on individual caution and professional skill an institutional response that the scale of harm no longer permitted. Information security governance was not built until the connectivity and vulnerability of digital infrastructure made reliance on awareness, policy, and institutional posture untenable at the scale of cyber risk.

The Systems Age built execution — the operational infrastructure that made the modern enterprise possible and that remains the foundation on which every enterprise at scale operates.

The next evolution must build judgment — the governance infrastructure that makes the exercise of consequential authority at scale accountable, defensible, and legitimate in the accountability environments that the next era will enforce. GD-II™ is not a luxury that well-resourced organizations may choose to pursue when circumstances permit.

It is not a trend whose institutional implications are cyclical and whose relevance will recede as the next operational priority claims organizational attention. It is the structural response to a world where decisions move faster, last longer, and are judged more harshly than at any previous point in institutional history — where the combination of AI acceleration, permanent records, expanding regulatory accountability, and institutional transparency has created conditions in which the absence of pre-execution decision governance is not merely a governance gap but an institutional liability that compounds with every consequential decision made without it.

Whether organizations adopt GD-II™ deliberately — through the recognition of structural necessity and the institutional commitment to building what the argument of this book establishes is required — or are forced into it by the accumulated institutional consequences of governance failures that cannot be managed through the retrospective mechanisms of the Systems Age will determine how those organizations are remembered.

Not by the operational sophistication of the execution systems they built. Not by the scale of the institutional impact they achieved. But by whether, when accountability arrived for the consequential decisions they made, they were able to account for those decisions — to demonstrate that the governance quality of the judgment behind each commitment met the standard that the institutional record of their era will eventually apply to the exercise of consequential authority at scale.

We learned how to scale work.

Now we must learn how to scale responsibility.

This is the work ahead.

The structural argument of this book does not depend on current events. The following appendix documents that current events have confirmed it.

The AI Employment-Governance Enforcement Landscape

Research-current revision prepared for publication;
status references are stated as of May 15, 2026

This appendix is a companion reference to *The Next Evolution: From Systems to Governed Decision-Intelligence* and is published separately from the primary text to preserve the structural integrity of the book's institutional argument. The argument does not depend on current events for its validity. This appendix documents that the structural condition the book describes is visible—in courts, legislatures, regulatory bodies, and among the builders of the most powerful AI systems in operation—and provides enterprise buyers with the current-state reference needed to connect the book's governance thesis to their immediate compliance and litigation environment.

It summarizes the principal legal and regulatory developments shaping the use of automated decision systems and artificial intelligence in employment and other human-consequential decisions. Its purpose is not to provide legal advice, but to identify the governance expectations emerging across these authorities: documentation, bias controls, notice, human oversight, vendor accountability, and contemporaneous records capable of explaining how consequential decisions were reached.

All entries are current as of publication. This appendix is designed to be updated in subsequent printings without modification to the primary text.

NFRASTRUCT®, Governed Decision-Intelligence™, Governed Decision-Intelligence Infrastructure™, GD-I™, and GD-II™ are trademarks of NFRASTRUCT, LLC.

I. Quick Reference: The Enforcement Landscape at a Glance

Enterprise buyers should not treat AI governance as hypothetical. The developments below show that employment-related AI and automated decision tools are already subject to active litigation, enacted statutes, agency rules, and scheduled compliance regimes. Where a law is scheduled, stayed, contested, or subject to replacement, that status is stated expressly.

Development	Jurisdiction	Effective/ Status	Primary Governance Requirement
Mobley v. Workday, Inc. — AI vendor agent-liability theory	U.S. Federal (N.D. Cal.)	Active litigation; no final liability ruling as of May 15, 2026	Pre-deployment governance; AI provenance; documentation of evaluation outputs, human authority, and vendor role
California FEHA / Civil Rights Council Automated-Decision Regulations	California	In force October 1, 2025	Anti-discrimination compliance for automated decision systems; recordkeeping; validation evidence; vendor oversight
Illinois HB 3773 / Public Act 103-0804 - Human Rights Act AI Amendment	Illinois	In force January 1, 2026; implementing rules under development	Anti-discrimination; AI-use transparency; notice and recordkeeping expectations
Colorado AI Act / SB 24-205 and 2026 replacement activity	Colorado	SB 24-205 enforcement temporarily stayed; legislature passed replacement framework in May 2026, expected to take effect January 1, 2027 if signed	Algorithmic-discrimination and consequential-decision governance remains active, but compliance architecture is shifting from the 2024 model toward revised ADMT dis-closure requirements
NYC Local Law 144 - Automated Employment Decision Tools	New York City	Enforced; subject to increased scrutiny following public enforcement/audit review	Annual independent bias audits; public disclosure; candidate notice
Texas Responsible Artificial Intelligence Governance Act (TRAIGA / HB 149)	Texas	In force January 1, 2026	State AI governance; prohibited intentional discriminatory uses; Texas Attorney General enforcement; no private right of action
EU AI Act - High-Risk Employment Systems	European Union	High-risk system obligations scheduled for August 2, 2026, subject to any enacted legislative delay or transition amendment	Risk management; technical documentation; human oversight; conformity assessment and registration obligations for in-scope high-risk systems
Executive Order 14365 - Ensuring a National Policy Framework for Artificial Intelligence	U.S. Federal	Signed December 11, 2025	Federal policy effort favoring a minimally burdensome national AI framework; directs federal review and litigation strategy against selected state AI laws

The Courts: Judicial Recognition of the Governance Gap

The most commercially significant AI-employment litigation development is a federal court's willingness to allow claims against an AI-hiring-technology vendor to proceed under theories that treat the vendor as more than a passive software supplier. The cases below should be read as litigation developments, not final findings of liability. They show why organizations deploying AI-assisted employment systems need governance records that document what the system did, what role it played, and which human authority relied on or overrode its outputs.

Mobley v. Workday, Inc. - N.D. Cal. No. 3:23-cv-00770

What It Is: A federal putative class and collective action filed in February 2023 by an African American plaintiff over age 40 with disabilities. The plaintiff alleges that he applied to numerous jobs through employers using Workday-powered applicant-screening tools and that Workday's algorithmic screening systems discriminated on the basis of race, age, and disability. The asserted federal theories include Title VII of the Civil Rights Act, the Age Discrimination in Employment Act, and the Americans with Disabilities Act. Workday denies the allegations, and no final liability determination has been issued.

Status as of May 15, 2026: Active and escalating. Key milestones include:

- **July 2024:** The court allowed claims to proceed on an agency theory, concluding that the pleadings plausibly alleged Workday performed functions that could make it directly liable as an agent of employers using its tools. The court rejected other theories, including the employment-agency theory, as pleaded.

- **May 2025:** The court conditionally certified an ADEA collective action for applicants age 40 and over whose applications were processed through Workday-enabled flows during the relevant period.

- **July 2025:** The litigation expanded to include discovery concerning HiredScore AI features and customers alleged to have enabled them.

- **January–March 2026:** The court continued to address the scope of claims and pleadings, including disputes over ADEA applicant coverage and amended state and disability-related claims.

- **As of May 15, 2026:** The case remains in active litigation and discovery; no final merits ruling establishes that Workday or any customer violated federal employment-discrimination law.

Why It Matters for Governed Decision-Intelligence Infrastructure™ (GD-II™): Mobley is one of the most consequential judicial developments to date concerning AI-assisted employment decisions. It demonstrates three governance exposures that GD-II™ directly addresses:

(1) organizations that deploy AI hiring tools must be able to explain what those tools evaluated, produced, or influenced;

(2) AI vendors may face direct litigation risk when their systems are alleged to perform traditional hiring functions; and

(3) the absence of contemporaneous governance records linking system outputs, human review, policy thresholds, and authority chains can create significant institutional exposure. The case is widely discussed as a bellwether for how courts may evaluate vendor and employer responsibility in AI-assisted hiring, but it has not yet produced a final liability rule.

Harper v. Sirius XM Radio - AI Hiring Discrimination Allegations

What It Is: A federal employment-discrimination lawsuit alleging that AI-assisted hiring tools used in the Sirius XM Radio application process discriminated against applicants on the basis of race in violation of Title VII. The plaintiff alleges he applied to 149 positions and that his qualifications met or exceeded the listed requirements for many of the positions at issue. The allegations remain allegations unless and until adjudicated.

Status as of May 15, 2026: Public legal commentary cites Harper alongside Mobley as part of a broader wave of AI-assisted hiring discrimination litigation. The case should not be described as establishing a final rule of law. Its publication-safe significance is that it illustrates that AI-hiring discrimination claims may arise directly against employers, independently of the vendor-liability theory being tested in Mobley.

Why It Matters for GD-II™: Harper illustrates that employer liability theories remain available even if vendor-liability theories are narrowed or rejected in other litigation. For enterprise governance purposes, the practical risk is the same: an organization using automated screening must be able to show how the tool functioned, what data and criteria were used, what human review occurred, and how protected-class discrimination risks were tested, monitored, and addressed.

The Regulatory Direction: From Voluntary AI Ethics to Enforceable Governance

The regulatory pattern is clear even though the details vary by jurisdiction. Regulators are not merely asking whether an AI tool is efficient. They are asking whether the organization can document how the tool operates, whether it creates unlawful disparate impact or algorithmic discrimination, whether affected individuals receive required notice, whether human oversight is meaningful, and whether records are preserved long enough to support investigation or litigation.

California FEHA / Civil Rights Council Automated-Decision Regulations

California's Civil Rights Council regulations, effective October 1, 2025, clarify that automated decision systems used in employment can implicate the Fair Employment and Housing Act. For employers, the governance lesson is direct: automated tools that assist hiring, promotion, selection, or other employment decisions must be treated as part of the employment decision process, not as external technology beyond compliance review. Employers should maintain records, validation evidence, vendor documentation, and adverse-impact analysis sufficient to show that their systems do not produce unlawful discrimination.

Illinois HB 3773 / Public Act 103-0804

Illinois amended the Illinois Human Rights Act to address employer use of artificial intelligence in employment decisions, effective January 1, 2026. The law makes AI-assisted discrimination actionable under the state's human rights framework and directs rulemaking to implement it. Publication-safe framing should state that Illinois imposes anti-discrimination and transparency obligations and that implementing rules remain important to final compliance mechanics.

Colorado AI Act / 2026 Replacement Activity

Colorado is the most cautious entry because its 2024 AI Act is currently in transition. SB 24-205 originally imposed duties on developers and deployers of high-risk AI systems, including obligations for risk management, impact assessment, notice, and anti-discrimination. As of May 15, 2026, enforcement of the 2024 law has been temporarily stayed in litigation, and the Colorado General Assembly has passed a replacement bill that would repeal and reenact the framework with a narrower ADMT-based model expected to take effect January 1, 2027 if signed. The safest publication position is therefore not that Colorado's 2024 regime is simply "in force," but that Colorado remains a major AI-governance jurisdiction whose operative framework is being rewritten while the policy direction toward consequential-decision transparency continues.

NYC Local Law 144

New York City Local Law 144 prohibits covered employers and employment agencies from using automated employment decision tools unless the tool has undergone a bias audit within one year of use, the audit summary is publicly available, and required notices are provided to candidates or employees. The governance requirement is not merely technical testing; it is public, recurring, and tied to notice obligations.

Texas TRAIGA / HB 149

Texas's Responsible Artificial Intelligence Governance Act, effective January 1, 2026, creates statewide AI governance obligations and prohibits specified harmful uses of AI, including intentional discriminatory uses. TRAIGA is enforced by the Texas Attorney General and does not create a private right of action. For enterprise governance, the critical point is that Texas has moved AI governance from policy preference into state-enforceable law, while retaining an enforcement model materially different from private employment-discrimination litigation.

EU AI Act - Employment as High-Risk AI

Under the EU AI Act, employment, worker-management, and access-to-self-employment systems are treated as high-risk when they fall within the Act's scope. High-risk systems are subject to obligations including risk management, technical documentation, recordkeeping, human oversight, accuracy, robustness, cybersecurity, conformity assessment, and registration-related duties. The principal high-risk obligations are scheduled for August 2, 2026, but publication language should acknowledge that EU implementation timing may be affected by enacted transition or delay measures if adopted before publication.

Executive Order 14365 - National AI Policy Framework

On December 11, 2025, President Trump signed Executive Order 14365, titled "Ensuring a National Policy Framework for Artificial Intelligence." The order states a federal policy favoring a minimally burdensome national AI framework and directs federal review and litigation strategy concerning selected state AI laws. Its publication-safe significance is not that it eliminates state AI laws; executive orders do not themselves repeal state statutes. Its significance is that federal-state conflict over AI governance has become an active policy and litigation issue.

Publication-Safe Conclusion

The enforcement landscape is no longer theoretical. Courts are testing whether AI vendors may face direct responsibility for employment decisions their systems influence. States and cities are imposing notice, audit, recordkeeping, and anti-discrimination obligations. The EU is treating employment-related AI as high-risk. The federal government is simultaneously attempting to shape a national AI policy framework and challenge selected state approaches. The common denominator is governance: organizations must be able to prove what their systems did, how those systems were tested, who had authority to act, what human review occurred, what records were preserved, and how discrimination risk was controlled before consequential decisions were executed.

II. United States State Law: The Patchwork That Is Now Enforceable

State regulation of artificial intelligence in employment and other consequential decisions has accelerated materially. The jurisdictions summarized below are among the most directly relevant to enterprise organizations using artificial intelligence in employment decisions. Taken together, they create a compliance environment in which organizations operating across multiple states face overlapping and, in some cases, materially different legal requirements.

California — Fair Employment and Housing Act (FEHA) Automated-Decision System Regulations

Effective: October 1, 2025

Issuing body: California Civil Rights Council

What It Requires: California's regulations expressly address the use of automated decision systems in employment. They define such systems broadly and clarify that employers may be liable for discriminatory outcomes associated with systems they use, including those provided by third-party vendors. The regulations also impose expanded recordkeeping obligations, including retention of data used in or resulting from the application, development, or customization of automated-decision systems.

Why It Matters for Governed Decision-Intelligence Infrastructure™ (GD-II™): California establishes one of the most comprehensive state-level regulatory frameworks governing automated employment decision systems. Organizations using AI in California employment decisions face heightened compliance risk if they cannot produce reliable documentation demonstrating how their systems were evaluated, monitored, and governed.

Illinois — HB 3773, Amendment to the Illinois Human Rights Act

Effective: January 1, 2026

Enforcement: Illinois Department of Human Rights; private right of action available under the Illinois Human Rights Act

What It Requires: The Illinois amendments make it a civil rights violation to use artificial intelligence in a manner that results in unlawful discrimination in employment decisions. The law applies across the employment lifecycle, including recruitment, hiring, promotion, discipline, and termination. Employers must provide clear and conspicuous notice when AI will be used in covered employment decisions and must retain required notices and related records for four years.

Illinois Artificial Intelligence Video Interview Act: Illinois separately enforces the Artificial Intelligence Video Interview Act, which requires employers using AI to analyze video interviews to provide notice, explain the general manner in which the technology works and the characteristics it evaluates, obtain consent, and comply with statutory data handling requirements.

Colorado — Artificial Intelligence Act (SB 24-205, as amended)

Effective: June 30, 2026

Enforcement: Colorado Attorney General; no private right of action

What It Requires: Colorado enacted the first broad state law specifically regulating high-risk artificial intelligence systems used in consequential decisions, including employment. The statute requires developers and deployers to exercise reasonable care to protect consumers from algorithmic discrimination and imposes obligations for risk management, impact assessment, documentation, and notice.

Why It Matters for GD-II™: Colorado establishes a formal statutory governance framework for high-risk AI systems. Organizations using AI in employment decisions must be prepared to document the controls used to identify, assess, and mitigate discrimination risks.

New York City — Local Law 144 (Automated Employment Decision Tools)

Effective: July 5, 2023

Enforcement: New York City Department of Consumer and Worker Protection

What It Requires: Employers and employment agencies using automated employment decision tools in New York City must obtain an independent bias audit within one year before use and annually thereafter, publicly post a summary of audit results, and provide advance notice to candidates and employees. The notice must inform affected individuals that an automated tool will be used and disclose the job qualifications and characteristics the tool evaluates, as well as information about requesting an alternative selection process or accommodation where applicable.

Why It Matters for GD-II™: Local Law 144 is the most established and actively enforced U.S. rule specifically targeting automated hiring systems and provides a practical benchmark for enterprise AI hiring governance.

Texas — Texas Responsible Artificial Intelligence Governance Act (TRAIGA)

Effective: January 1, 2026

Enforcement: Texas Attorney General

What It Requires: Texas adopted a statewide AI governance statute that prohibits certain discriminatory uses of artificial intelligence and establishes disclosure, oversight, and enforcement mechanisms. The statute includes a cure process for certain violations and authorizes multiple tiers of civil penalties depending on the nature and duration of the violation.

Why It Matters for GD-II™: Texas adds a major commercial jurisdiction to the emerging U.S. AI regulatory landscape. Its enforcement structure and substantive requirements increase the need for documented, jurisdiction-aware governance controls for organizations operating nationally.

Collectively, these state and local laws demonstrate that artificial intelligence governance in employment is no longer a theoretical issue. It is an active and enforceable compliance domain. The legal trend is clear: organizations deploying AI in consequential employment decisions must be able to demonstrate that they have implemented effective controls to identify, monitor, document, and mitigate discrimination and related risks.

III. The European Union: The August 2026 Compliance Deadline

The EU AI Act (Regulation (EU) 2024/1689) represents the most comprehensive artificial intelligence governance framework currently in force and applies broadly to organizations that place AI systems on the EU market or put them into service in the European Union, including organizations headquartered outside the EU. For many enterprises using employment-related AI systems, the most significant upcoming compliance milestone is August 2, 2026.

EU AI Act — Annex III High-Risk Systems: Full Compliance Obligations Apply August 2, 2026

Enforcement deadline: August 2, 2026 for most obligations applicable to Annex III high-risk AI systems

Penalties: Up to €35 million or 7% of worldwide annual turnover for the most serious infringements

Applies to: Organizations placing AI systems on the EU market or putting them into service in the European Union, subject to the territorial scope of the regulation.

What Annex III Covers: AI systems used in employment contexts are expressly classified as high-risk under Annex III, including systems used for recruitment and selection, evaluation and monitoring of performance and behavior, promotion and termination decisions, and task allocation. For these systems, the EU AI Act imposes extensive compliance obligations, including:

- **Conformity assessment:** Completed and documented before the system is placed on the market or put into service.

- **Technical documentation:** Comprehensive documentation regarding system design, data, performance, risk management, and governance controls.

- **CE marking:** Required following successful completion of applicable conformity assessment procedures.

- **EU database registration:** Certain high-risk AI systems must be registered in the EU database before being placed on the market or put into service.

- **Human oversight:** Mandatory measures enabling appropriate human review, intervention, and oversight.

- **Transparency and information obligations:** Required disclosures and notices to affected persons as specified by the Regulation and applicable law.

- **Ongoing monitoring:** Post-market monitoring and incident reporting obligations.

Phased Implementation Context: The EU AI Act applies in stages. Prohibited AI practices became applicable on February 2, 2025. General-purpose AI model obligations became applicable on August 2, 2025. Most obligations applicable to Annex III high-risk systems, including employment-related systems, become applicable on August 2, 2026. Additional provisions become applicable thereafter in accordance with the Regulation's phased implementation schedule.

Why It Matters for Governed Decision-Intelligence Infrastructure™ (GD-II™): The EU AI Act's Annex III requirements for employment-related AI systems closely align with the governance principles embodied in GD-II™, including structured human oversight, technical documentation, monitoring, and accountability controls. Organizations seeking to operationalize these obligations will require robust governance infrastructure of the type GD-II™ is designed to provide.

IV. United States Federal: The Preemption Battle and Its Governance Consequence

The federal government's posture on artificial intelligence regulation is creating a dynamic that enterprise compliance teams must carefully understand: federal policy initiatives have sought to reduce what the administration characterizes as unnecessary regulatory burdens. In contrast, federal courts and existing civil rights statutes continue to provide independent legal frameworks for AI-assisted employment decisions. These developments operate through different institutional channels and on different timescales.

Trump Executive Order — Ensuring a National Policy Framework for Artificial Intelligence (Dec. 11, 2025)

Signed: December 11, 2025

Status: In effect; implementation proceeding through agency action and subject to ongoing legal and policy debate

What It Does: The executive order articulates a federal policy favoring a nationally coordinated and relatively streamlined approach to artificial intelligence regulation. Among other actions, it directs federal agencies to identify state requirements that may be inconsistent with federal priorities, authorizes the Department of Justice to evaluate potential legal challenges where appropriate, conditions certain federal broadband funding on compliance with specified federal requirements, and calls for recommendations on possible federal legislation. As a matter of constitutional law, however, an executive order does not, by itself, preempt state law. State statutes and regulations remain in effect unless displaced by valid federal legislation or judicial rulings.

The Compliance Implication: Organizations should not assume that federal policy initiatives will suspend or invalidate existing state and local AI requirements. Applicable laws in jurisdictions such as California, Illinois, Colorado, and New York City remain operative under their own terms unless and until modified by legislation or a court decision. Enterprise compliance programs should therefore be designed to address the legal requirements currently in force in the jurisdictions in which the organization operates.

Why It Matters for Governed Decision-Intelligence Infrastructure™ (GD-II™): The interaction between federal and state developments increases the complexity of AI governance rather than reducing it. Organizations operating across multiple jurisdictions must be able to document how they identify, interpret, and operationalize overlapping legal obligations. GD-II™ is designed to provide jurisdiction-aware governance records and accountability controls suited to that environment.

EEOC Position — Existing Federal Civil Rights Law

While certain AI-specific technical assistance materials were removed from the U.S. Equal Employment Opportunity Commission's website in early 2025, the underlying federal statutes governing employment discrimination remain fully in effect. Title VII of the Civil Rights Act of 1964, the Americans with Disabilities Act, and the Age Discrimination in Employment Act continue to apply to employment decisions that use artificial intelligence or automated decision tools. Federal litigation, including *Mobley v. Workday, Inc.*, is testing how these established statutes apply to AI-assisted employment decisions and to vendors whose systems materially participate in the decision-making process.

The Compliance Implication: Changes in executive branch guidance do not eliminate existing federal civil rights obligations. Organizations using AI in employment decisions remain subject to established anti-discrimination statutes. They should be prepared to demonstrate that their systems and governance processes are designed to prevent unlawful discrimination.

V. Industry Signals: The People Who Built These Systems Are Raising the Alarm

The most significant non-regulatory evidence that the governance gap is real and structurally serious comes from individuals who have helped build and evaluate some of the most advanced artificial intelligence systems currently in operation. Their public statements and actions do not constitute legal requirements, but they provide important signals about governance concerns recognized by practitioners working closest to the technology.

The February 2026 Safety Researcher Departures — A Governance Signal

In February 2026, several prominent researchers at leading artificial intelligence companies publicly announced their departures and expressed concerns about governance, safety, and institutional decision-making. These events received substantial media attention and were widely interpreted as evidence that internal debates over safety and governance remain active within the organizations developing frontier AI systems.

Mrinank Sharma, who led safeguards research at Anthropic, publicly announced his departure in February 2026 and described deep concern about the risks associated with advanced AI systems and the difficulty of ensuring that organizational values consistently guide operational decisions.

Zoë Hitzig, a former OpenAI researcher, published a New York Times essay explaining her decision to leave OpenAI and expressing concern about the concentration of highly sensitive personal information within AI systems and the governance challenges associated with monetization and platform incentives.

During the same general period, public reporting noted additional senior departures from other frontier AI companies, reinforcing broader industry discussion regarding governance and safety.

Why It Matters for Governed Decision-Intelligence Infrastructure™ (GD-II™): These departures are significant not because they establish any specific legal requirement, but because they indicate that governance and accountability concerns are being raised by individuals with direct experience inside the organizations developing advanced AI systems. For enterprises considering AI-assisted decision-making with consequential human outcomes, these events underscore the importance of implementing governance structures that translate stated principles into operational controls.

Future of Life Institute — 2025 AI Safety Index

The Future of Life Institute's 2025 AI Safety Index evaluated leading artificial intelligence companies across multiple governance and safety dimensions, including risk management, transparency, and preparedness for severe misuse scenarios. The report concluded that no company received a grade above D in its existential safety category, highlighting concerns about whether current governance frameworks are commensurate with the ambitions and capabilities described by frontier AI developers.

Why It Matters for GD-II™: The AI Safety Index suggests that even organizations with substantial technical expertise and publicly stated safety commitments continue to face significant governance challenges. Enterprises relying on third-party AI systems should therefore conduct independent governance assessments rather than assume vendor statements alone are sufficient evidence of effective oversight.

Public Opinion — Majority Concern Regarding AI Risks

Multiple national surveys conducted by major research and news organizations in 2025 and 2026 reported that a substantial portion of the U.S. public believes that the risks associated with artificial intelligence may outweigh its benefits or is more concerned than excited about expanded AI use. While survey results vary by methodology and timing, they consistently indicate significant public concern regarding artificial intelligence.

Why It Matters for GD-II™: Public trust is an important governance and commercial consideration. Organizations deploying AI in consequential decisions affecting employment, credit, healthcare, and education operate in an environment in which many affected individuals already approach AI with caution. Demonstrable governance and accountability can therefore become a meaningful source of institutional trust.

A Note on Using This Appendix

This appendix is designed to serve two functions. For enterprise buyers — General Counsels, Chief Risk Officers, Chief People Officers, and Board Chairs assessing the immediate compliance and litigation environment — it provides the current-state reference that connects the book's governance thesis to active legal obligations and enforcement risk.

The primary argument of *The Next Evolution* provides independent confirmation without contaminating the structural argument of the book itself. The book's thesis does not depend on any of the developments in this appendix. It depends on the structural logic that produced them. The developments in this appendix are the institutional expression of that structural logic becoming visible in the accountability environments that govern how organizations operate.

This appendix will be updated at subsequent printings to reflect new developments. The structural argument of the book will not require updating because it does not depend on current events. It depends on the institutional architecture that current events are now enforcing.

ABOUT THE AUTHOR

NFRASTRUCT® is the originator of the Governed Decision-Intelligence™ category and the architect of a new approach to governing consequential enterprise decisions before execution occurs. The work behind this book draws from direct exposure to enterprise hiring, governance, and risk failures across regulated and high-impact environments, where accountability, defensibility, and judgment under pressure are not theoretical concerns.

Rather than approaching decision-making as a cultural, procedural, or technological problem, **NFRASTRUCT®** focuses on Governed Decision-Intelligence™ as an infrastructure challenge—one that must be designed deliberately to withstand scale, scrutiny, and irreversible consequence. This book reflects that perspective: not as commentary, but as architecture.

NFRASTRUCT® operates independently and does not function as a consultancy, advisory firm, or policy body.

A note on authorship: The Next Evolution is a publication of NFRASTRUCT, LLC, authored under the institutional brand. The work is the product of NFRASTRUCT® as an institution rather than of a named individual, reflecting the nature of the contribution itself: a structural and architectural argument for a governance category, not a personal memoir or attributed opinion. NFRASTRUCT®, Governed Decision-Intelligence™, Governed Decision-Intelligence Infrastructure™, GD-I™, and GD-II™ are trademarks of NFRASTRUCT, LLC. Published by Decision-Intelligence Press™, an imprint of NFRASTRUCT®.